Early Modern Writing and the Privatization of Experience

Also Available From Bloomsbury

Shakespeare, 'Othello' and Domestic Tragedy, by Sean Benson
The Renaissance Literature Handbook, by Susan Bruce and Rebecca Steinberger

Early Modern Writing and the Privatization of Experience

Nick Davis

B L O O M S B U R Y

LONDON • NEW DELHI • NEW YORK • SYDNEY

Bloomsbury Academic
An imprint of Bloomsbury Publishing Plc

50 Bedford Square	1385 Broadway
London	New York
WC1B 3DP	NY 10018
UK	USA

www.bloomsbury.com

Bloomsbury is a registered trademark of Bloomsbury Publishing Plc

First published 2013

© Nick Davis, 2013

British Library Cataloguing-in-Publication Data
A catalogue record for this book is available from the British Library.

ISBN: HB: 978-1-4411-6682-1
ePub: 978-1-4411-7359-1
ePDF: 978-1-4411-3438-7

Library of Congress Cataloging-in-Publication Data
Davis, Nick (Nicholas Mark)
Early Modern Writing and the Privatisation of Experience / Nick Davis.
pages cm.
Includes bibliographical references and index.
ISBN 978-1-4411-6682-1 (hardback) – ISBN 978-1-4411-7359-1 (epub) –
ISBN 978-1-4411-3438-7 (epdf) 1. English literature–Early modern, 1500–1700–
History and criticism. 2. Privacy in literature. 3. Individualism in literature. I. Title.
PR428.P68D38 2013
820.9'003–dc23
2013029082

Typeset by Newgen Knowledge Works (P) Ltd., Chennai, India
Printed and bound in Great Britain

For my mother, Marjorie Eileen Davis, 1909–1997

Contents

Acknowledgements

My first thanks are due to Julia Davis, Louise Davis and Gail Kenwright for giving me continuous support and encouragement in writing this. I have benefited from discussion of sections of the argument with Graham Atkin, Bernard Beatty, Nandini Das, Michael Davies, Alison Findlay, Raymond Frontain, Joanne Mitchinson and Bob Owens. I am grateful to the Dean and Chapter of Westminster Abbey, the Kunsthistorische Museum, Vienna, and the National Portrait Gallery, London, for permission to reproduce, respectively, the Westminster Abbey portrait of Richard II, Bruegel's 'The Peasants' Dance', and Daniel Mytens' portrait of the Earl of Arundel. Lorna Kenwright kindly helped to prepare the images in the text for publication. I also wish to thank, once again, colleagues and students at Liverpool University, and the inhabitants of the city of Liverpool, for helping to create an environment which favours enquiry.

Instruments of Change

It is possible to contrast two personal imaginings of self, one in which the self faces outwards towards and forms part of an environment consisting partly of other people, the other in which it has an existence to which *ego*, as the bearer of an individual consciousness, is felt to be central, and of which no other individual consciousness can have direct experience. I find that both are present to me as versions of what I am. The second, non-public 'me' may co-exist more or less equably with the outward-facing 'me', and for much of the time I may not sense the existence of a discrepancy between them. Nevertheless, these perceived 'me's' are differently constituted, given that each possesses a dimension which the other lacks: the first takes form in a field of shared experience which others beside the self inhabit and shape; the other takes form in phenomena of individual 'mind' known directly only to the one who has or is this 'mind'. It is possible to assign the two perceptible 'me's' different relative importance, setting more value on the first, or on the second; in effect, treating one as being more properly or definitively 'me' than the other. Behaviour observable in the modern world strikingly brings the principle out. If a modern Westerner is asked to point to where the 'self' is, she/he will almost certainly point to the middle of the chest; but if the same question is asked of someone Chinese or Japanese, she/he will probably point to the middle of the face (though Western influence is also locally modifying the practice).[1] Cultures can differ markedly, then, in their positing of a 'me', which may be located primarily 'within', or primarily in what an individual makes known or considers to be knowable within a shared human environment. The human subjective state in a subject's own registration of it is not *there* as a single phenomenon to be investigated and understood, but as one existing in diversity against varied backgrounds of cultural practice and expectation.

This book is concerned with a general cultural movement away from the placing of predominant trust in the self's shared, publicly acknowledged or mediated experience, and towards identification of a person's individual, self-scrutinizing mind, inherently invisible to others, as the primary locus of authentic perception, thought and feeling. Such a movement occurred, in an uneven and contested process, during Europe's early modern period, which for these purposes roughly spans the fourteenth and early eighteenth centuries. I shall be examining English writing, produced during a 100 years of this larger time span, which is caught up with and forms part of the cultural mutation. The writers who will be given principal attention are Spenser, Donne, the Shakespeare of the second tetralogy, *King Lear* and *The Winter's Tale*, Hobbes and Bunyan. One of the distinctive claims that I shall be making is that writing here, as well as registering and sometimes reflecting on processes of cultural change, is also in some respects instrumental in their production. This introductory section offers a preliminary characterization of these processes, going with a first account of written discourse's potential bearing on them.

*   *   *

Daniella Gobetti writes succinctly that 'Private refers to what is singular or hidden, public to what is shared or visible.'[2] This statement would, I think, be intelligible in most human settings: such a perception of difference between 'public' and 'private' spheres apparently corresponds to universals of cultural practice. To live as a member of more or less any community is to feel the force of a conceptual–practical distinction between what is shared with or available – including available as a thing perceived – to all, and what is possessed singularly by or available primarily to a given individual. Social life as we find it offers three primary models for the conceptual–practical demarcation of a sphere of experience which is private,[3] in this sense, from a public one: (1) Privacy accrues in the imagined interior of an individual's body, as activities of the individual 'mind', such as mute reflection on possible courses of action or the experiencing of unexpressed emotions, both of which are inherently imperceptible to others. Cultures differ on the physical location of the individual mind, or of aspects of it, distributing these, say, between head and heart,[4] but are not found to place the mind of a person outside that person's bodily boundary.[5] (2) Privacy can be found in some already demarcated space, such as the house where an individual lives, or a room within such a house, which are more or less sealed off from communal perception. Most cultures support, it should be said, the perception of some degree of congruence between a house and a human body, which partly aligns this category of privacy with the first. (3) Privacy is available in spaces that lie outside communal perception; most reliably, in some wild and unfrequented area or – as is typically to be found in a modern city – one making for individual anonymity in a peopled setting to which the perception of an individual's community does not extend. Some putting together of models 1 and 2 produces the conception of privacy as 'interiority', contrasted for thought with the outward-facing character of life offered to communal perception. The currency of model 3 reminds us at the same time that privacy is not necessarily or exclusively a phenomenon of the 'interior'.

As soon as one has said this, however, it becomes obvious that the concept of the private can carry very different meanings and connotations in different cultural environments. The preceding statement about cultural universals is intended to serve as background for what is primarily an account of cultural change. This book's title flags up a phenomenon which is generally recognized, while not being very well charted or understood, as a feature of the West's transition from the middle ages through early modernity ('the Renaissance') to modernity (the later seventeenth century and beyond). To privatize experience, in this argument's terms, is to accord it more worth and significance when it accrues in what has the appearance of being a private sphere – when it seems to accrue primarily for individual perception and understanding, and only secondarily or contingently for others.

I should immediately distinguish the conception of my account from some others which have contemporary currency and bear on this field of enquiry. The critical movement familiarly known as British cultural materialism – represented, in this context, by key writings of Francis Barker, Catherine Belsey and Jonathan Dollimore[6] – offers the idea that the early modern period saw the inauguration of individual self-awareness in the modern form. Belsey states without inflection that 'the inner space of subjectivity (. . .) came into being in the Renaissance.'[7] Barker is clear on the principle that people in the middle ages did not locate parts or aspects of their experience in a sphere of the personally separate, demarcated from the experience of the social group. To be a functioning member of 'pre-bourgeois' political society, writes Barker,

> does not properly involve subjectivity at all, but a condition of dependent membership in which place and articulation are defined not by an interiorized self-recognition (. . .), but by incorporation in the body politic which is the king's body in its social form.[8]

It is easy to see that Barker, Belsey and their critical associates are attempting both to take the measure of and also to supersede Jacob Burckhardt's highly influential account of a rise, occurring first in Renaissance Italy, of an *authentic individualism*. Burckhardt explains that

> in the Middle Ages (. . .) human consciousness (. . .) lay dreaming, or half awake beneath a common veil. The veil was woven of faith, illusion, and childish prepossession, through which the world and history were seen clad in strange hues. Man was conscious of himself only as member of a race, people, party, family, or corporation – only through some general category.[9]

Part of the thrust of the British cultural materialists' argument is that the attitudes of individualism which Burckhardt lauds – and it is the case that his account projects the values of the nineteenth-century middle classes on to the culture of a different era – are not part of an eternal human disposition but the symptomal forms of an ideology with specific historical origins, consisting in the affirmation of what Belsey terms 'the unified subject of liberal humanism'.[10] But, to the detriment of historical understanding, their account of pre-modern to early modern cultural transition receives into itself Burckhardt's conception of a fundamentally corporatist medieval subject, unaware of having a personal existence which is independent of that of the group. As Lee Patterson observes, it is ironic that 'a Marxist-inspired account of subjectivity, one that thinks to demolish Burckhardtian humanism by reversing the terms of its analysis' should 'in fact leave (. . .) the humanist master narrative all the more firmly in place.'[11]

Patterson comments shrewdly that the British cultural materialists, who can for these purposes be grouped with New Historicists in the school of Stephen Greenblatt, do not evince interest in historical change as such, but are concerned primarily 'to establish (. . .) the modernity of their enterprise, the claim that in their chosen texts they descry the present condition in its initial, essential form.'[12] Patterson for his part has done a great deal to explicate medieval consciousness, in several forms, of existing in a condition of tension or struggle between subjective self-recognition and the demands of public, outward-facing existence, understanding of which is mediated by the recognitions of others.[13] But how should one evaluate the claim – not, it should be said, one put forward by Patterson – that the degree and kind of importance given to private experience was much the same for medieval pre-modernity as it was for the early modern period? So much is suggested in an engaging piece of polemic formulated by David Aers, who underlines the emphatic medieval concern with inwardness – in this account a strong anticipation of the modern – which is readily discernible, for example, in the reception of Augustine's *Confessions* and other texts of internal dialogue,[14] in the traditions of mystical thought and teaching, and in the importance given to individual and private acts of confession from the thirteenth century onwards, as well as demonstrated by the dramatization of subjective states to be found in the era's lyrics and romances. Aers asks, *contra* the cultural materialists, why 'such a big deal [has been] made of Hamlet observing he has "that within which passeth show"';[15] where, according to Barker, for the first time 'an interior subjectivity begins to speak'.[16] I wish to argue – while accepting part of what Aers contends – that Hamlet's statement is, considered from a historical standpoint, quite a big deal, in that it can serve as one marker of a genuine shift in the ambient culture's account rendered and evaluation of what is experienced as private (I shall return to it in Chapter 2). I am indeed attempting to formulate what Aers terms, with disparaging intent, a story of transformation,[17] tracking changes in the culture, medieval to early modern to modern, by which special importance is transferred to the community-detached self as a locus of valued experience. The cultural materialists' failure to write this story in a satisfactory form does not count as evidence that there is not one to write.

But, shifting the ground of discussion a little, what exactly does one mean here by a story? I can begin to sketch what might be meant by pointing out, in the first place, that the cultural changes with which I am concerned took place very unevenly, across a long period, at shifting speeds which could include going into reverse, and as differently embodied in the behaviour of different social groups; they are not a simply describable unilinear progression. Hamlet's claim to have 'that within which passeth show' could not conceivably signal a temporally defined moment of concerted cultural change, because there was no such moment: the kind of perception which it projects must have accrued and receded many times against shifting circumstantial backgrounds. Nor should we attempt to accelerate the history of change by pre-emptively deciding that, say, the perceptions of these matters held by Shakespeare and his contemporaries must already have been much like our own. Cultural materialism and New Historicism have helped to entrench perception of the middle ages as a foreign country,[18] a non-precursor of modernity with which modernity does not have to recognize continuity in order to transcend. But, as Erica Longfellow reminds us, in a good deal of modern research there has been insufficient acknowledgement that certain aspects of the early modern past are themselves foreign to us, that a number of its typifying mentalities are distinctly non-modern.[19] Pertinently to the present account, its conceptions of privacy seem to have incorporated kinds of experience which we would not regard as private. David Cressy concludes from the study of church court records and similar social-historical documents that virtually all life in this period had or was perceived as having 'public, social, or communal dimensions'.[20] Examination of texts giving instruction on religious life reveals, according to Longfellow, that 'private devotion was not something separate from or to be protected from public worship, (. . .) but a necessary part of the whole of worship that prepared the individual to be with the community.' She notes too that, on linguistic evidence marshalled by the *Oxford English Dictionary*, the conception of privacy with which we as moderns are most likely to feel at home, 'the state or condition of being alone, undisturbed, or free from public attention, as a matter of right', does not appear in England until the early nineteenth century, being first documented in 1814.[21] This may carry the interesting corollary that women of the middling to higher social strata were typically less marginalized by and sequestered within domestic conditions of life in the seventeenth century than in the nineteenth. If we deplore medieval or early modern culture too readily for its lack of modernity, meaning lack of resemblance to what we have or know or value, we may be missing certain features of it which violate our characteristic constructions of the modern.

So – the cultural changes with which we are concerned occurred slowly, unevenly and as gathering major momentum, probably later than has been commonly supposed. But, saying this still does not take us to the heart of the problems posed by framing a history of experience's privatization. The central issue is that, to co-opt Bruno Latour's turn of phrase, in respect of such privatization *we have never been entirely modern*. While the apotheosis of a fully community-independent, entirely self-reflexive subjectivity has been recurrently envisaged, it has never definitively occurred; because the constitution of the human subject renders it unachievable, because there are flaws in the notion of a self capable of possessing agency while it subsists in utter detachment from the agency which it experiences in other selves. Key insights concerning the intersubjective formation of the individual subject emerged in several fields of early twentieth-century thought, perhaps most strikingly (1) in Freud's account of secondary narcissism, implying that the ego takes form in spontaneous self-identification with perceived others (elaborated in Lacan's discussion of the *image spéculaire* which is simultaneously oneself and an other), (2) in Mauss's study of the gift which brings out a fundamental reciprocity of relation between the constitution of society and that of individual selfhood, so forming one of the cornerstones of modern anthropological enquiry and (3) in the phenomenological postulate, first formulated by Husserl, that it is impossible to know the world without acknowledging the existence of others' perspectives on it, necessarily different from but in one respect equivalent to and exemplary for the self's because individually possessing their own egocentric standpoints.[22] These expositions of selfhood do not obliterate the individual subject, but situate its agency and self-knowing within an intersubjective field.[23] The intersubjective relation, however one wishes to inflect an account of it, defines an inherent and structural non-detachment from others of the individual ego; it implies that analysis of individual agency necessarily includes analysis of what the individual experiences as the agency of others. The functioning of intersubjectivity appoints a limit to the degree of exclusive self-reflexiveness which the individual ego can attain and remain an ego; that is, not tip towards psychotic fragmentation.[24]

Nevertheless, on the understanding that there is a kind of gravitational force which pulls in the opposite direction, it is possible to distinguish the different extents to which projects of selfhood, metaphorically resembling projectiles thrown, seek to validate self's perception of self in some degree of independence from that self's perception of its existence in relation to others. A history of experience's privatization will thus be in large part a history of devices, practical and conceptual, *making for* a sense of individually lived separation from the lives of others, fostering attitudes of individualism. Shifts in the norms of house design across the early modern period are instances of such devices in a very concrete form. In England, across the seventeenth and eighteenth centuries, it is possible broadly to document an increase in the amount of time which individuals from the upper social strata spent, by choice, in a degree of physical separation from other individuals, which was made possible in part by the replacement of an architecture favouring communal life by one allowing for periods of personal isolation. Commenting on changes in the lifestyle of the English upper classes across this period, Lawrence Stone observes that 'house plans allocated space to corridors, which now allowed access without intruding on privacy', and 'private rooms, like "the study", "my lord's chamber", "my lady's chamber", were built for individual seclusion.'[25] The early modern period also sees – a related and overlapping phenomenon – widespread provision of larger houses with closets, offset small rooms with lockable doors which might be used for prayer, study, conversation, sexual activities which were to go unacknowledged, or the sequestration of valued possessions.[26]

For a comparable practical device – operating at an only slightly lower level of tangibility – which made for experience's privatization, it is also worth considering the era's newly developed technology of print. Cecile Jagodzinsky has argued that the experience of private reading, which the dissemination of printed texts hugely facilitated, helped to produce an enhanced sense of individual separateness from the group, by promoting awareness of the difference between the self that reads – known in the first place only *to* itself – and the self known to the world, and by functioning to establish that the workings of this removed self *need not be* made known to others, that it exists independently of 'public' selfhood.[27] Here it is worth considering, for instance, the angling of Shakespeare's sonnets towards their reader. They were published in 1609, at a time when Shakespeare stood in high repute as a dramatist; his plays were quite often staged, and a number of them could be read in makeshift printed versions issued to meet public demand. In presentation and content, however, the *Sonnets* drive a wedge between the Shakespeare of the theatre, and Shakespeare the publishing poet, in this second persona known primarily for the narrative poems *Venus and Adonis* and *The Rape of Lucrece*. Sonnets 110 and 111 allude clearly to the author's public career as a playwright and actor in which he has, in their language, 'Gor'd [severely wounded, let bleed]' his 'own thoughts'[28] in offering them up as theatrical fare, made himself 'a motley to the view', and in general terms gained a living at the cost of being personally demeaned and diminished. The sonnet collection itself, headed on the title page 'SHAKE-SPEARES SONNETS / Neuer before Imprinted', is on the other hand to be understood as offering something more distinctive, personal and generically elevated than a crowd-pleasing play, something which, for author and reader, communicates more directly with significant experience which has been privately acquired. The narrative material of the *Sonnets* may be in large part or entirely fictional – there is no way of gauging its personal authenticity in this sense. Nevertheless, the relationship formed by this printed text with its audience is evidently assumed to be more personal and intimate than that formed by a play, and reading of it is taken to involve a cultivation of thoughts and feelings which are removed from the common sphere.[29] It is not very long after the inception of printing that books cease to present themselves as common intellectual property, which had been the ordinary status of texts circulating in manuscript; most gain an author's name on the title page, and characterize themselves as presentations of a discourse pertaining to that author with which readers, typically facing them in the first place as items on public sale, will now decide whether or not to become personally acquainted.

Individualized rooms, closets, books personally chosen from a stall – as things in use all could and, it seems, often did, raise the perceived value and significance of experience gained in privacy – though it should be noted at the same time that as artefacts they are available for different kinds of use:

withdrawal into a private space may be conceived primarily as self-preparation for public engagement,[30] the content of a book bought by an individual may be shared with others through reading aloud, conversation or storytelling;[31] and so on. From this point on, however, I shall transfer attention to another kind of device which, to a greater extent than a room or the printed word as such, *determines* the kind of awareness which it generates and in this sense the use to which it is put. Such a device is a literary construct which, in controlled fashion, conducts its reader through a series of perceptions and standpoints such that the world looks rather different in the text's final perspective when one sets this beside its first one (see dynamic treatments of the viewer–image relation in Baroque painting). Some of these managed shiftings of perspective – ones of high incidence, we find, in early modern writing – produce a re-conceptualization of private experience, of public experience and of the difference between them.[32] I shall explain what I mean with the help of a well-known poem by Donne.

'The Canonization', probably written in the 1590s, offers in sequence three different perceptions of private experience. I shall attempt to track the poem's line of thought before returning to separate consideration of these controlled alterations of view. The poem begins with the male speaker's vehement rejection of a piece of proffered advice: he has, it seems, been rebuked by a male friend or intimate for attaching too much significance to a private relationship of love. The first riposte, angrily defensive, suggests that the charge has in some degree unsettled him. Instead of rebutting the charge he shouts down his interlocutor, telling him not to broach this topic at all:

> For Godsake hold your tongue, and let me love,
> > Or chide my palsie, or my gout,
> My five gray haires, or ruin'd fortune flout.[33]

There are, he tells this bearer of unwanted counsel, plenty of other things to do which common judgement treats as valid behaviour in the common sphere: 'Observe (. . .) the King's reall, or his stamped face'; that is, 'Go to court, or make money.' There is evidently a lack of connection between what is true for the speaker in the private sphere, and what is commonly, publicly, taken or observed to be true; attempts to connect them produce absurdity. The second stanza elaborates fancifully on the idea that what the speaker does or suffers as a lover exerts no effects whatsoever on the wider world, and is in the world's perspective utterly innocuous: 'What merchants ships have my sighs drown'd? / Who saies my teares have overflow'd his ground?' The third stanza of this five-stanza poem functions, however, as a kind of hinge in the development of its thought, and it is worth pausing on the distinctive character of what now occurs.

This third stanza begins with what seems to be acceptance of an insult. But it transpires that this is a tactical move which allows the speaker to pursue a new and most unusual line of thought, leading towards the lovers' elevating transfiguration:

> Call us what you will, wee are made such by love;
>   Call her one, mee another flye,
> We'are Tapers too, and at our owne cost die,
>   And wee in us finde the'Eagle and the dove,
>   The Phoenix riddle hath more wit
>   By us, we two being one, are it.
> So, to one neutrall thing both sexes fit,
>   Wee dye and rise the same, and prove
>   Mysterious by this love.

Flies in this era project the idea of a sordidly familiar and unbridled sexuality, as in Lear's 'Yon gilded fly doth lecher in my sight.' Self-melting candles carry obvious phallic significance. The concluding couplet alludes to the repeatable *petite mort* of orgasm. But these evocations of very ordinary, implicitly 'low', sexual activity have become in this stanza, most remarkably, the armature of a symbolism pointing towards transcendence of and triumph over the ordinary. The references to the eagle, the dove and the phoenix, opaque in character and hieratically suggestive, intimates that the sexual union of the lovers embodies some high mystery; and there is agreement among the poem's commentators that these three birds link connotatively in the field of alchemical practice. Stanton Linden notes that they are 'among the most common symbols in alchemical literature and pictorial art and are often, as here, used to represent substances and stages in the alchemical process';[34] in other words, the avian passage in the stanza more or less inescapably alludes to alchemy's transformation of initially 'low' or relatively worthless physical material, as raising of matter towards a perfected state. The paradoxical assertion being made, then, is that precisely by sharing love in the ordinary sense the speaker and his loved one access a realm of experience which is of the highest value, and beyond ordinary reach. (This statement is not, it should be said, self-evidently true as articulated, but one of its governing ideas seems to be, that through freely attaching value to a common experience the lovers raise it decisively above the merely common: subjective affirmation creates its own kind of intrinsic worth.) The stanza's own metaphoric procedures are thus tantamount to an alchemical act of transformation performed on what was in the first place unelevated and unpromising material, the banal facts of sexual coupling.

The concluding stanzas celebrate an achieved reversal of perspective: the ordinary world is considered again, but from the new standpoint which the poem has attained, where the lovers are raised far above it. In the fourth stanza poems written in celebration of these lovers – presumably including the present one – are imagined as hymns addressed to them as saints, and the final stanza gives us the prayer which the world, now composed of their devotees, delivers to them. The experience which the lovers possess *à deux* is now taken to subsume, as the greater subsumes the lesser, the shared experience of all human beings. 'Countries, Townes, Courts', defining that public sphere whose importance seemed to mock the speaker in the first stanza, now offer nothing of value which the lovers do not already possess, and even possess through the simple act of beholding one another: a private experience of lovers can thus be treated as offering the collective experience of human beings in epitome.[35]

This performance by Donne bridges two very different, and indeed incompatible, intuitions concerning the nature of valid, self- and world-defining experience: it is found in 'countries, towns, courts', representing the shared world of collective life; it is found in a very private domain, in this case a domain of sexual union accessible only to the speaker and his lover. The form of the argument suggests that the second domain does not merely offer an alternative to the first, but positively replaces it by containing everything that it contains in a real and perceptible albeit miniaturized form.[36] A similar thought occurs in Donne's 'The Sunne Rising', where the sun is informed that in warming the speaker ('all Princes') and his love ('all States') he warms an entire world; this is the 'world' of the lovers which contains, making individually accessible, everything of value which to be found in a larger world that can now be ignored.[37] The argument of the poem has been pulled across a kind of lip or threshold, as a consequence of which privately gained experience gains a very enticing allure as well as a compelling authority which publicly mediated experience now patently lacks. 'The Canonization's' unabashed dealings in hyperbole convey even to modern readers the shock of the new. Its three organizing moments of vision are the following: (1) a registering of dissociation between what private experience and publicly validated experience affirm, where private experience has no assured value; (2) a highly unexpected discovery of transcendent value in the sexual acts which, though generically commonplace and demeaning in the world's ordinary view, are known in their commanding particularity only to these lovers; (3) a seeing of the entire world again from this newly discovered and newly affirmed subjective, community-independent standpoint. There is, then, a certain dialectical coherence to the poem's project, as placing in sequence an experiencing of self-separation from the group, an experiencing of this separated state as having worth, including worth as a conveyor of insights, for the individual which should also be acknowledged by all, and an experiencing of the public world as diminished in relation to a newly affirmed privacy. I ask the reader to bear these three kinds of experience, and their potential relation, in mind, because they sketch in preliminary form the concerns of this study's three main sections. The chapter which follows pursues the underlying question of cultural change.

The Private and the Communal – Degrees of Separation

I have written so far of public and private spheres of experience which can be differentially valued, and of devices, including poems, which can function in certain contexts to support or produce perception of private experience as possessing a special value of its own. This takes us a certain way into the topic, but begs a question concerning the nature of the cultural transition from the middle ages through early modernity to the modern era. I have drawn attention to an influential academic view, resembling Jacob Burckhardt's and standing in some continuity with it, according to which medieval culture did not recognize, perhaps did not even have, subjective experience as distinct from the collective experience belonging to individuals as the members of a group. Addressing these assumptions, David Aers and Lee Patterson have pointed out forcefully enough that they are untenable, that they do not survive minimal familiarity with the evidence: medieval literature and medieval culture in general are very pervasively concerned with forms of subjective experience.

Nevertheless, I wish to take the historical discussion a stage further by examining certain features of the early modern transition which have just been brought to a focus in discussion of Donne's 'The Canonization'. This poem certainly arrives at a perspective where private experience has acquired more lustre than public, outward-facing experience, projected in the first stanza as the perceptions of the typical courtier or person of business. But it achieves this as literary device on the basis of producing, in stages, a powerful categorical *separation* of public and private experience; this is by no means in place for thought at the start of the poem, where the speaker becomes rattled on being told what the world in general makes of his privately valued love. Plainly an attribution of distinctive significance to private experience, when set beside public experience, requires a capacity and disposition to view the two as different, as being relatively unlinked in their formation. But there were procedures of thought current in medieval to early modern culture whose effect, while not one of suppressing private experience or diminishing its perceived importance, was to produce a relatively 'light' conceptual polarization of private experience and experience publicly shared or affirmed.

Let us consider for a moment the medieval morality play (a modern term, of course), that genre of symbolic drama which is, in the common critical view, tilted a long way in the direction of experiential collectivism. It sometimes centres on a character who speaks as one generically human (*Humanum Genus*, Mankynde, Everyman), and whose course of life as affected by good and evil forces is meant to be received as typifying that of human beings in general. Nevertheless, on inspection these figures turn out to be *both* omni-representative *and* instances of the irreducibly individual. As V. A. Kolve points out, the central figure of *Everyman* is linguistically constructed simultaneously in the plural and in the singular: he speaks both for or as the 'we' of humankind, and as 'I', a man from the contemporary world who happens to have been crossing the space of action as Death looks on at the play's start;[1] the audience's registration of this man as a particular person or kind of person quite properly leaks into its registration of his character as Everyman, as well as vice versa. Mankynde (in the play usually thus named) and his spiritual counsellor, Mercy, seem to be a farmer and a friar from the performance's environs as well as persons typed by what their names designate. *Humanum Genus* in *The Castle of Perseverance*, as well as figuring Humankind in a generalized theological conception, is a prosperous burgher who fits well into the play's East Anglian milieu. The one form of perception obtains alongside the other, much as the donor of a church window from the period can be seen kneeling in the same visual space as the intercessory saint – no series of major conceptual reframings and adjustments seems to be required in making the transition in either direction between attunement to the distinctively individual and to the attributively universal.[2] There is something here that is alien to modern consciousness, in so far as for the latter thoughts of the individual are more strongly demarcated from thoughts of the individual's participation in shared life. I shall examine certain features of medieval to early modern culture which make for perception of some degree of contiguity, implying 'light' or unstrenuous conceptual differentiation, between subjective experience and experience attributable to a group. They will continue to have a bearing on this study, since they are put directly at issue in the texts which are to be examined in the chapters which follow.

Environments of influence, cosmomorphism

I shall begin with an influential environment of a kind posited by well-defined traditions of classical to early modern thought. For us, in watching a play it is easy to suppose that at certain moments all the members of the audience are having a fairly similar emotional experience. But the classical world defined a scientific framework within which it was considered possible to explain, invoking active though impalpable influence, how such uniform effects can be produced at once in a group of people. The principle which comes into play may be termed *pneumatism*, where *pneuma* is – in a first approximation – a universal spirit-ether, itself in some manner alive, which pervades and interconnects the components of the physical universe.[3] One of the intellectual attractions of *pneumatism* is that it purports to establish a bridge between spiritual and physical phenomena, so explaining, for example, how something that arises first in the imagination of one person can come to exert a powerful emotional effect on others. In the instance of theatre, let us consider the hypothetical path along which a special movement of *pneuma* (Latin *spiritus*) in the actor's mind[4] can be communicated by means of the universal *pneuma* medium to the actor's body, which becomes redolent of a certain emotional state, to the physical space around the actor, and so to the minds and bodies of the audience who are positioned in it.[5] As moderns we usually envisage such tranferences of psychic effects as taking place *via* the medium of perception. But here the transference overleaps perception – is occult, in other words – and therefore operates on and in the mentalities which are affected immediately, and therefore uniformly; subjective experience in such an account is not, in principle, an individually formed response to something perceived, but a state of mind produced by a field of influence directly, which takes more or less the same form for all the minds in which this production occurs.

I begin with classical to early modern *pneumatic* understandings of emotions' passage between separated minds, because they offer one of the more striking instances of an envisaged by-passing of individually formed responses in the establishment of a shared mentality, and because they introduce the idea that separated minds and bodies are connected by a pervasive though impalpable medium. *Pneumatism* was preserved as a principle through the transmission of classical natural philosophy, medicine and rhetoric, the idea of *pneuma*'s existence and activity (to which I shall return) having been given its fullest development by the Stoics. It may be compared with the notion of Ibn Sina (Avicenna), taken up in early modern Europe by Montaigne among others, that the immaterial soul of an individual endowed with sufficient power of will can, via forms arising in that individual's imagination, influence the bodies and minds of others, much as it can influence the individual's own body – say, in inducing processes of healing.[6] Platonic thought also puts forward the principle that the minds of individuals are connected with their environments, including the minds of others, outside processes of perception, because the components of the cosmos at all levels are interconnected in their activity by the internal relations of the World Soul (see *Timaeus* 34b–37c), partly perceptible in so far as they have a fixed configuration as relations of musical harmony.

It is worth dwelling for a moment on what cosmological theory in the broadly Platonic style, underpinned by the traditions of Pythagoreanism, does with the experience of the individual in the private and public aspects of its formation. The *Rule of St. Benedict* (c. 540), foundational for Western monasticism, prescribes, as John Jeffries Martin puts it, that

> the interior self (. . .) be fashioned to correspond to the language of the *Psalms* that punctuated the monk's daily life, as when Benedict counsel[s] monks to pray in such a way '*ut mens nostra concordat voci nostrae* – that our mind be in accordance with our voice.'[7]

The concord here is musical in conception. Alain de Lille, discussing the liturgy in the twelfth century, explains that *symphonia* arises through the coincidence of speech acts and mind.[8] Ficino writes in the fifteenth that 'no harmony gives greater delight than that of heart and tongue,' explicating this rather more fully in a letter on music which states that 'a man is not harmoniously formed who does not delight in harmony, (. . .) for God rejoices in harmony to such an extent that he seems to have created the world especially for this reason, that all its individual parts should sing harmoniously to themselves and to the whole universe.'[9] Ficino's language, matching that of earlier writers in the Platonic tradition, intimates that the *harmonia* or *consonantia* which is being lauded has a double aspect: it is between the subjective self (*homo interior*) and the outward-facing one made manifest to others in action and language; but it is also and more fundamentally between the self in both of these constitutions, internal and externally related, and the order of a harmonious universe which subtends them, making the achievement of harmony in individual life a possibility. Transmitted classical thought, especially Platonic and Stoic, recommends human integration with a cosmos which is already integrated in an optimal form, while more specifically Christian reasoning points to underlying human likeness to God, whose image the spiritual life bids to recover. In both perspectives, however, it appears both possible and necessary to consider the individual's subjective life and communal life, together and without priority, as frameworks for participation in the order of an extra-human reality. Martin contrasts this vision with one that elevates personal 'sincerity', as put forward by key Reformation thinkers; here reference to an enfolding order is stripped away, and the injunction laid on the individual who searches for salvation is to give inner thought and feeling suitable communicative form: how else could one come under the proper scrutiny of others, and of the self which renders to itself an account of what it is?

I have already drawn attention to the medieval to early modern period's most widespread manner of thinking which posits an interactive relationship of individual and cosmos, which is the one adducing the presence of an omni-connective *pneuma*. It gains additional strength in the latter part of this period by virtue of the recovery and widened dissemination of classical texts. Cicero, the principal transmitter of Stoic thought to later eras, states that we find in the world abundant evidence of 'affective sympathy, sharing of a spirit (breath), interconnection and kinship between things (*rerum consentiens conspirans continuata cognata*).'[10] The idea of a universal interconnective medium can also be situated within the frameworks of Aristotelian and Platonic philosophy. Ptolemy explains the functioning of the cosmic relations with which astrology is concerned by reference to

> a certain power emanating from the ethereal eternal substance [the Aristotelian
> fifth element or quintessence, which] is dispersed through and permeates the
> whole region about the earth, [and is] throughout (. . .) subject to change, since,
> of the primary sublunary elements, fire and air are encompassed and changed by
> the motions in the ether, and in turn encompass and change all else, earth and
> water and the plants and animals therein.[11]

The notion of the Aristotelian quintessence, a kind of materially exiguous all-pervasive ether, remained important for early modern alchemical thought, and was certainly among the available explanations of cosmic *sumpatheia* (sympathy, interconnection). For Ficino and Giambattista Della Porta, however, the envisaged medium of interconnection between separated things is Plato's already mentioned World Soul, the notion of which was elaborated in particular by the Neoplatonists: having a unitary soul, the world is to be conceived as a unitary body. Brian Copenhaver summarizes Ficino's position thus:

> Bound together physically and metaphysically, the parts of the world constitute
> 'a living thing more unified than any other', a cosmic organism. Since the limbs

and organs of any animal affect one another, the influence of every part of this perfect organism on all other parts will be even stronger, helping the World's Body to move, live and breathe. Its breath is the cosmic spirit which, when applied to our spirit, connects us to the animate heavens.[12]

Della Porta writes,

> Virgil calleth this Spirit [which draws the cosmos into unity], The soul of the World; The Spirit, saith he, cherisheth it within, and conveying itself through the inmost parts, quickens and moves the whole lump, and closeth with this huge body. (. . .) The parts of this huge world (. . .) are knit together by the bond of one Nature: therefore as in us the brain, the lights, the heart, the liver, and other parts of us do receive and draw mutual benefit from one another, so that when one part suffers, the rest also suffer with it; even so the parts and members of this huge creature the World, I mean all the bodies that are in it, do in good neighbour-hood as it were, lend and borrow each others Nature; for by reason that they are linked in one common bond, therefore they have love in common; and by force of this common love, there is amongst them a common attraction, or tilting of one of them to another.[13]

Della Porta here is thinking Platonically, while also invoking Virgil's 'divine mind' (*mens divina*)[14], and the love (*philia*) which in thought stemming from the pre-Socratics draws together and binds the potentially scattered components of the cosmos. Consideration of a style of thinking which manifestly stands at the confluence of several philosophical–ethical–scientific traditions encourages us to draw two important interpretative inferences.

Thinkers of the early modern period were not entirely consistent, or even necessarily self-consistent, in their explications of cosmic interconnectedness (there was no uniform 'world picture', of the kind which Enlightenment science would seek to define).[15] But they enjoyed a degree of improvisatory freedom in giving an account of such matters, because they shared certain intuitions about what such interconnectedness was or consisted in, and of why the idea of it merited acceptance. Specifically, they carried over from ancient, especially Stoic, thought the idea that what self-evidently applies in the body of man also applies in 'the body of the world' where human life is embedded.[16] As Plotinus expresses it,

> all things must be enchained; and the sympathy and correspondences obtaining in any one closely knit organism must exist, first, and most intensely, in the All.[17]

The spontaneous interconnectedness of the living body, such that the manner of functioning of any part of it bears immediately on the well-being of other parts, and of the whole, must also be that of the universe where the body is formed and has its life. Anglo-American academics have become overly accustomed to discussing thought of this kind under the heading of 'macrocosm-microcosm analogy'. There is agreement that the idea is widespread in early modern accounts of the human state, but little on the optimal means of bringing it to bear in critical examination of the era's art and thought. For present purposes I wish to emphasize not what the sense of a microcosm to be observed at hand draws into formal correspondence – given that the planes of potential correspondence, making for possible interaction, cannot in principle be exhaustively or definitively mapped[18] – but what it draws into assumedly active interrelationship, so making individual life and communal life simultaneously analogous to and aspects of a larger life attributed to the world.

Anthropology offers a term which may help us to sharpen conceptions of the collective human subject as entertained by important traditions of classical-to-early modern thought familiarly entertain: such a subject is 'cosmomorphic',[19] in the sense that it is seen as being constituted by shared human connectedness with an enfolding environment which is held to have a degree of integration or unitary life – the notion of a 'cosmos' implies as much – producing integration or unity in the collective subject itself. Cosmomorphism as I am defining it is an understanding of the individual self formed partly on the basis of its assumed continuities with the surrounding world, including that of human others, against a background of acceptance that the self subsists to a major extent *in* its nexus of world-self relationships; on which account individual selves and their experiences must have a good deal in common. One well-established form of such thinking occurs in typical classical-to-early modern medical, in origin Hippocratic and Galenic, constructions of the individual mind and body, whose constitution and disposition are considered to be related to and interlinked with those of the cosmos.[20] Peter Brown characterizes the humourally regulated bodies of this medical tradition as 'little fiery universes through whose heart, brain and veins there pulsed the same heat and vital spirit as glowed in the stars.'[21] Redolent in its internal make-up of the shared human life-world, the individual body is thus to be maintained in or conducted towards health through its exposure to and functional alignment with appropriate cosmic influences. Associated with this view is the Galenic tendency not to assign diseases specific aetiologies, but to explain them uniformly through the flow and balance of the humours, a continuing phenomenon of every body's individual existence. Early modern medical theory and practice is one of the obvious naturalizations of a cosmomorphic view of things, showing that it continued to influence enquiry. When William Harvey presents his highly innovatory account of the blood's circulation, he offers intuitive confirmation of its rightness not by explaining the properties of pumps, but by pointing to the familiar circular motions of the cosmos and adducing the principle of macrocosmic–microcosmic similarity.[22]

The collective human subject and its representations

I shall now shift attention to another form of cultural practice whose effect was to sustain the notion that individual perception can access that of a collective human subject. It will be helpful to begin with the specific example of events in which the notion came under hostile scrutiny; what we find here will also have a bearing on the argument of the sections which follow. I draw on Emmanuel Le Roy Ladurie's brilliant study of a carnival held at Romans, in south central France, between 1579 and 1580 with considerable social and political fallout.[23]

Ladurie examines the symbolizations and counter-symbolizations which were put into public view by the city's politically antipathetic groups. The interpretative issues to which they gave rise were drastically resolved, finally, in a patrician-directed massacre of craftsmen and agricultural workers. Much of the Romans carnival consisted of activities arranged by or focused on temporarily formed 'kingdoms' (*reynages*), made up of young to middle-aged men from the city. A *reynage* was usually established through the mounting of a foot-race, for which some bird or animal was the designated prize. The two *reynages*, respectively patrician and plebeian, which assumed the most overtly political roles in the events of 1579–80 were named after the partridge and the capon. The background for plebeian hostility to the patricians can be sketched in by saying that some of the latter had recently exercised a pretended aristocratic right to be exempt from taxes, producing widespread resentment. In one of their street dances the members of the plebeian Capon Kingdom expressed, in an oblique symbolism, their sense of a need for rectification through some imposition of justice – quite simply, groups wearing shrouds danced with rakes, brooms and flails. As Ladurie explains, these dances possessed both a traditional symbolic–mythic and an immediate politically aggressive significance: they mimed preparations for spring sowing and the growing of new crops, a matter of threshing the old crop and sweeping away (enacting the 'death') of useless straw and chaff; they also mimed – or, let us say, were understood by some to have mimed – the destruction of anti-social evildoers, in context the privileged and corrupt. The Capons also set up the cry of 'Flesh of Christians, four deniers the pound,' a carnivalesque 'world turned upside-down' joke where human meat is substituted for that of animals, but also conceivably an allusion to actual and impending human slaughter. The dances and the street cries were blackly humorous, where the humour seems to have been sharpened by certain suggestions of threat. What they *signified* in a drawing together of traditional and familiar images was broadly clear, a sweeping away of the old year's remnants in the interests of renewal. But what they *meant*, as an indictment of particular social groups and possible call to violent action, was not clear at all, and presumably not designed to be so: if they did issue a specific threat, its scale remained unspecified; these were still, after all, manifestations of carnival, which could within a customary framework be expected to lead only to more of the same. The Partridges responded in the event, however, not with countering acts of carnival symbolization but with organized slaughter of the Capons. This may be seen as a representative catastrophe of its times in that communal festivity, structured along traditional lines, became or was received as destructive of political order in a conception now moving into dominance, namely that of unremitting top-down control.

Considered as pieces of signification, the carnival dances of the plebeians at Romans possess a pronounced intertextuality; the dance with the flails, for example, places itself at a point of overlapping between 'winter corn-threshing' as necessary and familiar activity, more abstractly 'enactment of the old year's death', and perhaps, at a level of concrete implication, 'this is what we'd like to do to certain people.' The product of such overlapping is considerably instability of meaning; which has the corollary that registration of context will do a great deal to determine the meaning that is received (there had presumably been other years in which similar dances had not been taken to embody a drastic threat). Kristeva defines intertextuality as 'the formation of a specific signifying system (. . .)[24] as a result of the redistribution of several different sign-systems.'[25] Intertextuality is a characteristic feature of premodern collective representations, as it were the 'thoughts' of a posited collective human subject. Organized around focal images which typically have the human body at their centre, they function as fields for the collocation of discourses which can be brought into resemblance while lacking full conceptual alignment; they identify areas of possible correspondence – making for a degree of reciprocal mapping – between ideas of similar formation which have partly differing import. An instance would be the Pauline metaphoric armour of the Christian (*Eph.* 6:11–18), as superimposed on the concerns of actual warfare in the image of a warrior taking up arms. One might say that collective representations gain cultural currency partly *as a means of* mediating and organizing conceptual tensions of this kind. W. B. Yeats offers the comparable idea that in a given cultural context certain representations may be invested with 'emotion of multitude':[26] they are, in their phenomenological profile, for the many, because evoking through a compressed symbolism the multifariousness of ambient human existence.

The conspicuous setting in play of intertextual relationships is also characteristic of premodern literary practice. Walter J. Ong observes that, as compared with early modern print-centred culture,

> manuscript culture had taken intertextuality for granted. (. . .) It deliberately created texts out of other texts, borrowing, adapting, sharing the common, originally oral, formulas and themes, even though it worked them up into fresh literary forms impossible without writing. Print culture of itself has a different mind. It tends to feel a work as 'closed', set off from other works, a unit in itself.[27]

It is noticeable that printed texts tend to suppress or camouflage discursive dissonance as produced by intertextual relationship. Returning to what was said in the prefatory chapter, one of the marks of a printed text's envisaged lack of intertextual connection is its attribution – in the rapidly developing early modern practice – to a named *author*: the attribution of some degree of finality and context-independence in what is being presented, vouchsafed by this ostensibly personal assumption of responsibility for the text considered as statement.

Conversely, premodern literary composition freely cultivates the common-place, a recognized and much frequented 'locality' (*topos*) in discourse where otherwise dispersed fields of discourse overlap. These places in discourses are regarded as being places in shared experience. Ancient oratory had identified *koinoi topoi*, Latin *loci communes*, generally accepted propositions about 'the way things are' which can in principle be slotted into any number of particular persuasive arguments. They are given a prominent role, for example, in Aristotle's *Rhetoric*.[28] Ernst Curtius notes that, with the later classical dissolution of political and judicial rhetoric as an independent form, the practice of organizing discourse around familiar *topoi* 'penetrated into all literary genres'.[29]

Curtius' monumental *European Literature and the Latin Middle Ages* provides a very useful overview of themes, structured by relatively consistent formats of presentation, which are commonly taken up in the educated writing of the period. Nevertheless, it is necessary to make two practical modifications to Curtius' approach. A *topos* remains recognizable, self-evidently, by retaining some consistency of presentational format; but we should understand that it is kept in place not by the weight of tradition but because it stands at a confluence between several streams of active thinking. A representative example, and one which metaphorically defines a location in the ordinary sense, is the *locus amoenus* or delightful (physical-literary) place, a focal presentation of what is most pleasing about the natural world which became (and of course remains) rich in cultural connotation: for a writer or reader conversant with its possibilities it could evoke inter alia an Edenic or otherwise paradisal human state, sensual or spiritual bliss, the genitals, the luxuriance of natural growth, and the prolificness of literary invention itself.[30] Moreover, one may further adjust Curtius in noting that orientation towards the literary *topos* melded in practice with orientation towards the culturally focal image, which might be given definition in any medium. Obvious examples from medieval culture are the visual templates offered by a monarch enthroned, and by church architecture which combines allusion to, among other things, the form of Christ's body, and of a ship ('nave' = *navis*). A later section of this account will consider the importance of the medieval to early modern idea of *mirroring* – projected in many book titles of the period[31] – as defining the relationship between a culturally focal image and the beholder. What such a 'mirror' is to be imagined as reflecting is collective experience, extended in its delineation because laid down across space and time, in a form now made accessible to individual knowledge.

Medieval to early modern academic enquiry also possesses a non-visual counterpart to the culturally focal image which channels collective experience. It is another version of the figurative common place, an area of experience which has been explored by many and so made over for shared understanding. Academic study and reflection in the dominant Aristotelian tradition gave such understanding the highest epistemological credentials. Conceived anthropomorphically, it is the extensive experience of the collective human subject consolidated as reliable judgement. In the *Posterior Analytics*, part of his *Organon* or fundamental methodology of enquiry, Aristotle addresses a primary question about the acquisition of knowledge. Valid knowledge, so his argument runs, concerns what obtains universally, and it is on the basis of such knowledge that we construct larger inferences about nature or what is. But our given perceptions are of individual occurrences: 'it is impossible to perceive what is universal and holds in every case', and it is therefore evident that 'it is not possible to understand through perception.' By 'perception' (*aistheseis*) in this arresting statement Aristotle means, specifically, *individual* acts of perception. For this way of thinking the experience which yields knowledge of the universal arises in memory's synthesis of many perceptual acts: 'from perception there comes memory (. . .) and from memory (when it occurs often in connection with the same thing), experience (*empeiria*); for memories that are many in number form a single experience.'[32]

It is clear from context, as well as affirmed by the normative medieval to early modern reception of Aristotle, that synthesis of such memories as 'experience' should not be understood as a specifically personal activity. Rather, 'experience' arises out of humanly shared daily and traditional familiarity with the sort of thing that occurs, sometimes as defined in an authoritative statement – this is the domain of the 'probable', in its early modern sense of what is generally taken to be the case.[33] Valid knowledge is thus in its essence a synthesis of common perceptions of what has been undergone by the human collectivity.[34] A good deal of the period's formal enquiries, then, engage with the 'probable' as intrinsically shared or immediately shareable knowledge, that to which more or less anyone with a mind will give assent. In the sphere of natural philosophy, two such items of knowledge would be 'heavy objects fall downwards' and 'fire rises upwards', propositions which ordinary processes of living make self-evident. This epistemological stance is to be sharply distinguished from that taken by the experimentalism, stressing the production, scrutiny and analysis of individual occurrences, which is discernible in the scientific methodologies of William Gilbert and Francis Bacon and which gains greater intellectual prominence in later seventeenth-century Europe.

The culturally focal image performs a distinctive and prominent role under general conditions of illiteracy. We know that most Europeans in the fifteenth century were functionally illiterate. It is true that competence in reading became much more widespread with the arrival of printing, but this change occurred in a cultural setting substantially formed by illiteracy, and did not in the first place much disturb the collectivist sets of mind which were associated with it. Across much of the early modern period, extensive interlinkage between popular knowledge-organizing images and commonplaces of educated writing or speech, which were made more illustrious in their turn by the value which normative study placed on the 'probable', went on functioning to assign the subjective experience of the individual a significant embedding in experience which was assumed to be shared.

Play and the thinness of civilization

The final set of factors to be considered as bearing on cultural fashionings of the distinction between public and private come into play as a certain coincidence of content between aristocratic ideologies and those of peasants, burghers and artisans. We can sketch the area of coincidence by pointing out that all of these social groups tended to participate, at the same time and even with some degree of solidarity, in the communal festivals which were an important feature of medieval-to-early modern social life. Often but not exclusively occurring on holy days defined by the church calendar, these festivals had as their most obvious common feature the shared playing of games, and especially the taking of roles and acting by rules which were different from those of ordinary life.[35] Returning to Ladurie's examination of such a festival in later sixteenth-century France will be of help in establishing certain festive norms.

The wide currency of 'King' as an English surname is probably explained not so much by claims laid to royal connection or descent, as by the practice of assigning individuals the role of king or group-leader in games collectively played out. The primary function of such a temporary king is to assign and authorize the unusual, non-everyday conventions – sometimes termed 'misrule', though probably 'other rule' would be more appropriate – by which his temporary followers were expected to behave.[36] Sometimes festivities as conducted by a larger community would mobilize several such groups, as occurred at Romans. Temporary kings might be enthroned in parallel with temporary queens. Or, a woman of high social status might become an autonomous figure of special, interim authority; the practice is recalled in an episode from Malory's Arthurian cycle where the real Queen Guinevere assumes the role of a May Queen, decreeing that ten knights – her band of personal followers, who are to be clad richly in green for the occasion – will ride out Maying with her early one morning into the woods and fields beyond the court.[37]

Although the connection is unobvious in a modern perspective, such seasonal games and sanctioned role-playing abut conceptually on 'game' in the other senses of quarry hunted and the recreation of hunting. What the two kinds of play have in common is in the first place a placing in partial and temporary abeyance of the norms of everyday life. Festivity sanctions forms of behaviour which have somewhat different ground rules from the ones which ordinarily obtain; some festivities, especially those associated with the coming of summer, produce a relaxation of social codes and tempered movement towards wildness. The hunter is similarly drawn away from the ordinary social world by the requirements of entering a wild space and pursuing the creatures which inhabit it. Festivity and hunting impact in similar ways on the cultural imagination, as a keeping in view of collective fashioning of life in the interests of well-being: the civilizing order is itself seen, in the perspectives which they create, as a kind of interim organization placed on the natural energies from which human life is never entirely remote. If civilization bears a certain *resemblance* to play, as a submission of behaviour to rules which can at certain times be altered, it is divided by no insurmountable barrier from the wildness and anorder which are its conceptual antithesis.

The later fourteenth-century romance known as *Sir Gawain and the Green Knight*[38] is so designed as to project a notion of civilization's 'thinness', which comprises recognition of both its necessity and its precariousness with respect to the forces which it seeks to contain and subdue. The action of this narrative moves with extreme clarity between forest or wild zones, which Gawain first enters by making an arduous winter journey and his host at the unfamiliar castle enters by hunting, and zones of conspicuously civilized life, King Arthur's court and the stylistically *à la mode* castle in which Gawain finds (seeming) respite. Hunting in the wilds enables the lord of the castle to explore a state of labile transition between 'culture' and 'nature'. The hunts proceed according to explicit and fairly elaborate predetermined rules,[39] but allow for wild self-abandonment and, in the case of the boar hunt, a deliberate courting of danger. The carcasses of the lately hunted deer are rapidly transformed – on the spot, by expert huntsmen – into portions of meat suitable for gift-giving and exchange; part of the civilized prestige of such 'game' meat is that it directly recalls hunting in its character of archaic, quasi-feral act. Gawain, praying to Christ and Mary in acknowledgement of his human sinfulness, makes of the winter journey with its trials of physical endurance an act of penitence and spiritual self-emptying, involving a stripping away of familiar, habituated, socially supported modes of thought and behaviour.[40]

In these instances, the lord of the castle and Gawain both arrive at a kind of privacy by having dealings with what is relatively wild and contingent, at a distance from the shared spaces of communal life. Medieval romance offers still more radical exposition of 'wild' privacy in those episodes from the careers of the lover-knights Lancelot and Tristan where, driven by an anguish which alienates them from human association, they go to dwell in forest wastes. For a period they lead a barely human existence which includes a forgoing of sociable behaviour, even of language. The consolidation of this narrative motif is assisted in Middle English contexts by the phonic coincidence of 'wood', carrying its modern meaning of 'area with trees', and 'wood' meaning 'mad'. Going wild or mad is not, for Lancelot or Tristan, a therapeutic or otherwise constructive experience, but a making of deeper entry to state of disconnection from shared life which their sufferings have already produced. They are eventually discovered by chance, and led back to human and courtly surroundings where socially conformable behaviour is relearned, although the underlying personal and social difficulties remain. But, as well as defining conditions of 'wild' privacy which, as conceived by the culture, differ markedly from ordinary, sociable conditions of existence,[41] *Sir Gawain and the Green Knight* explores a different kind of privacy, that established between two people in a domestic space – in this case, a bedchamber – removed from general view.[42] Gawain, as the story's central figure, is troubled by the difficulty of establishing a relationship between what occurs here, in an (apparently) isolated transaction between two people, and what occurs before the eyes of the immediate community in transactions made in the course of shared merrymaking between him and the lord of the castle. This difficulty is compounded by awareness that what occurs in both spheres partakes of the character of play, and is partly governed by special rules which stand apart from those of ordinary life.

The romance is persistently ironic about claims which might be made for the civilized nature of what occurs in 'interior' privacy between Gawain and the lady of the castle. Gawain is flattered and otherwise pressured into viewing the 'love-talking' (sexually inflected courtly conversation) which the pair sustain on successive days as a kind of aesthetic-*cum*-moral achievement. But the lord of the castle, who has been aware of this by-play throughout (since he instigated it), removes from Gawain the satisfaction of viewing what has occurred in private between him and the lady as possessing value: true, he resisted her sexual advances; but he also became guilty of deceit in not handing over a gift which the lady has given him – a requirement of the game transactions made between him and the lord in communal view. What had looked to Gawain like an achievement of civilization, as implementation of *courtoisie* – courtly manners and virtues – is thus reclassified for him as a kind of wildness which has gone unrecognized as such. As it happens, the form of the narrative has already intimated as much by embedding the interior-private scenes, with their atmosphere of stealth and deceit, within scenes of hunting. What the lord of the castle finally offers the discomfited Gawain is a return to moral reliance on public transactions, preferably those made between men,[43] in a world where the stresses of communal life are offset by phases of self-dedication to absolute play, lacking in moral significance. The romance accords 'interior' privacy some intrinsic value – it is the space in which Gawain arrives at the knowledge of self which is required for the making of Christian confession[44] – but treats as perilous attempts to extend its scope in the management of life. *Exactly when* Gawain supposes that self-awareness gained in private is of the greatest personal use and benefit, it is feeding him false information; whereas, at least the self-examination required as preparation for confession can be guided by a priest.

Briefly, then, this fourteenth-century romance, an unusually sophisticated piece of writing but representative of the dominant social mentality of its era, differentiates the self of culture and cultivation not only systematically but also *lightly* from the uncultivated or 'wild' self; which carries the corollary that civilized selfhood requires recurrent reinstatement through acts communally performed or performed in general view. Nor does it perceive the civilized self as standing in any necessary connection with the self of 'interior' privacy. It is an important aspect of this way of looking at things that it does not seek to attain an *integrated* perspective on ordinary social selfhood, on festive social selfhood, and on private, socially remote selfhood. It would be for the shared experience of humankind to accommodate all of these modes of experience, while individually lived experience moves discontinuously between them. The knowledge that experience offers remains *specular* in the premodern sense that what artefacts called 'mirrors' reflect is, *ex definitio*, knowledge which the individual does not derive directly from immediate and personal experience. But the mentality which informs *Sir Gawain and the Green Knight* is not much separated in time and milieu from ones in which these assumptions are reversed.

Auspices of cultural change: A disciplinary revolution

The social theorist Norbert Elias, at work between the 1930s and 1960s, drew attention to a factor in early modern culture which made for much increased practical-*cum*-conceptual differentiation of private and communal life; what comes into effect here is consequential on an extension into social life of the functions of the state.[45] It is recognized that this era saw a widespread centralization of state power, going with a ramping up of the state's exercise of authority over the domains which it claimed to govern. This produced the emergence of a state overseen, legal-process-controlled public sphere, whose existence makes certain distinctive requirements of the behaviour of the individual. Active policing of a public sphere – albeit inconsistently put into effect[46] – made for firmer drawing of the boundaries of privacy, and also for the limitation of what one might call spillage from private action into the public zone. A new social regime fairly typical of early modern life, especially in the towns, enjoined and often enforced individual cultivation of self-control and the capacity to restrain unruly emotions' outward expression. An example of these would be emotions which impel preservation of personal honour through duelling; this was determinedly suppressed by early modern state authority in all of its forms, albeit with incomplete success. Elias identifies, with extensive documentation, a series of early modern shifts in prescribed etiquette which made for intensification of the distinction between an interior-private sphere – especially that of the individual body, often bracketed conceptually with the house or room – and a communal, public sphere. They include the covering of the body, emblematic of what is common to human beings, at all possible times, before one's intimates and even oneself, the use of cutlery and personal plates to delimit contact with food and produce personal distancing from the common act of eating, and the curtailment of collective pleasure-taking, as in periods of festival. One of the great merits of Elias' argument is that it connects these and similar shifts, actual or recommended, in individual behaviour closely with shifts in the conception and organization of social power.

Erasmus recommends, in the spirit of his era's disciplinary initiative, that children avoid farting in company and, as revealingly, that they avoid giving the impression that they might be doing so by rocking to and fro.[47] It is the case that farting in this period took on a charged cultural significance as a conspicuous infraction of the public-private boundary, an offensive releasing of something bodily produced into the communal zone. English developed a specialized term, 'foist' (derived from gamblers' use of the word to mean slipping someone an object without their knowing it which is then believed to be theirs), for farting silently, with the intention of disguising a fart's origin and allowing it to be attributed to someone else.[48] Keith Thomas notes that 'the early modern period betrays a continuous preoccupation with "the art of farting decently"', and that there was a cultural fixation on the embarrassment before others that might be caused by inappropriate breaking of wind. This second accrued somewhat ironically in a setting where medical opinion was unanimous on the dangers of seeking to contain intestinal wind inside the body.[49] The recurrent downward expulsion, often unintended, of a repulsive gas, likely to be smelt at once by those in the vicinity, is a fairly good representation of the bodily human as a thing which all inescapably find that they have in common. It is noticeable, however, that in the early modern period a distinctive anxiety often attends perception of individual connectedness with this very ordinary feature of alimentary functioning. And in more general terms the new preoccupation with the individual interior as a highly demarcated zone, qualitatively different from what is external to it, often has psychological consequence, mobilizing awareness of an individual separatedness which begins at the body's boundaries.

We should also take account of the early modern era's many technical innovations or instruments which made for the consolidation of domains of knowledge which are established *in* individual acts of perception as well as *given over to* individual perception, as in the accessing of collective knowledge. These are primarily the instruments and products of a burgeoning practical mathematics which includes the technical devices and operational procedures of navigation, astronomy, surveying, cartography and of image-making within the framework of geometricized vanishing-point perspective, and also the immediately numerical computational procedures of commercial reckoning and account-keeping.[50] It is an important part of my argument that some writing characteristic of the period similarly facilitates novel, individually centred consolidations of what feels like knowledge, while also at times encouraging reflection on the nature of this process.

Moreover, and as is widely recognized, important shifts in spiritual consciousness were bound up with the newly emphatic dissociation of the individual and private from the communal. It can be said, in a permissible generalization, that the Protestant and Catholic Reformations of the sixteenth century attached enhanced importance to personal spiritual states which were for the individual to cultivate, and to be considered in some degree of disconnection from the spiritual life of a community.[51] Jean Delumeau has probably done the most to characterize the period's increased attentiveness to the psychological interior, accessible in the first place to an individual's scrutiny, as the sphere of spiritual well-being.[52] We have been given many accounts of this cultural transition, whose broad features are generally known, though Anglo-American enquiry has tended to associate it too directly and specifically with Protestantism.

Attempting to explain the early modern disciplinary initiative, with its far-reaching if uneven effects, Charles Taylor points to the mutual reinforcement in the period of programmes for religious renewal, especially those set in place by the Protestant and Catholic Reformations, and programmes for civic renewal, broadly inspired by educated humanism with its turn towards classical thought and precedent.[53] The first is an initiative to make laypeople live by religious standards not dissimilar to those expected of the clergy, the two Reformations being the raising to a higher power of medieval initiatives for the securing of fuller lay religious commitment; the second is a decisive empowering of educated, *bien pensant*, professionally competent magistrates, humanism's poster children, who are in principle delegated by princes to administer the public sphere through enforcement of suitable legal codes with generally beneficial results. Where the two impulses coincide we find early modern 'civility', an agenda for the exercise of social power such that elites set about moulding the behaviour of the governed extensively in the interests of order and piety. Suppression of communal festivity in its interconnection with popular religious practice – a phenomenon which Peter Burke calls the early modern 'Triumph of Lent'[54] – stands at such a point of coincidence, and was one of the major initiatives taken up by civic authorities of the period. It was often accompanied, of course, by elite self-separation from such communal festivity as survived.

It is in sixteenth-century English that we find the first use of the word 'culture' to mean 'the cultivation of the mind, faculties, manners, etc.', and 'improvement by education or training'.[55] This goes with the conception of 'culture', *qua* 'cultivation', as a continuing and unremitting project, quite distinct from medieval prizing of that in culture which stands in self-aware proximity to 'the wild'. James Snead observes, while identifying the singularity of modern Western *mores*, that culture understood in this way

> always also means the *culture* of culture: a certain continuance in the nurture
> of those concepts and experiences which have helped or are helping to lend
> self-consciousness and awareness to a given group. Not only must culture be
> immanent now, but it must also give the promise of being *continuously* so.[56]

The programme of such 'culture' at the individual level is unremitting self-surveillance and self-government in the interests of personal improvement along designated lines; which, as Taylor points out, implies a human subject which should be limitlessly capable of refashioning what it is through a taking of methodical, disciplined action.[57] As brought to bear on the physical world it implies continuous reshaping of the naturally given to meet humanly determined requirements, a project quite alien to that of classical–medieval *techne* which is, of course, embraced by the natural philosophy of Francis Bacon. There is, then, a degree of structural conformity and practical connection between Baconian science, with its transformatory designs on nature, and early modern cultural designs on human material, itself considered to be indefinitely susceptible of improving change.

This returns us to the raised cultural value of 'interiority'. An interior-private space – perhaps a room which can be closed off from the more communal spaces of a household – can be readily conceived as a space which is under the individual subject's control, and in which he/she can shape the experience for which it is the imagined container, one in which things of value will predictably accrue. This coheres with the conception of the mind itself as a sort of container which is at the subject's disposal in a different way from what lies outside it. Jagodzinski argues that print culture made a significant contribution of its own to conceptions of the mental interior as a sort of work-space standing outside the shared human domain. [58] The mind of modernizing thought is a *concentrationnaire* institution, generically similar to the spaces of surveillance and correction in which, as Foucault's first well-known writings point out, the deviant of early modern Europe were increasingly placed. The conception comes to a head philosophically in Locke's account of an individual mind which entirely oversees and manages its own formation: here mind itself has become a fully 'interiorized' phenomenon, *qua* agency that can operate quite independently of its environment, taking charge of its own constitution. The interior-private as seen here is a space where projects of 'culture' can, in principle, be realized *more fully* than in an outer world of relative disorder, cluttered with the insistent presence and activity of others. Erasmus behaviourally predicted the future in his preference for eating alone. Descartes captures a new theme of civilized reflection in stating that most of the troubles of the world arise because people don't know how to sit quietly in their own rooms.

Nevertheless, a self-inconsistent and incomplete revolution

The larger sections of this study will be concerned with (1) the fracturing of cosmomorphic mentalities, (2) the dismantling and replacement of traditional collective representations and (3) the establishment of reflective positions on communal play where it is becoming or has become perceptibly 'common' in a pejorative sense. All can be treated as manifestations of early modern culture's disciplinary transformation, in its role of enforcing replacement of relatively collectivist by relatively individualist mentalities. Nevertheless, in examining what occurs in these areas of thought and practice it is necessary to be continuously aware of the gap between reforming design and what was pragmatically achieved, and of latent incoherencies in the reforming designs themselves. What I term, broadly following Elias, the disciplinary revolution is a project which cannot by its nature be fully accomplished; primarily since, as was noted earlier, it is psychically impossible for an individual finally to become the self-shaping, self-determining monad of Enlightenment thought – though she/he can certainly *imagine* her/himself as having attained this form of existence. It is true that the religious reformations of the sixteenth century sought, in general terms, to promote in the individual mentalities of focused self-awareness going with practices of self-improvement. But churches of the two major formations also acted in certain respects to *restrict* the scope of individual spiritual autonomy, a characteristic requirement being first-person, individually 'owned' statement of some relatively uniform profession of faith or credal formula. The medieval Mass probably offered laypeople more space for private spiritual activity than the post-Tridentine one, which enjoined specified forms of participation. The Protestant churches not only promoted individual reading of the Bible, rejecting the exegetical traditions of Catholicism, but also institutionalized and resolutely enforced *correct* practices of reading.[59] These ostensible anomalies are not atypical of the era. In the areas of culturally significant change to be examined by way of their literary articulation and consideration, we shall find that cultural change is an imbricated process which tends to re-deploy in altered form some of what it may appear to have swept away.

Part A

Introduction

Cosmomorphic Fracture: 'For every man alone thinks that he hath got / To be a Phoenix'

I am calling *cosmomorphism* the conception of the human state such that man and the world share a common life and form a living unity, one aspect of which is that cosmic and natural processes form an *analogue* for related processes in the individual. Cosmorphism involves an understanding of the self formed partly on the basis of its assumed continuities and connections with the surrounding environment, including human others, in a setting of belief that important parts of the self's existence are bound up in its nexus of self-to-world relationships. In the perspectives of anthropology this is a very widespread way of looking at individual existence, in which it is taken for granted that, while some significant parts of the experience of self's existence are separated off from this assumed experience of an enveloping whole, other significant parts are indissociable from it. One experiences the world partly on the basis of personally being an instance or locus of the collective human, because collective human life itself is embedded in a powerfully formative and otherwise influential world environment – something organized and as-if living, a *cosmos*. The organization of the cosmos – generally seen as instancing both sameness and alteration across time, as in the motions of the heavenly bodies – thus hypothetically extends to or includes or otherwise affects or models for understanding the organization of societies, of lower-order relations between individuals, as within family groups, and probably the condition of the individual body with its interacting organs and faculties.

Cosmomorphism of outlook is of very wide geographical diffusion, and has arisen with special predictability in societies whose mainstay is agriculture. Nevertheless, in post-classical Europe and neighbouring regions several factors made for its contestation, and sometimes its marginalization. In particular, the three Abrahamic religions acted to promote its very thorough rethinking, though in general terms without obliterating it. For what is meant by this last statement we may consider the ferocious debates over astrology which are entirely characteristic of medieval to early modern European culture. These debates tip inescapably between 'astrology is a rational putting to use of understanding of the cosmos', and 'astrology denies the sovereignty of God's will';[1] in practice a degree of closure is sometimes imposed on them by *politique* placing of certain kinds of prediction off limits,[2] or by an acceptance of cognitive inadequacy: 'astrological causation is probably real, but human beings are incapable of understanding it.'[3] But scientific enquiry in the emergent modern style constituted a more radical challenge in tending towards a complete discounting of the force of cosmomorphic hypothesis and belief. It is easy to recognize as one of its entering wedges the mid-seventeenth-century 'mechanical philosophy' which purports to make all causation intelligible and scrutable as the effects of collision between particles; causal action at a distance is no longer a tolerable hypothesis.[4] In broader cultural terms, and in a way which helps to contextualize the new practices of science, cosmomorphism of outlook tends to be displaced by the rise of urban life and of manufacturing as a source of wealth.

The prestige widely enjoyed by cosmomophism in the early modern period, and also instances of its drastic loss, raise intriguing questions about the operation of loose intuitions about the world alongside explicitly formulated precepts in the sustaining of a cultural mind-set. It is not helpful to say that early modern Europeans believed that the cosmos was interconnected by an ethereal, influence-transmitting medium making for constant interaction – let us say, the Aristotelian *quintessence* – and therefore thought cosmomorphically, in the way that can be inferred, for example, from much of their medical practice. This is rather like saying that people believe in gravity and therefore do not float away from the earth's surface. Rather, cosmomorphism was embedded in a great deal of early modern cultural practice, so constituting an intuitive reality or generally accepted 'ground' of thinking, and therefore those of educated background who pondered on these matters turned to such explanatory hypotheses as that provided by Aristotle's quintessence. By the same token one can view early modern alchemy, theoretical and practical, as a highly evolved and intellectualized version of the era's prevalent common sense.[5] This is not the same as saying that the era's prevalent common sense is pervaded by alchemical reasoning (a person who brewed beer became a magus . . .). Nevertheless, the two stand in a cultural continuum, as the design of Jonson's *The Alchemist* clearly demonstrates. In considering cosmomorphism's questioning and displacement we are dealing not only with specific outcroppings of intellectual unease, but also with a disturbing of some deeply laid intuitions which are far less readily brought to conscious scrutiny.

The section that follows is concerned with writing that registers a fracturing of, or even itself tests to destruction, the early modern period's cosmomorphic manner of thinking. For a description of a human world and of a widely found mentality, constitutively inimical to cosmomorphic thinking, one can hardly do better than turn to a well-known passage from Donne's *First Anniversary*:

> 'Tis all in pieces, all cohærence gone;
> All iust supply, and all Relation:
> Prince, Subiect, Father, Sonne, are things forgot,
> For euery man alone thinks he hath got
> To be a Phoenix, and that there can bee
> None of that kinde, of which he is, but hee. (ll. 213–18)[6]

The ethical stance taken by the speaker here is that cosmomorphic thought construction *should* take place as we try to envisage fundamental human relationships, but now on account of forces found to be in play does not and cannot; the most readily available mode of self-perception being that of absolute personal separateness and uniqueness, whose insistence is caught in the thumpingly emphatic 'got' of line 211. Donne is being hyperbolic, but he is also examining a real cultural phenomenon. In this section I shall examine a body of writing, Donne's poems (mainly earlier ones), and a play, *King Lear*, which in various ways address what in the culture threatens the integrity and survival of ordinary, street-level cosmomorphism, at the same time making their own potentially transforming scrutiny of this mentality, one which is in the pessimistic perspective of Donne's *Anniversaries* already a lost cause. These texts are in important respects *about* the transformation of cultural belief, giving it appropriate status as a thing wonderful, portentous or terrible for thought (*deinos*). My approach to these literary dealings with the cosmomorphic vision, and what makes for its disruption, gives some prominence to an examination of one detailed feature of each text's implied scientific-cum-medical reasoning and reflection. Here I shall be considering Donne's self-definition as a melancholic, which he connects with special aptitudes for creativity, and *King Lear*'s profoundly troubled exposition, necessarily inconclusive, of the relationship between human existence and the visible cosmos.

'That Dark Sun': Donne and Melancholic Individuality

Donne is concerned across the range of his writing with discovery of unity in the world or cosmos, with what might impede such discovery, and also with the possibility that this looked-for unity does not exist or, as in the *Anniversaries*, has ceased to exist. I shall begin by considering the opening of 'Satyre I', probably among his earliest poems, which brings together a characteristic assemblage of intellectual motifs by which Donne's writing is made immediately recognizable. The passage evokes the chaotic life of a city's streets, into which the speaker imagines himself being led by a suitable denizen, another young man – apparently a kind of *alter ego* – whom he characterizes as a 'fondling motley humorist'[1] and addresses as 'wild uncertaine thee'. It also evokes this city life's ostensible converse, the physically static, withdrawn existence of one who habitually communes with books in his solitary chamber, an existence compared to imprisonment and being 'coffin'd' like a corpse. And it also evokes the virtual presence of these books' writers, 'constant company' (ll. 1–12) in the sense that they are continuously there to be consulted, but not exactly constant as an influence if we consider the disjunctions of thought which serial reading of them produces:

> Here are Gods conduits, grave Divines; and here
> Nature's Secretary, the Philosopher;
> And jolly Statesmen, which teach how to tie
> The sinews of a cities mistique bodie;
> Here gathering Chroniclers, and by them stand
> Giddie fantastique Poëts of each land. (ll. 5–10)

We already find ourselves dealing with two kinds of cognitive dissonance. It is found in the resistance to conceptual organization which chance street adventures and eclectic reading have in common: the speaker's envisaged companion and his social behaviour are obviously 'giddy', but then so too are his chosen poets (or perhaps poets generically) and, for that matter, the experience of reading across texts with such different angles on the truth. But it is also found *between* knowledge of life as a thing found by immersive participation in it, and the kind of knowledge which can be offered or suggested by more abstractive thinking: chaotic though city life seems to be, might not the grave divines, the philosopher, and the 'jolly [some texts: wily] Statesmen' be right in thinking that its 'sinews' can be tied in such a way as to form a 'mistique bodie', a spontaneous unity like that which Platonic thought attributes to the cosmos? The 'philosopher' most directly referenced may be Plato, as the pursuer of analogy between the underlying form of a city and that of a soul in Books 2 to 5 of *The Republic*.

The speaker leaves hanging this thought of a city's being drawn into unity, and we notice that the passage leaves him, in effect, divided into three people: he is the 'motley humorist', given to following random impulse, who relishes and wishes to be part of this city's turbulent life; he is the bemused and detached observer, not only capable of enjoying varied reading in 'coffin'd' seclusion, but also capable of following a wild city companion to see where his antics lead; but he is at least open to the idea that all this disorientating experience, gathered from both life and books, might tend towards some sort of unity, supposing that one could conceive or actively shape this city as a 'mistique bodie'. The passage and what follows in the satire is representative of Donne's poetry in that what one might call centripetal and centrifugal kinds of thinking are going on at the same time: it whirls off into scattered observations and thoughts; it holds present, like Isaiah Berlin's hedgehog, the notion that there is One Big Thing which, supposing one knew it or could put it into effect, would enable one to make sense of everything else.[2]

Where does this locate the most valued experience of selfhood? 'Satyre I' is intriguing on the issue, in that it leaves pointedly unreconciled the self which exists in some degree of integrality with the group through wise action or reflection (the aspiration of the 'hedgehog'), and the self who attempts to do the same through headlong participation (the way taken by the childlike 'fox', this hedgehog's counterpart, who seems barely to differentiate himself from other people and their perceptions of him),[3] while distinguishing both from the self who stands apart to savour the incongruities in what he observes and finds himself privately thinking. Each of these selves probably accesses a kind of truth, but it is not a truth which would be accessible to the others.

Having identified this complex of thoughts in 'Satyre I's' explicatory presentation of it, I shall turn to a more closely defined mentality of individual-from-group detachment which produces enhanced percipience at certain costs. This is the mentality of melancholia as Donne distinctively understands it. The understanding can be brought to a first focus by means of a portrayal of him, made presumably under his direction, in the character of a melancholic. We are considering the Lothian portrait, thought to have been executed when Donne was in his mid twenties (c. 1595), which has become since its recovery in 1959 the best-known contemporary representation of him. It contains a surprising figurative detail which has been only lately revealed (in the cleaning of the painting under the supervision of the National Portrait Gallery), and which helps to define the larger conception of the portrait, as well as carrying important implications for Donne's mid-1590s sense of what it is to be a thinker and poet. It will be useful to examine some other features of the portrait before returning to this detail's significance.

In general acceptance the Donne represented in the portrait has the thoroughly recognizable attributes of a melancholic as the period conceived that condition; these include the folded arms, the collar in disarray and the intent look suggesting preoccupation with inner thoughts. But it should be said that the figure whom we see is a very smartly turned-out melancholic – something a little surprising in context – and also apparently a healthy one. In particular, his flesh tone is not darkened, as would have been expected in the complexional melancholic, one whose humoural state is inherently tilted towards the 'cold' and 'dry'.[4] In the medical thought of the era one could be a complexional melancholic without necessarily suffering from melancholia and, conversely, suffer from melancholia without necessarily being a complexional melancholic.[5] The Donne of the Lothian portrait is a melancholic of this second kind.

On these and some other grounds, to be identified shortly, it is possible to classify the Donne whom we are shown as a love-melancholic – one who suffers from 'lovesickness' or erotic melancholy or *amor hereos*[6] – lovesickness being in the view taken in this period one of the most familiar and widespread forms of melancholia.[7] The portrait's clearest pointer to love melancholia is the inscription which overarches the sitter's head, 'Illumina tenebr[as] nostras domina (Lighten our shadows, lady).'[8] The lovesick were not usually regarded as complexional melancholics, but as people in whom love itself, taking the form of mental fixation, produces the physical–psychological phenomena of melancholia. Ficino influentially explained that

> the anxious care by which vulgar lovers are vexed day and night is a certain species of madness. As long as love lasts, they are afflicted first by the burning of the bile, then by the burning of the black bile, and they rush into frenzies and fire, and as if blind do not know where they are being precipitated.[9]

Donald Beecher and Massimo Ciavolella, introducing Jacques Ferrand's early seventeenth-century *Treatise on Lovesickness*, point out that in the era's understanding

> the depraved judgements and imaginations of lovers came about as a result of the cloudy soots and vapors generated by the adustion [burning, parching, dessication] of humours, for it was the burning by the passions that provoked the decline into states of depression or mania. Yet it was the fixing of the will upon the beloved object that first stamped the imagination, imprinting it with an image that displaced all other considerations, that dried and chilled the brain and brought on the illness.[10]

'Depraved' here carries its medical meaning of 'deflected from ordinary or natural functioning'. It will be useful to bear these accounts of a *pathology* in mind as we assess the implied condition of Donne as portrayed.

I return to the figurative detail which has just come to modern attention. Tarnya Cooper, who curates at the National Portrait Gallery, describes it as a 'vertical white brush stroke rising from John Donne's chest'. It looks like a small plume of smoke or steam, issuing from concealment by the sitter's clothing and becoming invisible as it fans out in the region of the neck. The portrait's recent cleaning has made the detail visible, and at the same time established that it forms part of the original painting, that it is not a later accretion. Cooper comments, 'whether we interpret this as John Donne's rising spirit or something more profane needs further consideration, but it is an interesting feature for a man whose haunting poetry links spiritual and physical love.'[11] This is helpful, and judiciously leaves conclusions open; nevertheless, it is possible to arrive at a fairly certain interpretation, integrating what the plume signifies with other ideas informing the portrait.

Here is something that is most unusual in any context, a representation of *the vapour of melancholy*, conceived as emanating from the sitter's chest and rising to the region of the head where it will be inhaled or otherwise absorbed.[12]

This interpretation of the brushstroke's significance is strongly supported by a passage in Donne's *Devotions Upon Emergent Occasions* (published 1624) where he describes the melancholic – whose condition is his own – as being personally disposed to produce, as a bodily exhalation, the vapour in the absorption or breathing of which melancholia is further intensified. It is worth quoting these statements in full:

> What will not kill a man if a vapour will? How great an Elephant, how small a Mouse destroys! (. . .) [T]hat that which is but a vapor, and a vapor not forced, but breathed, should kill, that our Nourse should overlay us, and Ayre that nourishes us, should destroy us, but that it is a halfe Atheisme to murmure against Nature, who is Gods immediate commissioner, who would not thinke himselfe miserable to bee put into the hands of Nature, who does not only set him up for a marke for others to shoote at, but delights herselfe to blow him up like a glasse, till shee see him breake, even with her owne breath? (. . .) [W]hen our selves are the Well, that breaths out this exhalation (. . .), who can ever after this, aggravate his sorrow, by this Circumstance, That it was his Neighbor, his familiar Friend, his Brother, that destroyed him with a whispering, and a calumniating breath, when wee our selves doe it to our selves by these same meanes, kill our selves with our owne vapors? (. . .) [W]hat have I done, either to breed, or to breath these vapors? They tell me it is my Melancholy; Did I infuse, did I drinke in Melancholly into my selfe? It is my thoughtfulnesse, was I not made to thinke? It is my study; doth not my Calling call for that? I have don nothing, wilfully, perversely toward it, yet must suffer in it, die by it.[13]

This was probably written some 30 years after Donne sat for the Lothian portrait, and focuses on thinkers', not lovers' melancholy, but there is no reason to believe that his ideas about the physical course taken by non-complexional melancholia, as such, had radically changed; they also stand, as we have seen, in continuity with the ordinary medical reasoning of the period while placing a personal construction on it.

In the argument of the *Devotions* the self-produced and self-absorbed vapour of melancholia becomes a central intellectual exhibit, because it counts as strong evidence that there is *something fundamentally wrong with* the natural human state as the writer experiences it. In the psychological–pathological sequence which he describes human beings can spontaneously, simply by being what they are and using their minds as they do ('It is my thoughtfulnesse, was I not made to thinke?'), give rise to an exhalation which, in its recycling through the body and as a self-compounding process, harms or destroys them. The earlier portrait seems to be representing a very similar pathology consisting of melancholia's vapour-mediated self-potentiation and self-reinforcement. The Donne who can be assumed to have supervised the portrayal seems to be particularly concerned with the labile interconversion of mental and physical states, of the discursive and the somatic, with which melancholia can be readily associated. One of Eliot's famous pronouncements on Donne seems uncannily attuned to this very Donneian conception: 'A thought to Donne was an experience; it modified his sensibility.'[14] In the *Devotions* the conception defines an intensely experienced state of personal misfortune and unhappiness. But the emotional tone of the portrait is, of course, entirely different, and this very presentable-looking young man seems not to have fallen into some deadly psychophysical trap: Donne's costume has a sombreness about it, but the style is modish,[15] his demeanour suggests composure rather than compulsion, and there is chutzpah in the semi-blasphemous appeal to the 'lady' who will 'lighten our shadows'.[16] Donne as shown here seems to be *settling into* a state of melancholia as one might settle into the enjoyment of a cigar.[17] The relatively young Donne, the Donne who developed a highly individual poetic style, on this evidence prized and even cultivated melancholia in a manner that the older Donne, at least in his own account, decidedly did not.

How is it possible to take a relatively upbeat view of melancholia? The answer to this question is provided by a medical–philosophical conception originating in the classical world, one which endows the melancholic with a special capacity for inspired or otherwise brilliant thinking. The idea is formulated by a follower of Aristotle who implicitly connects the mental distraction or alienation of the melancholic with the inspirational divine frenzy (*mania*) of Platonic thought:

> Why is it that all those who have become eminent in philosophy or politics or poetry or the arts are clearly melancholics? (. . .) Wine and the melancholy temperament are of a similar nature. (. . .) Those who possess much cold black bile become dull and stupid, whereas those who possess much hot bile are elated and brilliant or erotic or easily moved to anger and desire, while some become more loquacious. Many too are subject to fits of exaltation and ecstasy, because this heat is located near the seat of the intellect; and this is how Sibyls and soothsayers arise and all that are divinely inspired. (. . .) Maracus, the Syracusan, was actually a better poet when he was out of his mind.[18]

The Platonic connection is made explicit in the writings of Ficino – it is substantially as a result of his influence that melancholy becomes the temperament of genius for the sixteenth century.[19] The medical thinker Guainerio had already come up with the idea that melancholic genius perceives by direct intuition, *sine discursu*, in a way unmediated by natural perception or conventional understanding which derives from it: it has its own knowledge-generative resources.[20]

It should be said at this point that early modern melancholia rather poorly maps modern 'depression' or one half of modern 'bipolarity'.[21] It is of particular relevance to Donne that the conception of it can span pathology, an inspirational epistemology, and an unhitching of mental process from relationship to natural perception. Orsino in *Twelfth Night*, who considers himself to be suffering from erotic melancholy or *amor hereos*, takes this last position: 'So full of shapes is fancy / That it alone is high fantastical' (1.1.14–15).[22] Jacques du Bosc – who seems to have been reading Montaigne, hence the mention of gaining access to a 'private room' within the mind – points to that standing apart from absorption in the outer experiential world which typifies the melancholic mentality:

> Wee may not wonder, that the Melancholy are so constant, and never seene to be troubled, even when they are forced to yeeld by necessity, since they always reserve in themselves a privat roome, where to the tempests of Fortune cannot reach. There it is, where the soule retires, (. . .) where she gaines an absolute command upon her judgements, and where she solitarily entertaines her self, even in the midst of companies. (. . .) In this solitude of the upper part, the spirit is fortified. (. . .) [W]ho can praise enough this noble musing of the Melancholy, since by it the soule seemes to abandon when she list, the clamorous commerce of the senses; And that we consider with an attention lesse distracted, what we are, when our imagination represents to us ourselves, then *Narcissus* saw himself in a fountain. (. . .) We cannot find ourselves indeed, but in ourselves.[23]

Du Bosc's neoStoic lauding of an achieved inner constancy is of course alien to Donne; but the idea of a radical inner-mental separateness and autonomy bears strongly on his thought.

What might the nature-independent – in a medical sense, 'depraved' – contents of the melancholic imagination look like? Albrecht Dürer bids to answer this question directly in the remarkable, widely circulated *Melencolia I* (1514), which is probably the period's most fully articulated and revealing, as well as startling, exposition of a partially unwelcome mental state which is also potentially one of genius.[24] According to Robert Burton, Dürer here represents Melancholy

> like a sad woman leaning on her arme with fixed looks, neglected habit &c. held therefore by some proud, soft, sottish, or halfe mad, as the *Abderites* esteemed of *Democritus*: and yet of a deepe reach, excellent apprehension, judicious, wise and witty.[25]

Sometimes characterized as an angel who has forgotten how to fly, the engraving's central figure is maximally alienated from ordinary, given natural experience: what the whole composition shows is an *other*, non-natural space of thought – consider the figure's intense though undirected gaze – shown as such explicitly by the presence in its sky of a black sun, a kind of anti-sun whose effects transpose the ordinary properties of what is sunlit and what is in shadow (the lit side of an object is the side facing *away* from it). It is interesting to note that the poet and dramatist Vondel, writing in 1634, refers to Donne himself as 'that dark sun (*die duistre zon*)',[26] apparently connecting him and his poetry

directly with Dürer's well-known composition. The objects that surround the central figure are, in the main, either instruments of thought, especially mathematical, and of construction, or, more strangely, projected ideas, entities like the polyhedron which thought itself has brought into existence.[27] This thought-world of distracted–abstracted insight lacks the hierarchical and teleological organization which was generally attributed to the cosmos itself.[28] The melancholic mentality as given form here is inherently *insubordinate* with respect to nature, a kind of parallel *sui generis* cosmos.

Melancholic thought in what one might call its surreal aspect lacks an operational distinction between ideas and objects, since its objects, in so far as it can be said to envisage them, are idea-equivalents: in *Melencolia I* a perplexing geometrical solid and a closely observed dog (which probably connotes persistence or 'doggedness') inhabit the same space on what seem to be the same terms. By the same token, there appears to be no outer limit to what thought can envisage; for example, a negative sun is something pretty hard to conceive of. But the price of such expansiveness is thought's self-isolation, or discovery of inward connection with *itself* at the cost of becoming disconnected from its environment. In *Melencolia I* a ladder leads upwards and out of the frame, which seems to function perversely as an index of the figure's mental self-confinement: the melancholic will not climb it – there is to be no *Melencolia II*.[29]

Awareness of the melancholic imagination's attributed properties – especially, we can follow Vondel in noting, as Dürer represented them in a scene paradoxically illuminated by a black sun – immediately throws into relief two characteristic features of Donne's poetry. These are the construction of heterocosms which transpose and reorganize elements drawn from natural perception within a newly constituted frame, as occurs in 'The Sunne Rising' or 'The Flea', and the construction of anti-worlds, where the vital interconnections of nature have been removed from the field of experience, as in 'A Nocturnall upon S. Lucies day' or the *Anniversaries*. The second form of writing purports to issue directly out of melancholic vision; the first manifestly does not, and is often euphoric in manner, but it emphatically instates and develops thematically upon the world-apartness of the kind of imagination which melancholia is alleged to fashion. It is on the basis of this sort of self-generating, self-sustaining perception that, as in the celebratory language of 'The Good Morrow', a 'little room' can become 'an everywhere'; and it is, *pari passu*, easy to see why Donne is drawn to the map and the convex mirroring surface, often that of the eye, as means of giving form to a finite visual field which seems to reconstitute and by that means contain the world around it.

What is at stake in both kinds of poetry is the potential *otherness* of an individual mind's hypothetical contents with respect to what arises in 'natural' perception oriented to the outer world which the individual inhabits. We have seen in the prefatory chapter how 'The Canonization' takes natural perception through a kind of everting transformation, such that it is now included along with more or less everything else that the world contains in a vision belonging uniquely to the speaker and the one loved, as an aspect of the private mentality which they share. This is a suitable juncture at which to return to the famous declaration which Hamlet makes while exhibiting the behavioural traits of a melancolic: 'I have that within which passeth show.' In its more limited sense, it is a claim of a kind that an individual might make in more or less any cultural setting: 'There is a difference between what I can know about myself through introspection, and what can be observed of me from outside.' Perhaps some kinds of feeling resist outward, immediately shared expression: Seneca's Phaedra comments, in this spirit, that 'Light cares can speak, huge cares are dumbfounded (*Curae leves loquuntur, ingentes stupent*).'[30] Cordelia in *King Lear* objects to the glibness of her sisters' protestations of love, on the principle that sincere and strongly felt emotions do not necessarily find a ready articulation. We infer from the rest of the play's action that Cordelia has already given ample *demonstration*, over time, of her feelings towards her father; Goneril and Regan on the other hand are *declaring* love, on cue, in compressed, exaggerated utterance. If Lear were acting sensibly at this juncture he would certainly go on attributing greater worth to Cordelia's long-term demonstration of love, a making outwardly manifest of an inward mentality, than to his other daughters' sudden protestations.

I labour the point in order to differentiate ordinary tongue-tiedness or decorous reticence from what Hamlet claims with the self-conferred authority of the melancholic: he has 'that within which passeth show' – which I take to mean, some of his most significant inner thoughts *could not even in principle* be transposed into an intelligible and otherwise acceptable form of public expression; the two are incommensurable, like circle and square.[31] The comparison which Hamlet makes with an actor's or hypocrite's performance (his visible demonstrations of grief 'are actions which a man might play') helps to clarify what is distinctive about his claim: whatever might be made manifest in speech, gesture and so on, to others is *already* non-identical with and inadequate to the interior state which might be taken to correspond with it.[32] Hamlet's claim, in other words, points to the existence of a not only huge but unbridgeable disjunction between what can be affirmed of personal experience, and what can be known of the self given to public scrutiny.[33] Polonius judges from the tenor of Hamlet's behaviour at court and his known sexual interest in Ophelia that he is suffering from love-melancholy. Polonius is wrong about this, but Hamlet is certainly thinking like a melancholic in one of the period's understandings of that state; the melancholia just happens to have a different cause.

In Donne, however, and especially the Donne of the *Songs and Sonets*, a knowledge shared with the reader of melancholia's power to yield both *heightened* and *altered* imaginative vision, serves to enframe poetic assertion that, as Achsah Guibbory puts it, 'personal fulfilment can only be found in love, and that the realm of sexuality is autonomous, private, self-sufficient.'[34] I have said, I think, enough to substantiate this; and will now transfer attention to another conjunction in Donne's writing between the idea of melancholia and the discovery of individual separateness. This is registration of human-to-cosmic fracture in an account of its personally experienced effects. George Williamson pointed some 60 years ago to the relation between early modern melancholy and the period's preoccupation with nature's decay, which sometimes issued in full-dress theological-scientific debate.[35] Cosmomorphism is, we recall, the conception of the human state such that man and the world share a common life and form a living unity, one aspect of which is that observable cosmic and natural processes form an *analogue* for related processes in the individual. I shall consider 'An Elegie upon the death of the Ladie Marckam'[36] as a representative Donne poem which begins with an instatement of the cosmomorphic vision before developing this in the direction of experienced fracture:

> Man is the world, and Death the Ocean
> To which God giues the lower parts of man,
> This Sea invirons all, and though as yet
> God hath sett marks, and bounds twixt vs, and it,
> Yet doth it roare, and gnawe, and still pretend,
> And breakes our banck when ere it takes a friend.

Thinking on the largest geographical–historical–typological scale, the passage adduces an analogy between the sea's constant, destructive assault on the land – as elemented of earth, 'low' with respect to the other three elements, including water[37] – and death's predation on man's 'lower parts', those which are least spiritual, primarily the body. Both processes, we are told, have divinely appointed and to some extent observable limits – the 'marks, and bounds' set for the sea in l. 4 seem to refer to the known shapes of coastlines and land-masses, including navigational 'marks', as well as God's promise in *Genesis* 9 that there will not be another general Flood.

The lines' envisaged integration of 'man' and 'world' has implicit consolatory force, since it distinguishes sharply between what is best about human beings and what death takes away. But that is not the direction of the poem's development.

If cosmomorphism is an understanding of the self on the basis of its integrity and continuity with the world, including other human beings, and intently considers inter-human connection as an aspect of the individual-to-cosmos connection, it becomes clear as soon as we say this that the 'Elegie on the Lady Marckam' moves in its initial development *away from* cosmomorphism's integration of 'man' the collectivity and 'world', traversing individual perceptions that dismantle it. The first of these occurs in the pointed subjectivism of l. 6: sea-resemblant death 'breakes *our* banck when ere it takes a friend' (my emphasis); the flooding land becomes a correlate for the speaker's individual suffering and those of a circle of fellow-sufferers. The lines that follow introduce experience undergone, through grief occasioned by *this* particular loss, equivalent at the personal level to destruction by water, but one produced instead from the land, as tears, and in its effects in the individual a greater undoing of divinely appointed order than the biblical Flood:

> Then our land-waters (teares of Passion) vent;
> Our waters, then, aboue our firmament [see *Gen.* 1.7–8; what is happening here
>   violates the fundamental template of creation],
> (Teares which our Soule doth for her sinn let fall)
> Take all a brackish tast, and funerall. (ll. 7–10)

Subsequent lines make it clear that these tears are optically delusive, 'false spectacles' through which 'we cannot see / (. . .) what wee are, nor what shee' (ll. 15–16). There is, then, a proffered formal similarity between the 'sea's' (death's) relentless erosion of the 'land' (what in us is mortal), and grief's erosion of the first-put forward, integrated, cosmomorphic imaging of 'man' as 'world' and 'world' as 'man'. What remains as the deposit of this process is an isolated individual's conceptually unaccommodated experience, the 'brackish' taste of tears, unmistakably sincere tokens of grief which also figure spiritual disorientation and a lack of access to final truths.

Donne's writing does not characteristically refute, reject or even register scepticism concerning cosmomorphic images of Man, like that presented at the beginning of the Marckam elegy. As melancholic or tilted towards melancholia, it does not, however, characteristically sustain them,[38] but takes them instead through an unpredictable, dismantling transformation.[39] In the case of the elegy a more personal application of the death-as-invasive-sea metaphor becomes, so to speak, written over the first, cosmomorphic application, before the metaphor itself is turned inside-out through a further personalizing identification of 'inland' tears as waters that are more destructive than the biblical Flood. These ideas considered in their presented sequence are, needless to say, highly discontinuous, but the having of them *is* melancholic individuality, the mental inhabiting of that space which thought alone creates and whose contents are nothing other than its deposits. Melancholic individuality typically discovers – or, from a non-melancholic standpoint, posits – the disconnectedness of people from people, of people from macrocosmic world, and of what one thinks from what is usually taken to be the case. But what it finds in the process of discovery is uniquely its possession and uniquely defining of it, like the elegy's brackish-tasting tears.

*   *   *

The assessment of Donne that has just been offered somewhat resembles one which is already in the field: his writing, in the style which we have learnt to call 'metaphysical', feeds off and draws energy from the dissolution during its era of thought which conceives of a profound integratedness of world and human life; Donne converts natural philosophy into spiralling metaphor, since traditional natural philosophy is his time is becoming little *but* metaphor. A drafting of this view occurs in Dryden's lastingly influential critical account of Donne, which implies that the philosophical ideas referenced in his poetry would have been hard to take entirely seriously even in his own time:

> He affects the metaphysics, not only in his satires, but in his amorous verses, where nature alone should reign; and perplexes the minds of the fair sex with nice speculations of philosophy, when he should engage their hearts, and entertain them with the softnesses of love.[40]

'Nice' suggests affected and contrived, while the 'speculations' which 'nice' qualifies are placed as remote from the natural and appropriate. Dryden in this passage projects later seventeenth-century educated scepticism about cosmomorphic ontologies onto the mentality of Donne's era.

Examination of some of the forms taken by melancholic vision in Donne has, however, taken us down a different path. Donne is not a proto-modern scientific sceptic in relation to the normative natural philosophy of his era; though, as some of the letters show, he is willing to assess aspects of it critically – which is to say that he participates actively in his own era's intellectual life. His poetry, of which I am treating the Marckam elegy as representative,[41] not only procedurally takes the cosmomorphic account of 'man's' integration with 'world' entirely seriously, but also envisages this authentic order's dissolution. The dissolution can be a matter of distorted perception – in the elegy it is a compelling though misleading effect of grief – but can also occur, as some other poems have it, *in re*, as the world itself decays and falls into entropic disorganization. Williamson is undoubtedly right to flag up the relation between acceptance of world-decay as a cosmological hypothesis, and melancholic imagination in this era's conception of it. Pervasive dissolution is an inherently pessimistic theme on which melancholia, in so far as it tilts towards pessimism, is likely to seize (see Jacques in *As You Like It*: 'And thus from hour to hour we rot and rot'). Nevertheless, I have also drawn attention to the extreme world-apartness of the Donneian melancholic imagination, going with his sense that an individual's processes of thought can channel powerful energies without requiring the corroboration of natural perception. We find that, in Donne, the entropic skewings and disjointings of imaginative vision that melancholia is considered to produce exert more sway over the intellect than anything similar which perception of the cosmos might put into effect.

The 'Anniversary' poems are, as is generally recognized, self-aware hyperbolic performances, which seem to have annoyed Ben Jonson on these grounds. They ask us to accept as our premise of enquiry and cueing of vision that the world as we have it is 'Sicke (. . .), yea dead, yea putrified' (l. 56), an internally contradictory proposition and one to which the most ardent theological-scientific dissolutionist would have refused assent, but one which melancholia, arising from the departure of a 'rich soule' (l. 1), can entertain as genuine. Melancholia looks on to the disjoined and entropic, and it is an aspect of this looking that it does not include a categorical distinction between the manner of looking and the actuality of what is being looked at. In this reading the Copernican construction of the planetary system, treated in *The First Anniversary* as an account of cosmic fragmentation (see the famous passage about lost cosmic 'coherence' cited in the preceding section of this study), is not a given form of contemporary scientific knowledge whose effect is to induce melancholia, but is in itself a form of melancholic vision which the speaker builds into his own because it is ready to hand.[42]

The poem is, then, in a particularly radical sense a performance of mourning, and thus a seeing of the world under the aspect of melancholia. Here is melancholic truth: there is no Platonic World Soul, or Aristotelian

Quintessence, or Paracelsian Balm – which are, of course, in a non-melancholic perspective conceptually non-aligned but comparable ways of conceiving the interconnectedness on which the life of the cosmos depends – but only the discrete object-concepts of thought, commanding intellectual presences in their wayward intricacy. A related melancholic truth is that there is no common human condition, implying human-to-cosmos and human-to-human connection, but only what is to be seen from the standpoint of the isolated, paranoiac solipsist; it is worth invoking once again the statement, 'For every man alone thinks he hath got / To be a Phoenix . . .'; ll. 217–18). And here, of course, the melancholic hits on a truth of general application,[43] since the world as we have it is not short of individual isolation, solipsism and paranoia. The 'Anniversary' poems thus go on confronting their reader with the genuinely open question, 'How witty's ruine?' (l. 99): as melancholia conceives of the world, disorder, not unlike Spenser's Mutabilitie, appears to be in charge of what it is; and, mental conditions of 'ruine' in any case define the melancholic state. These poems catch the sheer *contingency* of individual experience when set against the solidarities and maintained continuities which are to be found in the experience of a group.

3

King Lear and the Death of the World

You'd have to be really
   greedy for life
if you didn't want to die when the whole world's
   dying with you.

Chorus in Thyestes[1]

This chapter examines *King Lear*'s handling of a double action; not the 'Gloucester and his sons' plot as juxtaposed with the 'Lear and his daughters' plot, but the unfolding of a human action in significant relation to that of a cosmological action which is also part of the narrative world of the play. The cosmological action is an unusual celestial event, the occurrence of coincidental lunar and solar eclipses. These are coincidental not in the sense that they occur simultaneously (which is physically impossible),[2] but that they occur in direct sequence across roughly half the period of a lunar month, as the moon moves orbitally between two places of eclipse alignment. Shakespeare had an obvious model for the incorporation into one dramatic design of a cosmological action – an eclipse action, in fact – and a human action. But Shakespeare's creative use of this model, like the place of eclipses in *King Lear*'s design, has for contingent reasons received no modern critical attention.[3] The dramatic model here is Seneca's *Thyestes*. By any objective reckoning this was the classical play which had the most pervasive influence on Tudor-Jacobean drama; most obviously because it was the template for revenge tragedy, and so the begetter of a sturdy genre which includes *The Spanish Tragedy*, *Hamlet* and innumerable plot threads in other surviving or referenced plays.[4] We also know that the educated of early modern Europe held Seneca's plays in very high regard. Here the judgement of Cinthio, critic and author of plays and *novelle* (from which as it happens Shakespeare adapts the plots of *Measure for*

Measure and *Othello*), is representative: 'In almost all of his tragedies [Seneca] surpassed (in so far as I can judge) all the Greeks who ever wrote – in wisdom, in gravity, in decorum, in majesty, and in memorable aphorism.'[5] The artistic influence of Seneca's plays in France, the German-speaking countries, Italy and Spain was as great during this period as in England. Nevertheless, the reasons for Seneca's contemporary critical neglect, which extends to willed non-recognition of his formative influence, are not far to seek. Since the later eighteenth century and the Romantic era the drama of ancient Athens has been Europe's absolutely unchallenged *classical* drama, while the repute of Roman literature not produced in the so-called Golden period – that is, under Augustus – has, at least for a general humanities audience,[6] fallen almost irretrievably. And, to come to basics, it is convenient to have a body of densely conceived writing with a potential bearing on the texts which one studies declared off-limits. I am directing attention to the cosmological action of *King Lear* not merely because it's there, but because it is crucial to the design of the play; and attending to Seneca's *Thyestes* can help us to understand what this design is. Cosmomorphism is, as I have tried to explain, a partly intuitive and culturally widespread way of thinking about the human-to-cosmos relation on a basis of reciprocal modelling, where the dominant idea is that of the spontaneously unified body. As in the individual body, as people in general inhabit and experience it, so in the world at large: such is the phenomenon of life, understood on the model of bodily life, that the kind of relation which obtains between my organs, limbs and faculties – such that, say, the healthy functioning of one bears immediately on the welfare of the others – also obtains between the widely scattered but also co-ordinated and influentially connected components of the cosmos, of which living human beings also form a part; and as a corollary, the immediate environment or cosmos may be taken to exhibit a life comparable to and related to that of human beings. Cosmos- or body-like wholes thus come to be consolidated for perception, through an application of familiar conceptual procedures, in accounts of human social organization at several levels, potentially including those of the kin-group or household, village, city (as in Donne's 'Satyre I'), and realm, in the explanation of phenomenal occurrence over time, as in analogies drawn between the human life cycle and the cycle of the seasons or the earth's life across successive ages, and in understanding of cosmic organization, such as that of the earth with (in the Aristotelian account) its four vertically self-arranging elements, or of the earth and planets. Clearly, what such thinking *can* put as issue is the nature of relationship as such. To bring the definition

of this issue nearer to the action of *King Lear*, is the relation between a child
and a parent simply *there* and operative, like that between breathing and being
alive, or between moon, earth and sun in the era's common thought, or *there*
only in the sense that it obtains between any two objects which happen to be
in one vicinity, and whose movements can accordingly be charted against one
another? What is a 'bond' between human beings, as in Cordelia's 'I love your
Majesty / According to my bond' (1.1.82–3)?[7] – or is the question intractable
and its posing improper, the dangerous breaking of a taboo, as the destructive
development of the play's opening action might be taken to suggest? In being
about cosmos *King Lear* is also – very immediately, as a function of the thought
of the era and the play's own distinctive narrative-dramatic organization – *about*
human relationship, and thus concerned with givens of thought so intimately
'ours' that we ordinarily resist bringing them to conscious scrutiny. It is this
distinctive organization which the account that follows is intended finally to
lay out for appraisal. I shall begin by considering debates about cosmology, in
particular debates over astrological influence and determination, which for
contemporaries provided part of the frame for the play's reception.

* * *

In 1577 Queen Elizabeth had a memorable face-out with a comet. According
to Henry Howard, Earl of Northampton, who claims to have witnessed the
event, the queen, then at her palace in Richmond, was advised by her courtiers
not to have a window opened so that she could look at the comet which had
lately appeared in the skies. In wide acceptance comets – unpredictable in their
arrivals, visually diverse – were ominous, especially for monarchs; in Marvell's
'The Mower to the Glo-worms', for example, comets by their nature portend the
downfall of the great, 'princes' funerals'.[8] On such grounds, presumably, it was
suggested to Elizabeth that she avoid encountering this one. Elizabeth, however,
interpreted her queenly role differently:

> With a courage answerable to the greatnesse of her state, she caused the
> Window to be set open, and cast out this word, *Iacta est alea, The Dice are
> throwne.* Affirming that her stedfast hope and conscience was too firmly placed
> in the prouidence of God, to bee blasted or affrighted with those beames which
> eyther had a ground in nature whereupon to rise, or at least no warrant out of
> scripture, to portend the mishaps of princes.[9]

I take '*Iacta est alea*' to be Elizabeth's own words, and what follows to be
Howard's account of what he takes her to have meant in speaking and acting

as she did. What is striking about the episode, apart from Elizabeth's feistiness, is that no one present seems to know quite how to deal with the celestial manifestation, or how a comet's malign powers are supposed to come into effect.[10] If the queen is being advised not to look at the comet, is this treating it as an unwelcome guest to whom she can administer the royal snub? Do its 'beams', perhaps the projection of its influence across cosmic spaces, directly harm those on whom they fall (which is perhaps the underlying rationale of her courtiers' advice), or might their agency be psychological and purely a function of being seen, as consisting in a power to 'affright'? – both of which hypotheses sit uneasily with the idea of prognostication, for which the comet is primarily a sign to be understood. The words glossing Elizabeth's '*Iacta est alea*' contain the contradictory suggestions that comets occur by process of nature, and as spontaneous prodigies; if this second were true, it might confer on them diminished *explicability*, accompanied however by enhanced powers of *signification*. And on what convincing authority are comets to be feared in any case, given that the scriptures offer no account of them? It is possible to say, however, that in choosing to confront the comet, while invoking as precedent Caesar's crossing of the Rubicon, Elizabeth as reported is in her own view doing something both risky and decisive: reading over the story from her standpoint, one might well conclude that celestial determination of events is real, *and* that resolute action can (probably) counter or modify its effects.[11]

In examining early modern cosmology and speculation about the 'disastrous' – in the root sense, what is brought about by the malign influence of a star or planet – it is useful to recall that intellectual construction in these matters was unstable, and also that people who thought about such things were quite capable of putting to themselves rather different explanatory accounts at the same time. We can avoid having to say, 'c. 1600 everyone believed that . . .,' while at the same time acknowledging the general incidence of what I term cosmomorphic thinking, often interwoven in some degree with scepticism and doubt. Nicholas Culpeper declared in a republican spirit that the major solar eclipse of 1652 (occurring on what came to be known as 'Black Monday') portended the general downfall of monarchy, but also wrote in the same place, 'What harm will it do *Princes* to prepare for the loss of a kingdom, though it never come? Is it not the way to teach them *humility*?'[12] The antiquarian Ralph Thoresby confided to his diary in 1682, 'I am not unaware that (. . .) meteors [startling objects appearing in the heavens] proceed from natural causes, yet [they] are frequently also the presages of imminent calamities.'[13] This last takes us in the direction of Gloucester's thoughts about celestial determination, voiced near the start of *King Lear*:

> These late eclipses of the sun and moon portend no good to us. Though the wisdom of nature can reason thus and thus, yet nature finds itself scourged by the sequent effects. (1.2.97–100)

Eclipses occur naturally, in ways that we can readily explain, and yet are also anomalies in cosmic functioning, disruptive of natural process. I shall return to Gloucester's statement, which introduces a narrative of eclipses into the narrative action of the play, but am for the time being flagging up its frank acceptance of the intellectually semi-contradictory. To invoke Lévi-Strauss's phrase, against a background of cosmomorphic intuition anomalous celestial phenomena such as eclipses are likely to be found 'good to think with (*bons à penser*)'; saying which does not predict the precise character and direction of the thinking.

Portentous eclipses identify a field of significant overlapping between the action of *King Lear* and that of Seneca's *Thyestes*. Long before Seneca a disturbing of the sun in its orbit had become integral to the story of Thyestes' feast: so terrible is a father's eating of his own children that the cosmos itself flinches in response. In the early modern period eclipses had, as compared with comets, a rather more clearly defined astronomical–astrological profile. A comet is generically anomalous as a 'long-haired star (*aster kometes*)', and the appearance of every comet is a singular, unpredictable event.[14] Eclipses on the other hand have similar visual forms and effects, and they could in the early modern period be predicted reliably, with calibration of the degree to which the sun would be obscured. Nevertheless, a major solar eclipse, producing a general darkening and even the sudden visibility of the stars, is a spectacular and extraordinary cosmic occurrence. The almanacs of wide early modern printed distribution give some prominence to a year's impending eclipses, placing special emphasis on solar eclipses of appreciable magnitude where such were to occur.[15] The Christian scriptures for their part accord eclipses a good deal of narrative and symbolic weight. Most conspicuously, in Matthew and Luke's gospels a solar eclipse coincides with the Crucifixion. Luke's is particularly explicit:

> And it was about the sixth hour, and there was a darkness over all the earth until the ninth hour. And the sun was darkened [*eklupontos* = 'was failing', 'was being concealed'; Vulgate: *obscuratus*], and the veil of the temple was rent in the midst. (23.44–5)

The Crucifixion was considered to have taken place at Passover, and therefore to have coincided with a full moon. And yet, as commentators noted, a full moon, facing towards the sun, would not eclipse it, in order to do which the moon would have to be new – that is, on the other side of the earth with respect to the sun. This is the culminating and climactic observation made in what remained into the early modern period the best-known account of 'the machine of the universe' (a phrase deriving ultimately from Lucretius), the treatise *Of the Sphere* written in the thirteenth century by an Englishman, John of Hollywood (Johannes de Sacrobosco). Having described the intelligible workings of the cosmos in some detail, John concludes:

> It is also evident that, when the sun was eclipsed during the Passion and the same Passion occurred at full moon, that eclipse was not natural – nay it was miraculous and contrary to nature (. . .). On which account Dionysius the Areopagite is reported to have said during the same Passion, 'Either the God of nature suffers, or the machine of the universe is fallen into pieces (*aut machina mundi dissolvetur*).'[16]

This miraculous solar eclipse is an event which eludes the kind of conceptualization which the rest of John's treatise provides; his ending on it is a gesture of intellectual humility.

Christian scripture also accords major significance to *coincidental* lunar and solar eclipses – coincidental not, however and merely, in the sense explained at the start of section, but in the sense that they are actually simultaneous. The passage occurs in *Revelations*: 'And I beheld when [the Lamb] had opened the sixth seal, and, lo, there was a great earthquake: and the sun became black as sackcloth of hair, and the moon became as blood' (6.12); this answers to Luke 21.11 and 25: 'And great earthquakes shall be in divers places'; 'And there shall be signs in the sun, and in the moon, and in the stars.' Again, the suggestion, enhanced here by the co-occurrence of an earthquake, is of a kind of paroxysm in the cosmos, alien to its ordinary functioning. Coincidental eclipses in the naturalistic understanding are endowed with ominous astrological significance in the *Centiloquium*, one of the influential Hermetic writings: 'In the world many evils will happen, when in one month there shall happen an eclipse of both luminaries; chiefly in those places subject to the [zodiacal] sign in which they happen.'[17] Texts associated with Hermes Trismegistus were, in early modern Europe, often accorded signal authority, for some parallel to that of the Bible.[18]

Eclipses are referred to quite frequently by Shakespeare, as for example in Sonnets 35, 60 and 107, of which the last is the most astrologically rich. But the idea of a double eclipse, treated as a particularly strong portent, is put forward in *Othello*: the hero, having strangled Desdemona, states, 'Methinks it should be now a huge eclipse / Of sun and moon, and that th'affrighted globe / Should yawn at alteration' (5.2.98–110).[19] The yawning can be taken to be an opening of fissures by disturbances of the earth; Pliny's *Natural History* notes a natural coincidentality of earthquakes with eclipses,[20] in an account carrying different philosophical weighting from *Revelations* 6.[21] Varied thoughts about prodigies seem to underlie *Macbeth*'s remarkable listing of disruptions in the cosmos which mark the murder of King Duncan, as attested by the conversation between Ross and the Old Man at 2.4; these are a huge storm, a solar eclipse, an explosion (perhaps), an earthquake, the crying of an unrecognized bird, the killing of a falcon by an owl and cannibalism in horses. We are beginning to identify a spectrum in the potential classification of cosmic portents, which may be taken to be less or more susceptible of naturalistic explanation. The cosmological manifestations attending Duncan's murder push, it seems, towards the 'unnatural' end of this spectrum, but not unequivocally (perhaps we should, with Pliny, *expect* an earthquake to coincide with an eclipse), while the solar and lunar eclipses of Gloucester's account push, perhaps, towards the 'natural' one – but still inspire awe, and are 'unnatural' in their causal fallout. It will be helpful to bear in mind such perplexities about ascribing 'naturalness', implying comprehensibility to the human observer, or lack of it, to occurrences of the kind as we turn to the relationship between *King Lear* and one of its most important intertexts, *Thyestes*.

The major celestial phenomenon in the action of *Thyestes* is in the genre of solar eclipse – it is an occurrence affecting the sun, the day is darkened – though the mechanism of solar eclipse is not mentioned, and the mythic trope used to evoke the phenomenon is that of a deflection from its regular course of the sun's chariot. The literary archetype for representation of such an occurrence was a famous, much anthologized passage from one of Pindar's odes,[22] and the narrative language of the play is broadly faithful to it. The play's eclipse, as we may reasonably call it, is referred to by speakers no less than seven times over the course of the action, beginning with the Fury's statement that the sun is hesitating to begin the day (see ll. 120–1),[23] part of nature's general recoiling from the horrors which impend (see ll. 48–51, 103–21). We gather that disturbance of the sun's ordinary, natural bringing of daylight continues for the action's duration. As emerges with particular clarity in Katharina Volk's recent account,[24] the five-stage figures who speak of the sun's darkening offer differing conceptualizations of the phenomenon, which project different understanding of the human-to-cosmos relationship, these differences being integral to the play's design. The most significant contrast is that between the imaginative cosmologies of Atreus, and of the Chorus, who bear witness to but do not participate in the events which unfold.

Let us recall that the play's pivotal event is Atreus' tricking of his brother, Thyestes, into devouring the flesh of his own sons; this is one of a sequence of outrages, extending beyond the time-frame of the play, which the feuding brothers perform on one another, and in context an act of revenge (Atreus is the grandson of Tantalus, whose Ghost is brought onstage at the play's start, and father to Agamemnon: the cycle of atrocity and retribution characterizes a dynasty). The beginning of the action at the human level is Atreus' inception and development of his plan. He proceeds to butcher Thyestes' sons and feed them to their father under the pretence of providing a welcoming feast. Atreus gloatingly reveals the crime to his brother, one in which Thyestes is of course perpetrator as well as victim. Thyestes requests of Jove that a thunderbolt strike him down, and concludes the play by predicting that retribution will fall on Atreus.

The play's most grotesque and in its way powerful, though not per se convincing, instatement of cosmomorphic vision comes as Atreus rejoices at the success of his plot: Thyestes has eaten his sons, and is about to be told as much.

> Peer of the stars I stride, out-topping all, my proud head reaching to the lofty sky. *Now* I hold the kingdom's glories, *now* my father's throne. I discharge the gods (*dimitto superos*): I have reached the pinnacle of my prayers. This is good, this is ample, this is enough now, even for me. But why should it be enough? I shall go on, and fill the father with the death of his sons. Lest shame should present any obstacle, daylight has withdrawn: go on while heaven is empty (*dum caelum vacat*)! Indeed I wish I could stop the gods fleeing, round them up and drag them all to see this feast of vengeance. But it is enough that the father see it. Even though the daylight is unwilling I shall dispel from you the darkness that conceals your sorrows. (ll. 885–96)

The postulation of an empty heaven, specifically a heaven made empty by human action, recalls a motif from Seneca's *Medea*. Although Medea in that play is a powerful sorceress (and uses these powers to dispose of Jason's new bride), she takes her climactic revenge on the Jason who has betrayed her by stunningly *natural* means; that is, by killing her and Jason's young sons with a knife. This atrocity – performed, as we are made fully aware, on herself as well as on her betrayer – seems to confer on Medea a kind of praeter-natural status. In the play's almost untranslatable final line Jason admonishes Medea thus: '*Testare nullos esse, qua veheris, deos* (Bear witness where you go to the knowledge that the gods are not / Bear out [through being what you are] the knowledge that where you go, the gods are not)'.[25] In taking a knife to her children Medea seems to have stepped outside the constraints which make human beings part of an interconnected world, a cosmos to which the power of the gods usually gives some order. As for Seneca's Atreus, he is a more Nero-like figure who sees himself as stepping through drastic self-assertion into the gods' place. As Volk puts it, 'describing himself as moving among the stars, Atreus takes on the role of the sun that he has driven away'.[26] The self-conferred apotheosis continues in his taking of purpose to 'dispel the darkness' which for the time being conceals from Thyestes the misery of his own state. In his own imagination Atreus is becoming a figure with god-like solar powers, having set the gods themselves, including the sun-god, in flight.

We may contrast this, however, with the reflections of the Chorus on the sky's unnatural darkening. This comes just before Atreus' speech of manic self-glorification, and the speeches inescapably contextualize one another. All through the play a bearer of reflective wisdom, the Chorus arrives its own explanation for what is taking place. In Stoic scientific philosophy the cosmos passes periodically – through withdrawal of its *pneuma*, its living interconnective medium – into a condition of violent, fiery dissolution, the *ekpurosis*, after which a new cosmos takes form. (Given the syncretism of much classical to early modern thinking, this could be taken to resemble, and in some sense correspond to, the Jewish and Christian Day of the Lord, occasion of the world's apocalyptic destruction.) According to the Chorus in Seneca's play, the strange darkening of the sky which they witness is probably the beginning of the *ekpurosis*, the self-extinction of the world. They move gradually towards this conclusion in a very substantial speech of lamentation and questioning. With Caryl Churchill's dramatically expert translation placed beside the original, here is the mid section of the Chorus's considerably longer statement, and its ending:

> Sed quiquid id est, utinam nox sit!
> trepidant, trepidant
> pectora magno percussa metu,
> ne fatali cuncta ruina
> quassata labent

iterumque deos hominesque premat
deforme chaos
iterum terras et mare cingens
et vaga picti sidera mundi
Natura tegat. (. . .)

Nos e tanto visi populi
digni, premeret
quos everso cardine mundus?
in nos aetas ultima venit?
o nos dua sorte creatos,
seu perdidimus solem miseri,
sive expulimus!
Abeant questus, discede timor:
vitae est avidus quisquis non vult
mundo secum pereunte mori. (ll. 828–34, 875–84)

(Whatever this is
I hope it is night.
I'm struck with terror
in case it's all collapsing,
shapeless chaos crushing gods and men.
        No winter, no spring
no moon racing her brother, planets
        piled together in a pit. (. . .)

How have we been chosen
out of everyone
somehow deserving
to have the world smash up and
fall on us? Or have the last days come
        in our lifetime? It's
a hard fate, whether we've lost the sun
        or driven it away.
Let's stop lamenting.
let's not be frightened.
You'd have to be really
        greedy for life
if you didn't want to die when the whole world's
        dying with you.)[27]

Broadly, the Chorus comes to accept its perceived fate, that of dying with a dying world, in a spirit of Stoic composure. Awareness of being caught up in a general, and even in some sense natural, process does not, however, resolve questions of responsibility. Is the Chorus deserving of (*digni*, l. 876) this destruction, and have they played a part in driving the sun away, perhaps merely by being coeval with Atreus and Thyestes, or is what is occurring pure misfortune? It is also necessary to point out that, in hindsight which the audience possesses, the Chorus's philosophical–scientific conclusion is incorrect: Thyestes' feast did not coincide with or produce an *ekpurosis*. Moreover, on the basis of what has occurred there is no possibility of assessing the causal relationship, or even the question of whether a causal relation exists, between atrocious events at the human level and this disturbance of the sun in its course; all we know is that the two have coincided. There seems to be more to trust in the Chorus's statements, reflective in manner and redolent of hard-earned wisdom, than in Atreus' manic improvisations. Nevertheless, in encountering these two very different visions of the human-to-cosmos relationship, we are in both cases made simultaneously aware of an urgently felt human *need* for cosmological thinking, and of the precariousness of such thinking's epistemological foundations. Thomas Rosenmeyer writes revealingly of Senecan tragic figures' always defeated or never assuaged 'rage to embrace nature':[28] they wish, as they inform us, to be incorporate with natural process while lacking the insight into self and world that would make such a thing possible.[29] An aspect of the experience of *Thyestes* which carries over into the experience of *King Lear* is that of participating in the collapse or fragmentation of a comprehensive vision, one which integrates understanding of what human beings are with an account of their known conditions of life.

*   *   *

We turn now more directly to Shakespeare's play and some features of its immediate context. Major eclipses of the moon and sun took place on 17 September and 2 October (that period's reckoning) 1605. They were a lunar eclipse which covered the whole of the moon in the earth's umbral or penumbral shadow and, as seen from London, an eclipse covering nine-tenths of the sun.[30] The eclipses have often been used by modern scholars to date the composition of *King Lear*, in view of the remarks made by Gloucester which insert such a phenomenon into the world of the play.[31] Astronomers had long predicted these eclipses, and their seemingly enhanced prognostic significance

as *coincidental* eclipses – the phenomenon referred to by Othello – had not
escaped attention. John Harvey, brother to Gabriel, had referred to them in a
discussion of astrology published in 1588.[32] The tendency of Harvey's argument
is to question or diminish their prognostic significance; which is part of a
tactical move to uphold the value of certain astrological predictions by casting
doubt on that of others.[33] Almanacs covering 1605 refer to the eclipses of that
year with apprehension, as one might expect. One Himbert de Billy, in a French
pamphlet released in English in 1604, places them in the decade's close-packed
sequence of eclipses, to which he gives apocalyptic significance:[34]

> I cannot tell how it hapneth, that so many great Eclipses (especially of the
> Sunne) do fall in so few yeeres, wherby greuous and wretched accidents are
> presaged. Perhaps these be the latter days, when as all piety and charity shall
> ware colde, trueth and iustice shall be oppressed: and all things else shall be
> mixed, disturbed [sic], and turned upside downe, and the forepart set behind
> by torments and seditions: and finally nothing else shall be expected, but spoyle
> and ruine of the common society.

De Billy is particularly concerned with the major solar eclipse: 'When as the
Sunne is Eclipsed, it can not be (unless God appoint otherwise) but some great
accidents is [sic] to be expected in the world, according to the quantitie of the
Eclipse;' among the possible sequent effects are 'the death of some great King or
Prince, seditions, warres, famine, and pestilence.' He also applies the Hermetic
Centiloquium's principle that the effects of eclipses are determined partly by the
zodiacal signs in which they occur:

> O Kings and Princes which are borne under the signes of the Ballance and the
> Ramme: also the Prouinces & Cities which are subiect unto the first quadrangle
> of the Zodiack, and to the signe of Scorpio, Many greuous euils are foreseen to
> fal upon, extreme miseries are euen at hand.[35]

We may compare the tone of this, however, with the very measured one
adopted by an English almanac writer with official *imprimatur*, John Dade,
who directs attention to the eclipses and their possibly dire significance but
avoids issuing specific predictions; he suggests, moreover, that in so far as they
live in Christian obedience under godly rule the inhabitants of the country
should have nothing to fear.[36] I shall not, he writes, speak of the eclipses'

> signification (. . .), onely beseeching God to direct vs with his holy spirit, that we
> may live as true Christians, faithfully professing the Gospel of Iesus Christ: and
> hartily praying for the preseruation of our most excellent & renowned Iosias,

our good Queene, with his Maiesties royal offspring, and the happie state of his most honourable priuie counself, and the true and faithful subiects of this Land.[37]

It is clever in context to style James the modern counterpart of Josiah, in scriptural narrative an exceptionally pious monarch who averts the divine punishment which threatens Judah by instituting religious reform.[38] The tone of Dade's account is one of Protestant confidence, and its purposes are emollient.

On the other hand, Robert Pricket's poem of prophetice commentary on contemporary events, *Times Anotomie* (sic), published in 1606, while expressing confidence in James ('But God hath sent to us a virtuous King'), pronounces that the recent mutually abutting lunar and solar eclipses must carry dire significance:

> And if the sunne should but some signe bewraie,
> Might no man dare gainst such prediction saie.
> And now shall heaven both fier and bloud presage,
> And we not thinke they chide this sinfull age [–]
> Eclipses strange both of the Moone and Sunne,
> When strangely they, on heapes together come [?][39]

Unlike de Billy, Pricket refrains from drawing specific prognostic inferences but, taking a position rather more anxious than Dade's, considers it wise to receive the eclipses as a serious warning addressed to a 'sinful' word.

The coincidental eclipses of 1605 evidently produced contemporary concern, and will have been a talking point as they approached – Gloucester's statement, in other words, had a referent in the contemporary world of which audiences will have been aware. At the same time these eclipses seem not to have become an astrological *cause célèbre*. I would say that this suited the purposes of Shakespeare and his company: the eclipses were known, but they did not have a distinctive profile; they can become focal in the play on the basis of the differing significances which characters attach to them. An obvious contrast here is with the 'Black Monday' solar eclipse of 1652, maximally incident in London, which was marked by large swathes of public panic. The difference is explained not by the degree ('severity') of the latter eclipse but by the fact that, in the aftermath of a monarch's execution, collective guilt and fear of punishment were readily stirred up. The uproar over 'Black Monday' seems to have been triggered by a royalist tract's assertion, made in the preceding year, that a nation of regicides was about to experience God's wrath. Republican ripostes produced by William Lilly among others did more to compound than allay the going anxieties in offering counter-prognostications of their own.[40] The tenor of public discussion and behaviour in 1652, set beside that of 1605, makes it clear that eclipses *could* potentially take on fearful purport; but also that this did not necessarily happen.

To return to Gloucester's account, which it will now be useful to cite in full: The Gloucester who speaks in play's second scene has lately been present at the terrible unravelling of Lear's abdication ceremony and, in the scene itself, just read Edgar's supposed letter of treachery:

> These late eclipses in the sun and moon portend no good to us. Though the wisdom of nature can reason thus and thus, yet nature finds itself scourged by the sequent effects. Love cools, friendship falls off, brothers divide; in cities mutinies, in countries discords, palaces treason, the bond cracked between son and father. Find out this villain, Edmund. It shall loose thee nothing. Do it carefully. And the noble and true-hearted Kent banished, his offence honesty – strange, strange. (1.2.97–105)

'Sequent effects' here can be readily glossed: astrologers generally considered the effects at the earthly level of such cosmic manifestations as eclipses to take place across a period of time – perhaps one of several months – following the manifestation itself. Gloucester's account begins, as has been noted, with an instatement of naturalistic explanation. He is saying, in effect, hooray for Hollywood: thanks to his treatise and others of the kind we can fully understand the cosmic motions which produce eclipses. *But* we find nonetheless that eclipses portend disturbances in the order of nature – In the light of this reasoning events in Gloucester's world become *legible* to him, and he can place the supposed villainy of his legitimate son in the same explanatory system as the outbreak of realm-threatening discord at court and banishment of loyal Kent. A little before, Gloucester has doubted the evidence of Edgar's treachery ('He cannot be such a monster'; l. 89); but, with some assistance from reading of the heavens he now moves beyond epistemological hesitation, as the image of a comprehensible world returns. Here certainty, even certainty about something appalling, is found preferable to conceptual irresolution.

There immediately follows, with Gloucester's exit, the speech of Edmund in which he scorns the uses to which human beings put the notion of astrological determinism, especially in seeking to evade personal responsibility for what they are and do;

> as if we were villains by necessity, fools by heavenly compulsion, knaves, thieves, and treacherers by spiritual [Folio: spherical] predominance, drunkards, liars, and adulterers by an enforced obedience of planetary influence; and all that we are evil in by a divine thrusting on. (ll. 109–14)

This is cogently stated, and hard not to find refreshing when set against a non-sceptical habit of mind which has been manipulated into dangerous credulity. Nevertheless, there is a certain undertow in Edmund's scornful tirade. His conclusion sounds like hyperstatement of personal disconnection from cosmic order, as if this were a bastard's equivocal privilege and stigma: 'Fut! [cf. *Fout!* = Fuck!] I should have been that I am, had the maidenliest star of the firmament twinkled on my bastardy [Folio: bastardizing]' (ll. 118–20). Nowhere does Edmund deny the reality of cosmomorphic connection: more simply and crudely, it is not for him, the manner of his begetting assigns him elsewhere. Conversely, the Gloucester whom Edmund presents to the audience as a fool is not necessarily that. His statements fit the (apparent) situation, and lack irritating Polonian sententiousness, while the mental dependence on finding an explanation-*cum*-solution and un-self aware brutality of turning against a son have a disturbing ordinariness about them; Gloucester's is a fairly representative mentality of its times, prone to respect for conventional ideas, which happens to have been fed a lying story.

There is beginning to shape up a debate and dialectic which is thoroughly embedded in the action of the play, and is for many purposes indistinguishable from it; its terms are fundamental relationship, human-to-cosmos and human-to-human, where the two may be entirely continuous. To cite Thomas Rosenmeyer's excellent phrase, the 'rage to embrace nature' takes several forms in the working out of the play's action; and this defines, I venture to say, one half of a very large conceptual antithesis. Such 'rage' is apparent, for example, in Edmund's several arias performed in the character of *Bastard*, including the one just discussed, and in his compulsive, parodic evocation of a cosmic vision which assigns him no place. A telling instance of the latter occurs only in the Folio text. As the just-discussed scene continues, Edmund pretends, now with a view to duping Edgar, to give much the same account of the eclipses' astrological decipherability as his father: 'O these eclipses do portend these divisions' (1.2.123). But as we set him beside Gloucester there is a difference: 'Mine is [Folio: my cue is] villainous melancholy' – Edmund is taking on the culturally familiar role of the melancholic (see the preceding chapter's discussion) who observes and also participates mentally in cosmic conditions of dislocation and misalignment. The 'divisions', now taken in the sense of 'musical intervals', which the eclipses have portended are rendered by Edmund as the gratingly discordant musical notes which he proceeds to sing, 'Fa, sol, la, mi' (Folio: 1.2.124–7). (In the Quarto version he reels off an account of dire astrological predictions which he claims lately to have read, so amusing Edgar: 'How long have you been a sectary astronomical?' (l. 137) – a *true believer* in astrology.) But we begin to understand the animus which drives Edmund as one diminished by or excluded from a cosmomorphic account of universal interrelatedness, and one who therefore becomes in counter-fantasy an autonomous natural force, granted a goddess Nature's personal protection (see 1.2.1–21). Here a wounding of the assumedly normative relationship of man and man and man and cosmos seems to have called into play a furious will to reinstate it on a personally chosen, personally arbitrated basis.

But the 'rage' is also apparent at times in members of Lear's affective party. Kent is, especially in the Quarto version, in the nature of a self-appointed maintainer and upholder of cosmomorphic vision: relationship *is*, or is *there*, unconditionally, in solidarity with a cosmos and human world of given structure: asked by Lear on returning in disguise whether he knows him, Kent gives a response which offers instruction in seeing the world thus: 'No, sir, but you have that in your countenance which I would fain call master' (1.4.24–5). Kent snaps, however, on finding himself obliged to deal as messenger facing rival messenger with the Oswald who serves Regan while he serves the king, and who in Kent's vision of things lacks the minimal requirements of humanity: Oswald is not to be included in an account of 'nature' which Kent finds acceptable, and which he becomes desperate to reinstate.[41] Here, having physically attacked Oswald for want of other remedy, he becomes placed in the impossible epistemological position of attempting to *talk into being* a living of or in fundamental relationship which has no conceptual reality for those whom he addresses. A good deal of the invective which he produces edges, for accountable reasons, towards flat nonsense ('A plague upon your epileptic visage! / Smile you my speeches as if I were a fool? / Goose, and I had you upon Sarum Plain / I'd send you cackling home to Camelot'; 2.2.75–8). We know that this sort of thing is not going to work, that the desperately improvised remedy is a compounding of the problem.

It is necessary to recall, however, that it is Lear's rage which brought us here, and that this rage too is for a reinstatement of nature. Shakespeare's Lear carries with him some of the archaic pretensions of monarchy, such that a vital and active connection exists between ruler, realm and cosmos; for a similar sense of the ruler to realm relation one might compare Shakespeare's Richard II's 'favouring' of the soil of England by gathering it in his hands.[42] Lear on the heath will *act like* someone who is unleashing the power of the storm:

> Blow, wind, and crack your cheeks! Rage, blow,
> Your cataracts and hurricane, spout
> Till you have drenched the steeples, drowned the cocks! (3.2.1–3)

Lear at this point wants to see the whole human world destroyed, in parallel to his own. A little before this he has said threateningly to Goneril, 'I do not bid the thunder-bearer shoot' (2.4.197) – as it were, 'I do not intend to release Jove's thunderbolts' – with the apparent confidence of one who can do just that. In the sweep of action that runs up to the storm Lear's attitude to the cosmos seems to be rooted in the conception that the monarch is or is equivalent to a cosmic force, comparable in majesty of action to one of the celestial bodies. In the opening scene Lear, his sense of *what is* much disturbed by Cordelia's 'Nothing', acts to sever given, cosmically grounded connection with this until-now cherished daughter. Invoking the inexorability of the cosmic motions, he attempts to give his judgement rendered on Cordelia the same kind of irresistible force: this is, in Lear's conception, a mighty, quasi-godlike action which exceeds the ordinary human constraints. Lear's characterization differs strongly, needless to say, from that of Seneca's Atreus; nevertheless his attitude here is similarly that of someone godlike or at a level with the gods, who can shake and reshape the world.

The specific analogy which the play offers for the reciprocal actions of Cordelia and Lear at this juncture is that of lunar and solar eclipses. The 'eclipse dragon', the astronomers' charting of nodes in the lunar orbit which makes eclipses predictable, based in ancient notions of a prodigious creature who recurrently devours the sun,[43] is referred to twice in *King Lear*; in Edmund's lewd joking ('My father compounded with my mother under the Dragon's tail'; 1.2.115–6 – which simultaneously evokes the eclipse dragon and the constellation Draco[44]); and, in the play's opening action itself, in Lear's warning to Kent as Kent tries to check him: 'Come not between the dragon and his wrath' (1.1.111). The royal dragon of British heraldry fuses in these words with the cosmic dragon whose movements define the conditions of eclipse.[45]

Prior to uttering these words Lear has, in pronouncing judgement on Cordelia, pledged himself to what he states 'By all the operation of the orbs / From whom we do exist and cease to be' (1.1.101–2); Lear speaks, that is, until broken by events as one who has the grand motions of the cosmos as his personal point of reference. We may, moreover, see the unfolding Lear-Cordelia action as shadowing an 'eclipses' plot.[46] Brian Rotman's account of the play brings out the significance which its action confers on mathematical zero, the 'cipher', an object of frequent reflection in Shakespeare's writing.[47] A central feature of the zero in Shakespeare's evocation of it is that it does not articulate conceptually with the Roman system of numeration, which during this period is still in predominant practical use (partly because interlinked with use of the abacus) and, to most people, more readily comprehensible. The zero is in the early seventeeth-century cultural setting a considerably more paradoxical thing than any of the Roman numerals: it not only multiplies value, but also stands for its absence, and lacks the Roman numerals' simple integrality.[48] We should at this point recall the era's standard classification, along well-established traditional lines, of the moon as feminine and the sun as masculine. Cordelia's very powerful and disruptive 'Nothing' (1.1.79), as uttered in the first scene, is to be projected visually as the zero's signifier, a blank circle. Its utterance immediately *darkens* the solar Lear, after the manner of an eclipse, on which he bids to eclipse *her* as 'moon' by removing her importance and lustre: to the astonishment of all present he declares her a thing without value. Cordelia's banishment and Lear's ensuing dependence on her sisters diminishes *him*, in due course producing madness; and so on (we shall return to the sequence). In other words, one of our templates for conceptualization of the play's action is an astronomical period, like that of 1605 and surrounding years, when eclipses happen sequentially, hard on one another's heels.

Lear, as has been said, participates in this action by relating what he does or finds himself doing to the huge, relentless movement of a cosmic body, meanwhile inviting others to do the same. This suggestion of a personal human-to-cosmos affinity has three shifting semi-consonant aspects: (1) the coming into effect of what Lear says or does is to be as inexorable as that of the grand motions of the cosmos (his pledge is 'by all the operations of the orbs . . .'); (2) Lear's actions *are* the grand motions of the cosmos (fixated on the object of his wrath, he is the dragon); (3) his actions, being those of a king, affect others *as if they were* the grand motions of the cosmos (he produces a huge upheaval in the human world at whose centre he stands). The second of these positions is the one to which, as we have seen, Atreus aspires, and implies a capacity utterly to destroy or remake human relationship; Lear oscillates around this position, as attractor, at the eventual cost of full madness. Lear will, of course, reject the afflatus of 'natural' or 'cosmic' monarchy; in his most succinct statement of this, 'they told me I was everything; 'tis a lie, I am not ague-proof' (4.6.102). In the same scene Gloucester, once a convinced star reader, accepts incapacity to read anything at all: recognizing that he has erred grievously over the respective natures of his sons, blind, faced with a piece of writing (probably imagined by the deranged Lear), he responds 'Were all the letters suns [in hearing, also 'sons'], I could not see one' (4.6.134). For both, the cosmomorphic kind of intuition, once overvalued, is discredited in a process that involves considerable suffering: in undergoing this *pathos* of knowledge both confront a fundamental failure of human relationship, in which failure they have participated, and a correspondent disappearance of 'nature'; it has become for them a thing not, apparently, to be reclaimed or remade.

What antithesis is set up in the play to a destined-to-defeat, positively destructive rage to embrace nature; which is precipitated, as is made clear, by wounding of unselfconscious at-oneness or at-homeness with what has been *taken* to be nature? Like *Thyestes*, the play defines more than one way of mentally representing and so living in relation to human beings' natural or cosmic conditions of life. And, a good deal more fully than *Thyestes*, with its Chorus of bystanders or witnesses who are without a role in the central action, it makes the establishment or testing of these visions structural to the entire action's development. Here, however, important discrepancies between the Quarto and Folio texts suggest that we are approaching an area of instability in the play's relation to its ambient culture, registered in its composition.

As we look across its two main extant versions, we find that *King Lear* sets not one but two counter-mentalities against the rage to embrace nature, which one might also call revanchist formulations of a cosmomorphism more safely left to custom and intuition. These mentalities are projected to some extent in both versions of the play, though each has a discernible tilting towards one or the other. One of the mentalities has a certain resonance with an emergent tendency in the era's philosophical enquiries into nature.

(A) Ancient thought, some of it associated with the semi-mythic Pythagoras, had posited a musically organized cosmos. As Edmund's burst of discordant singing implies, one of the early modern era's perceived manifestations of cosmic interconnection is musical concord, while discord betokens cosmic breakdown; Dryden would, in a brilliant phrase, characterize the final, apocalyptic dissolution of the cosmos as 'the untuning of the sky'.[49] The Quarto version of *King Lear* has Cordelia bring Lear back to sanity partly through the force of music which, taking effect alongside other medicines, retunes what he is with the order of the cosmos. This is in accordance with the era's astrological, *sumpatheia*-orientated conceptions of medical practice; in the Quarto a doctor is present to direct Lear's cure, reintegrating the activity of his mind with the orderly cosmic motions. Cordelia and her responsiveness to Lear's sufferings, which will issue in the finding of this practical remedy, are, moreover, enframed in the Quarto version by a significant statement from Kent which formally counterbalances Edmund's scorning of the principle of astrological determination. Kent is mentally comparing Cordelia with her sisters:

> It is the stars,
> The stars above us govern our conditions,
> Else one self mate and make could not beget
> Such different issues. (4.3.29)

In both extant versions of the play Cordelia seeks, and possibly has, a personal affinity with what is beneficent in nature. Speaking before the doctor (in the Folio, a 'Gentleman' attendant) prior to the restoring of Lear's mind, she utters this entreaty:

> All blest secrets,
> All you unpublished virtues of the earth,
> Spring with my tears, be aidant and remediate
> In the good man's distress! (4.4.15–18)

This recalls in miniature the prayer uttered by Ovid's Medea prior to her accomplishment of a similar feat, the medical–magical rejuvenation of Jason's father Aeson (see *Metamorphoses*, 7.192–219). We should not be surprised by this glancing reference to the great classical sorceress, who is a morally ambivalent or unplaceable figure as distinct from an evil one, and whom early modern accounts sometimes present entirely favourably.[50] Strongly in the Quarto version but less so in the Folio, Cordelia's personal qualities, words and actions serve to consolidate the image of a fundamentally good or harmonious natural order existing in full integrity and continuity with the life of human beings, with the effect that fundamental bonds between human beings are never in fact broken; as an agent within such a cosmos she can channel and exert medical–magical curative powers. There is also a touch of modernity in Cordelia's and the Quarto doctor's restorative procedures. The earlier action of the play contains suggestions of humoural imbalance, and Lear has looked like one surrounded by the familiar complexional types (Cornwall, 'the hot duke', is choleric; Albany is phlegmatic; Kent with his perpetual eagerness of manner is probably sanguine; the Gloucester family with its affinity for reflective thought inclines towards melancholia). Now, however, no mention is made of humoural correction proceeding along the familiar Hippocratic–Galenic lines, and Cordelia, like Paracelsus, goes directly for the cure.

(B) Edgar, on the other hand, takes an entirely different view of the human-to-cosmos relationship and of fundamental human connection; and implements this view in practice, moreover, with a ruthlessness which can be found disquieting. Why, in particular, does he take so long to reveal who he is to Gloucester, his now-blinded, psychologically crushed and despairing father?[51] A reason can, I would say, be quite straightforwardly given. Having gone through a kind of personal extinction and interim self-recreation as Mad Tom, Edgar entrusts himself and the life of those around him to what is *made* by chosen action, as distinct from received and consolidated as a natural given. Faced with Gloucester as he now finds him, tipping towards despair and its remedy in suicide, it seems clear that Edgar's response is not at all to console but to remake his father, as one who has moved beyond despair to belief that he has a place in the world; one of the intended purposes here is, I take it, that of forming a new relation with his altered father in due course. It does not matter to Edgar that Gloucester's newly instilled belief in the benignity of the gods (see 4.6.72–4) derives from a fiction, given that there was no fall from a cliff, no miraculous survival. One can believe about the cosmos what one likes, it seems, provided that this allows for the taking of suitable action within it. Human beings, for the very pragmatic Edgar, know adequately and act optimally in relation to only what they themselves have set in shape or brought into existence; in which case the intuitions and projections of cosmomorphism become, supposing that one wishes to entertain them, a potentially useful fantasy, no less, no more – a radical individualization of ostensibly collective experience if ever there was one. Edgar's constructivist position on valid human knowledge rhymes with that being advanced in the play's era by Francis Bacon.[52] The play seems to be giving this mode of thought its due, at the same time holding it up as an object of possibly troubling reflection. It is inimical to the naturalist position on knowledge which is associated in the play particularly with Kent. In the Folio version it becomes more prominent, not because it is given more forceful statement, but because here statement of the naturalist position is comparatively subdued. The Folio entirely excises the scene in which Cordelia becomes Kent's access to the vision of a *good* cosmos. In including the Fool's joking about prophecy at the end of the first storm scene (see 3.2.80–95), the Folio ridicules the idea that the cosmos has an integral life and history, organized for the discerning across time. In the scene of Lear's recovery it removes the curative music, redolent of harmonious cosmic form, along with the ministering doctor, in whose place we merely have a concerned 'Gentleman' who stands back to let Cordelia take charge of her father's welfare. I would say that this brings to the fore the precariousness of human relationship, imagined separately from any possible cosmic embedding: the relation between Cordelia and Lear becomes more exclusively what takes form *now*, in what passes between them.

Nevertheless, and as has been said, both these modes of thinking, which I am terming naturalist and constructivist, are operative to some degree in both the versions of *King Lear* that we have, an aspect of the play's Senecan rawness and openness of philosophical vision. One of the effects of their co-presence is to intensify the mental ordeal with the audience undergoes in witnessing the play's concluding action. To return to represented events which continue to shadow an 'eclipses' plot: In the final scene of the play Lear enters with the body of Cordelia in his arms, addressing onlookers thus:

> Howl, howl, howl, howl! O you are men of stones
> Had I your tongues and eyes, I would use them so
> That heaven's vault should crack. She's gone for ever.
> I know when one is dead and when one lives.
> She's dead as earth. Lend me a looking-glass;
> If that her breath will mist or stain the stone,
> Why, then she lives.

The three highest-ranking figures present now respond as choric witnesses:

Kent	Is this the promised end?
Edgar	Or image of that horror?
Albany	Fall and cease. (5.3.250–7)

Contextualized by the action's continuous probing of the human-to-cosmos relationship, the scene's apocalyptic symbolism is powerful. Shakespeare once again finds a way of bringing onstage, through a use of human avatars, the kind of eclipse action which is instated by description only in *Thyestes*. The moon here, as has been said, is female, and the sun male. We are looking at a dying sun, who howls in pain and holds in his arms an already dead moon – in the language of Sonnet 107 a 'mortal moon' who has not 'endured' eclipse – and is himself on the verge of dying through the ensuing, inescapable effects of grief. As Lear, bearing Cordelia's body, advances across the stage the pair are, in Kent's vision of them, enacting full cosmic dissolution, in the characters of a ruling sun and moon heading towards extinction. Kent asks 'Is this the promised end?' In *Thyestes*, we recall, the Chorus similarly takes the play's eclipse to be a sign of and occurrence in the world's ending. Kent in *King Lear*'s final scene believes that he is witnessing the world's destruction, and is prepared to die: 'I have a journey (. . .) shortly to go; / My master calls, and I must not say no' (5.3.313–4). Edgar on the other hand, opting for a mentality of survival, advises more cautious interpretation of what we have before us: this humanly enacted double eclipse is an 'image of that horror', the world's end; not the end itself, but an intimation of the terrible thing which it will be. It is well known that *King Lear* was only performed in an ameliorated or 'lightened' version where Cordelia does not die from the later seventeenth to the early nineteenth century. The horror which the play inspires in its original form has to do with the suggestion that, in its appalling represented conflicts and mutual damagings of human beings, the world itself is reeling towards destruction.

Part B

Introduction

Collective Representations, Symbolic Narratives

The chapters of this section are concerned centrally with *The Faerie Queene* and *The Pilgrim's Progress*. The approach which I take places them in, and also explores the possibility that they contribute to, a broad cultural development which is in several respects a privatization, a transference from trust from what seems to have been established by the group to what seems to have been established by the individual. The idea of a collective representation was introduced in Chapter 1 and can, as was suggested there, be captured quite readily in metaphor. A collective representation, often treated as if it *could* be a figured visual presentation and often given actual figured visual form,[1] projects a 'thought' which can be imagined as belonging to a collective human subject: 'us', 'we' – where 'we' can be one's immediate social group, one's forebears, one's co-believers, one's nation, *et alia* – have over the course of time and as refracted through the mentalities of many individuals shared a certain kind of experience, giving rise to a way of thinking about a reality which can, as a representation, be offered to the perception of any individual composing the 'we'. I have given the example of the *locus amoenus* or delightful place, in early modern European thought often redolent of Eden. The delightful place, conceived as bringing together several of the natural world's most pleasant features, can be presented to 'me', incorporate for these purposes with a 'we', as the kind of thing of which 'we' already have latent knowledge, a knowledge already *there* and mediating shared insight which can be refurbished for the individual perceiver at any time. I have suggested that the upholding of collective representations, seen as giving communicative form to valid knowledge, is fairly characteristic of premodern European culture. In a simple but reasonably viable definition an allegorical narrative, in such a context, is one that enables the beholder/hearer/reader to encounter – as it were to re-encounter and bring directly before individual consciousness, since 'we' already have knowledge of them – a series of 'scenes' and 'actions' partly made up of such visual mediations of collective experience and collective insight. A much explored collective representation, as it were a common 'place' in discourse, like the *locus amoenus*, will take on for its culture-rich symbolic valency, and is obviously susceptible of use or development ('cultivation' as if it were a piece of shared land) for many different individual purposes. An allegorical text which deploys collective representations resembles any other communicative text in being obliged to set up its own working relation between the already-familiar, therefore readily intelligible, and the novel or particular, therefore less readily intelligible though probably of greater immediate interest; but in the case of deployments of collective representations the novelty or particularity may, perhaps, be entirely a function of a familiar 'thought's' contextual placing, as in the case of the folkloric dances at Romans which on a particular occasion and in a particular angling were received by some as threatening political violence.

The represented actions of *The Faerie Queene* and *The Pilgrim's Progress* sometimes traverse figurative–discursive common places – conspicuously including the *locus amoenus* – and are themselves constituted in part by action motifs of traditional, commonly understood valency, such as the arming of a hero in preparation for necessary combat. Nevertheless, as soon as we note this we also note that these fields of common experience and knowledge, notionally shared by 'us' all, are treated by both texts with persistent or at least recurrent suspicion – to the point where a narrative agent's acceptance of a common motif's obvious and familiar meaning as symbolizing a reality can often function as a trap: one thinks, for example of the Redcross knight in Spenser's first book taking up with, in Duessa, the relatively conventional (-looking) version of a romance knight's lady, having fallen out of relationship with the more inscrutable Una, who is a figure harder to know or suppose that one knows generically. A good deal of such suspicion directed to the 'common' and received is, we could say, a function of both texts' Protestantism:[2] Protestant religious reform is often manifestly a sweeping away of familiar cultural representations, often specific images or kinds of image, which have in some degree oriented collective thought until the taking of such measures, and would presumably go on doing so if not removed from general access. The characteristic aim of early modern church reform, Catholic as well as Protestant, is certainly to draw collective, culturally received representations more fully within the scope of individual scrutiny and individual critical examination: ideally, one should *understand*, be able to conceptualize adequately, that to which as believer one *looks* – in the attempt to promote which faith ideal a detailed, extensive monitoring of individual religious thought and practice comes fiercely into play. Nevertheless, there are many fields of cultural representation which do not fall straightforwardly, or fall at all, within the designated terrain of ecclesiastical reform – one such being the *locus amoenus* itself; and our texts' broadly 'reformist' attitude to received cultural representations – their will or willingness to deliver them over to potentially devastating individual scrutiny and critique – is bound up with larger cultural transformations of which Protestant church reform and Catholic church reform are themselves components. I do not wish to explain the texts' 'reformism' away at an early stage in the enquiry, but to consider pragmatically what it is, and what it does – and also how far in particular instances it extends, since a narrative of purportedly general symbolic valency which summarily rejected, or placed in sceptical quarantine, every received collective representation whatsoever would have sawn off the branch on which it is also required to sit. In discussing Spenser, Bunyan and obvious precursor texts such as Langland's and Chaucer's, my concern will be to identify the formal resources of narrative allegory, with a view to tracking processes of generic change.

Readerly Isolation and Subjective Freedom in *The Faerie Queene*

Keats placed as epigraph to his 1817 *Poems* a quotation from Spenser's *Muiopotmos, or The Fate of the Butterfly*:

> What more felicity can fall to creature,
> Than to enjoy delight with liberty?[1]

There is a distinctive experience offered by reading Spenser, one of being given space for individual response and choice in the exploring of a virtual world, to which I wish to give special attention in the present chapter.[2] In Spenser's allegorical poem about a butterfly, writing highly regarded by Keats and his contemporaries, it is figured in the creature's free exploration and enjoyment of its world, and present in what occurs as the reader encounters and metaphorically takes or makes a way through the defiles of a complex, therefore spacious, literary construct.[3] Spenser's narrator expresses a similar idea in the Proem to Book Six of *The Faerie Queene* at a point where he, and presumably the reader, must be aware of having made their way deeply 'into' the poem as intricate structured form, one which encourages and rewards exploration led by desire and curiosity:

> The waies, through which my weary steps I guyde,
> > In this delightfull land of Faery,
> > Are so exceeding spacious and wyde,
> > And sprinckled with such sweet variety,
> > Of all that pleasant is to eare or eye,
> > That I nigh rauished with rare thoughts delight,
> > My tedious trauell doe forget thereby;

>   And when I gin to feele decay of might,
>   It strength to me supplies, and chears my dulled spright. (6.Proem.1)[4]

This bids to identify a distinctive experience of reading: if the 'waies' offered here for taking are 'spacious and wyde', this might only have the effect of increasing the experienced *longeurs* of travel; but the prime effect of this expansiveness is, on the contrary, to afford widened access to 'rare things' which lift the imagination and spirits. I shall over the course of the present chapter attempt to explain how this provision of readerly 'delight', bound up with the enjoyment of a kind of freedom, emerges as a feature of symbolic narrative design in *The Faerie Queene*. This will be the upshot of an argument which begins by considering some of the resources of narrative allegory, and the layout of the 'waies' which are there for reading to follow in gaining access to the spaces of the poem.

*   *   *

Symbolic narrative dealing in collective representations has obvious uses for the idea of a *way*, known or knowable to human beings in general as a function of shared experience. This is susceptible of a finite number of narrative figurations, which helps to establish their intelligibility. It can be a way optimally taken, an idea well defined in the Hebrew and Christian scriptures,[5] and therefore a way lost or a way refused or a way abandoned; which may also be taken to imply the existence of a contrary way taken with evil consequence – from which, however, in some conceptions it might be possible to depart – like the one which Paul characterizes, in a common reception of the text, as the 'way to destruction' (I Cor. 1.18).[6] In a philosophical fable attributed to Prodicus, roughly contemporary with Socrates, Hercules when young is required to choose between the path of virtue and the path of pleasure, where the taking of the second implies moral descent into vice.[7] *Or*, there are more pluralistic conceptions of a way, based on the notion that the choosing of a particular metaphoric route in life, as in the selection of a path at a point of routes' divergence, has by its nature differentiating consequences which are not necessarily polarized as good and bad; thus Book Three of *The Faerie Queene* distinguishes between individual ways taken in dealing with the force of love, several of them defined as ethically good, including Belphoebe's dedication to chastity, implying mental self-containedness, and her sister Amoret's to faithful erotic love.

If there one *way* which is optimally taken, a feature usual in Christian allegory though not confined to it, then the business of symbolic representation is to conduct the beholder/ hearer/ reader (from now on, for mere convenience, the reader)[8] along it. In respect of this the discursive constitution of a *way* takes on a dual aspect: (1) The narrative and argumentative development of a symbolic text can itself be the giving of definition to a *way*, independently of the representation at a 'literal' or 'vehicle' level of a path or journey. (2) And the figured taking of a path or making of a journey can also provide cognitive mapping of this development by offering what one might call 'signposts' to a right 'route' which the reader knows of or can be brought to recognize because it is validated by shared experience – such a 'route' obviously pre-exists the individual's taking of it. We find that symbolic narrative often negotiates in practice between the priority of representing a path or journey ('signposting'), useful perhaps for the offering of explicit guidance in the making of choices while grounding these choices in the attributed experience of the group, and the requirements of *being* the path or journey which the reader takes by becoming mentally caught up in and affected by its development. Chaucer's dream allegory known as *The Book of the Duchess* concerns the possible taking of a *way* of mourning (as occasioned by bereavement, by loss in love . . .) available to human beings in general, and attested in its value by common experience. The poem sets the dreamer on a represented path through symbolic settings and includes, in the man wearing black whom the dreamer encounters, one who seems to be immobilized by grief, but who is drawn into conversation and acts of remembering; which is to say that it lightly defines at the literal level a path leading towards grief's alleviation, while being in some degree *itself* such a path – the dreamer, for his part, begins as one stultified by grief and ends as one who relishes the prospect of writing a poem.

Langland's *Piers Plowman*, another significant intertext for *The Faerie Queene*,[9] shows however that it is possible to set up a provocative tension between a development of thought that may be 'signposted' in the making of a journey, and other features of what a narrative text can provide. In the second vision of *Piers Plowman* Langland's omni-representative 'folk', who have just heard Reason's inspirational sermon and received instruction from Repentance, set out on a journey, a kind of pilgrimage patterned on real and familiar ones, whose goal however is Truth; that is, not the sort of objective or discovery at which an ordinary pilgrimage aims. Experiencing difficulty in finding the way, they sense the need for a guide; at which point there arrives in the narrative a ploughman, named Piers (the name very distantly evokes the apostle Peter), who offers to take on that function. Here it is worth recalling Chaucer's morally idealized ploughman in the Prologue to *The Canterbury Tales*, invented at about the same time.[10] In the texts' shared conception the small farmer who goes dedicatedly about the business of being one, thus providing for others as well as himself and helping to constitute an interlinked community, may well count as a practical instance of one who lives in goodness.[11]

This serves to bring out, however, a significant tension in the narrative conception of Langland's Piers. Figuring in the narrative of a journey towards Truth, he is or should be a guide who indicates the path. But as one who lives the good life, standing in a relation to Truth where practice and understanding are fused – 'I know him as kindly [naturally, directly]' claims Piers, 'as a clerk knows his books' (see 5.538)[12] – he is more simply and directly a personal example to be imitated. But pursuit of this thought tends to remove the promise of textually produced travel and discovery: the folk are to find Truth or become close to Truth by *being like* Piers – in the symbolic scene which now takes shape, by working voluntarily alongside him in his half-acre field – and not by moving into new terrain under his guidance, which would figure the accessing of some *other* kind of experience and self-awareness. If Truth is to be found, it ('he') is apparently to be found *here*. At one point, Piers offers guidance about a journey; but this journey-guidance is nothing other than a recalling of basic morality, causing the allure of a metaphoric journey to disappear. 'You should proceed', Piers tells the would-be pilgrims, 'by way of a brook called "Be-Mild-Of-Speech" / Until you find a ford, "Honour-Your-Parents"' (see 5.566–7), and so on. This move in the poem seems calculatedly irritating: the reader presumably wants and expects the guidance of a potent, evolved symbolism, organized around the motif of a journey, but all she/he gets is rote instruction of the kind that might be offered to a child – as if to say that the reader needs to 'follow' Piers in grasping the rudimentary before attempting anything more sophisticated; or perhaps that there is no 'more sophisticated', on the principle that the goodness of Christian moral teaching is not a sophistication.

There is, then, a certain inimicality or lack of fit between the giving of definition to a *way*, and the representation of an example for the reader to imitate in life. If the example is a convincing and successful one, then the *way* takes care of itself: supposing that one has become like Piers, one is already, it seems, in the sort of motion which is oriented towards Truth. Setting forth the purely exemplary tends to subvert the offering of guidance concerning the phased accomplishment of a progressive development. When such subversion is taking place, what becomes of the symbolic narrative in hand? Piers seems not to be a proper or satisfactory participant in the narrative which we have been discussing, since he provides no active accommodation of the metaphor of journey.[13]

The issue emerges again in the poem as the second vision's would-be pilgrims, now temporarily detained or indeed stuck in Piers' half-acre field, encounter the figure called Hunger. He is, as it were, Piers' monstrous counterpart, whom Piers has summoned in the first place in a desperate attempt to cow and discipline the work-force. Hunger speaks, in his fashion, for truth, but under the aspect of natural necessity: his is the rasping voice *of* hunger, projecting a mentality that is likely to emerge in people subjected to the threat of famine or experiencing its pangs. Hunger's social ethic is brutal (roughly, 'If people don't work, let them starve'), and probably, as Piers soon notices, decidedly un-Christian. There is dark humour in the poem's wheeling on of Hunger as purveyor of moral instruction: subjected to his 'teaching', the folk find themselves removed even further from intuition concerning goodness, and for that matter from the prospect of making a progressive journey. To experience the world as this second vision has it is, it seems, to approximate increasingly to the condition of Hunger, an immobile figure who suffers and rants. The development of a symbolic narrative that defines a *way forward*, by any means or at any level, has by the phase of the Hunger episode completely stalled.[14] This is an effect of the introduction into it both of a Piers whose 'teaching' is, primarily, lived example, and of a Hunger whose still more vivid 'teaching' is that of pain which gnaws the belly. But as negative and admonitory example, that of one whom Langland and many of his contemporaries will sometimes have found themselves to be like, to their detriment, Hunger is a considerable success.

Within the episode, summarily, Piers as exemplary figure critiques by his presence and potential effects a familiar cultural mentality of pilgrimage, while the commanding projection of a symbolic journey exposes the limitations of a vision dominated by Hunger as raw registration of naturally occurring need. The episode also intimates, pertinently to the procedures of symbolic narrative in Spenser, that while the pragmatic-*cum*-conceptual solutions to these impasses are not going to be readily found, the impasses themselves nevertheless require determined definition.[15] Considering the functions of an example helps us to understand what, within a symbolic narrative design, can work *against* the self-definition of a text as the pointing up of an already recognized, independently established route to be taken. The exemplary is an anomalous feature of a text conceived as constituting a *way* in its own development: by entering the text in the form of the exceptional or novel and, in principle, setting the reader in a kind of text-independent motion, it actively negates or at least questions the idea that the text is a useful traversing of the collectively known and recognizable.

This helps us to understand important features of design in Spenser's 'Letter to Raleigh', printed with the poem from the first edition of 1590, as they bear on the poem's shaping of the experience of reading. Purporting to describe 'the general intention and meaning' of the text, characterized as 'a continued Allegory, or darke conceit',[16] the 'Letter' is partly concerned with the tension between symbolic narrative as reminder of the collectively known, and as means of mobilizing for the individually receptive reader new forms of thought and action. The 'Letter' projects the difference between the two kinds of literary formation at more than one level. The first half of the 'Letter' is substantially concerned with the poem's foregrounding of exemplary figures. There is prince Arthur, portrayed as 'a braue knight, perfected in the twelue private morall vertues'; which explicitly takes up the *Nichomachean Ethics*' distinction between private and public (political) virtues.[17] Spenser names among Arthur's literary predecessors Tasso's Rinaldo, viewed as projecting 'the vertues of a priuate man', and his Godfredo, viewed as projecting the political ones. The rationale given for setting an exemplary human figure before the reader is that instruction 'by ensample' is inherently 'more profitable and gratious' than instruction 'by rule', where an instance given of the second is Plato's theoretical account of an ideal commonwealth's structure in *The Republic*, and of the first, Xenophon's fashioning (a term to which we shall return) 'in the person of Cyrus and the Persians (. . .) a gouernement such as might best be'; in Sidney's parallel account Xenophon's *Cyropaedia* 'bestow[s] a Cyrus upon the world' in such a way as to 'make many Cyruses',[18] which is different from providing an axiomatic exposition of good rule. Spenser's and Sidney's point is that the reader is more likely to find ethical improvement in imitating such figures which, as Aristotle suggests, occurs with psychological spontaneity,[19] than in attempting to apply to the business of living tabulated rules and precepts.

The 'Letter' moves on to give the poem's 'shadowing' of the Queen – 'shadow' in the era's language covers 'reflection in a mirror' as well as the word's ordinary modern sense – an exemplary aspect, in that its Belphoebe, corresponding to one of her 'persons', is 'a most virtuous and beautiful Lady'. *But* in her other 'person', that of monarch, Elizabeth is said to have as her correlate in the poem the Faerie Queene, by whom, writes Spenser, 'I meane glory in my generall intention', while her realm's correlate is the 'Faerye land' which this mirror-queen rules. Glory is that to which Arthur and the other poem-knights aspire (Arthur has in its fictional conceit himself fallen in love with the Fairy Queen), while its represented Fairy Land is the space of adventure, in romance's generic understanding of 'adventure', where they work out their individual destinies – this term and this name point to a narrative of becoming, where the experience of reading should also be one of progression. It is in keeping with this other thought that the second half of the 'Letter' concerns itself largely with the narrative development of the poem's underlying feigned history, which begins offstage at the Fairy Queen's court; and that, in its trailering of them, the main line of adventures becomes 'intermedled, (. . .) rather as Accidents, then intendments' with yet other adventures. These are said to include 'the loue of Britomart, the ouerthrow of Marinell, the misery of Florimell, the vertuousness of Belphoebe' and 'the lasciuiousness of Hellenora'; which is to say that they comprise, as the reader can know independently of the 'Letter', most of the material of Book Three. The 'Letter' tilts, then, in its development, more towards a profiling of narrative journey, and of discovery made over a span of adventure/ reading, than the opening argument, with its decisive recommendation of the perfected example, would have led one to expect.

The 'Letter' also introduces from an early stage an intellectually provocative language of 'fashioning'. What is probably its most loaded statement runs, 'The generall end (. . .) of all the booke is to fashion a gentleman or noble person in virtuous and gentle discipline.' As A. C. Hamilton points out, 'the poem's subtitle, "[Disposed into twelve books,] *Fashioning* XII. Morall vertues", indicates that the poem fashions a virtue by showing a hero fashioning or fashioned by it.'[20] So, fashioning (moulding, constructing) can be of *a virtue*, presumably as a mode of behaviour which requires explication, and also, in the light of what the 'Letter' claims about presented examples, of *a virtuous figure* in representation, one who takes action within the framework of the narrative. But it can additionally be, given that the 'Letter' has just referred to the misreadings endemically produced by an ill-disposed mind ('gealous opinions and misconstructions'), *of the virtuous reader* whose bringing into conceptual–practical existence this poem has as its declared purpose. Such threefold fashioning can be considered under the aspect of result, and under the aspect of process: the 'fashioned' reader in the first aspect is a kind of perfected creature who can with profit exit from reading into living; but the 'fashioned' reader in the second is one who submits in the act of reading to sequential and not necessarily end-directed self-discovery and self-change. One finds a similar duality in the 'Letter's' description of individual knight-heroes as the 'patron[s]' of their book's focal virtue. 'Patron' is linguistically cognate with 'pattern'; a knight in movement through the narrative would thus present the finished model of a virtue transposed into a mode of action. But a patron is also the defender or upholder of someone or something,[21] which may here include overseeing the making, as a conceptual–practical structure, of a virtue and its development of in themselves and in others: the patron in this other sense oversees and participates in a work in progress.

The 'Letter to Raleigh' thus helps to put form to the poem's self-awareness as a mediation of the culturally known and the newly established; for example, the poem's 'realm' as shadowed in its fictional Fairy Land – roughly, Britain under Tudor rule – is conceived both as a repository of tradition and collective awareness, and as a locus for emergence of the valid new; let us say, under the auspices of humanistic study and enquiry, going with widening of cognitive horizons, of global connection through discovery, trade and colonization, and of the Protestant reform of worship. The poem's central ideological warranty is the reformist Tudor state, much as the *Aeneid*'s is the newly inaugurated empire of Augustus. In its general tenor this is obvious; but what has been less obvious to commentators is the specific strategy of symbolic mediation between the shared and received, and what is emerging specifically *now*, allegedly in the ambient culture, even in *these* acts of writing and reading.

From now on I shall be concerned, for expository convenience, mainly with the poem as first issued in 1590. No 'straighter' in its thinking procedures than *Piers Plowman*, The Faerie Queene establishes a complex and shifting relationship between the producing or enacting of progression, and giving of definition to the exemplary. The poem's symbolic mediations of this relationship take strikingly different forms in its first three books.

Book One incites considerable suspicion of the way generally taken, while also dwelling on the dangers of losing one's way altogether. Redcross, Una and the dwarf become lost, of course, after seeking refuge from a storm in a densely treed wood which has the characteristics of a 'labyrinth'; for example, the path that seems nearest to an 'end' turns out to furthest from it. There is a certain ambivalence of value to the most 'beaten' path (1.1.10–11) which they select as the most promising of several (in an actual maze, of course, the path showing the signs of greatest wear is not necessarily the correct one): it leads them to Error's cave – but, then again, encounter with Error (literally, 'wandering') may be inescapable in what Una terms 'the wandring wood'[22] (13); the 'beaten' path (28) subsequently followed without deviation does lead Redcross and party out of the wood, but also to an encounter with Archimago 'vpon the way' (29; more on these disorientations shortly). Approach to Pride's palace is made by 'a broad high way (. . .) / All bare through people's feet', littered with corpses and the dying, along which many pass 'day and night' (4.2–3). Redcross's quest shows some features of a search-and-destroy mission: in romance a knight on adventure of self-proof characteristically destroys monsters and suppresses evil customs, defeating or killing their instigators (see Artegall in the opening cantos of Book Five); symbolically, Redcross's business is to rid the common mind of its 'monsters' and other evil denizens, an obvious example of the first being Error. But the Error episode suggests nonetheless that straightforward confrontation, issuing in combat, is not necessarily the optimal strategy. In fighting Error, Redcross falls into the monster's sinuous clutches, confusing its body parts with his own and only narrowly breaking free when Una shouts encouragement. It also transpires that Archimago can readily manipulate a mentality of virtuous confrontation.

The first book's Arthur is an exemplary figure, in some respects bearing out what is stated in the poem's accompanying 'Letter'; he is an idealizing representation of secular power as exerted to instate the good. But he is also a dazzling or numinous figure, possessed of certain inexplicable powers and magical attributes, as distinct from an imitable behavioural model. Redcross's career is exemplary in so far as English history becomes that in a roughly Foxeian assessment; that is, subservience to false religion, and the evil consequences of the same, brought to reflection, increase capacity to recognize the true one. In the first vision of *Piers Plowman*, similarly, Lady Mede (reward, bribery) is found to have been substituted for Holy Church as an object of veneration, with the possible consequence that careful inspection of a simulacrum will re-establish conditions for perception of what is genuine. But the strategy in Langland seems a risky one, and placing of trust in it arises by default: the Dreamer, finding Holy Church's manner remote and her teaching elusive, even incomprehensible, has desperately asked to be presented with something with which he can find a personal affinity, and therefore begin to understand (see the start of Passus 2).

In *Book Two*, by contrast, Guyon from the start offers an imitable example, but it and the manner of its offering are pedestrian – literally so, because Guyon at this point lacks a horse and proceeds circumspectly on foot. The idea that living in temperance equates with finding a middle way between presented extremes (see Aristotle, *Ethics*, 2, 7–9) is schoolbook simple, and generates some of the poem's flattest symbolic narrative. Here Medina, for instance, behaviourally projects a middle way between the lascivious forwardness of her sister Perissa and the scornful aloofness of her sister Elissa. But the book also introduces from an early stage the considerably more subtle and demanding idea that temperance is arrival at a proper 'mixing' or reconciliation of the passionate and the considered; in other words, that the passions are to be placed fully under wise direction *and* at the same time fully needed. Much of the book is Guyon's cumulative, though also fitful and uneven, education by experience. He is provided with a vantage-point from which to re-examine known features of the culture, as in the instances of its attitude to money and fungible wealth (Mammon's cave) and to bodily well-being as cultivation of pleasure, confused in the poem's perspective with the philosophers' *eudaemonia* (the Bower of Bliss).[23] Guyon, then, is in some limited respects an exemplary figure; his adventures are also so shaped as to submit familiar features of shared life to a searching re-evaluation.

But *Book Three* (especially, but not solely, if approached by way of reading books One and Two)[24] has markedly troubled dealings with going cultural representations. Book One in due course defines a *way*, primarily that of Protestant-Christian church-formation, having confronted perplexing alternatives. Book Two is founded in a case for and conceptions of ethical temperance which present acceptable philosophical credentials. The poem's third book, on the other hand, lacks epistemological drawstrings. It deals extensively in and with received conceptions of sexual love, but without the prior establishment of a cognitive high ground (and Arthur here finds himself out of his psychological depth; see 3.4.47–61). Its aim, as I shall attempt to explain further below, is to produce subjective disengagement from certain cultural representations which, sealed off as they from reasoned argument and even pragmatic evaluation, can look highly compelling. Its quest, in so far as it gives symbolic definition to a *way*, is for a *means* of understanding and taking suitable action in relation to what diverse experience of love presents. The central figure, Britomart, is so completely and dynamically in action as not to establish an imitable pattern for life and the making of choices – though, as I shall go on to suggest, her manner of being a narrative agent makes her exemplary to different effect. The book's climactic action bids to remove the enchantment – the given but magically inexplicable allure – of a powerful nexus of cultural representations, while Britomart here acts out of contrary powers, placed as elemental,[25] as one not rationally cognizant of what she does.

I wish, then, to keep a close eye on roles which are assigned to the reader as one caught up in a collectively registered process of cultural change, but also as one who encounters the new and formative as a phenomenon that can take shape in her/his particular act of reading. Three snapshots of episodes from and aspects of the 1590 three-book poem will have to serve in the place of a continuous account. I shall consider the beginning of Book One, the Alma allegory from Book Two, and Book Three's narrative landscaping.

*   *   *

As has been said, one of the key tasks self-assigned to the poem as a work of reformist ambitions is submitting to critical examination and, where suitable, putting into abeyance and/or replacing givens of common sense, representations which mobilize common feeling – as in the case of Duessa and the traditional loyalties which she can bring to a focus – and familiar constructions of the (old sense) probable. Given that the poem is substantially a work of narrative, the commonplaces of books One to Three are given realization primarily as common places, pieces of virtual topography or the imagined ambiences of figures in movement such as Una and Archimago. Appraisal of these places is a dangerous business, since as terrain and milieu they commonly mislead perception, appearing to offer cognitive–practical security when they do nothing of the kind.

Shortly after the reader first encounters them Redcross, Una and the attendant dwarf find shelter from a sudden storm in a wood where, entering one of the common places of georgic poetry,[26] they find instructive images of human life in the properties and uses of different tree species:

> The Laurell, meed of mightie Conquerours
> And poets sage; the Firre that weepeth still:
> The Willow, worne of forlorne Paramours;
> The Eugh, obedient to the bender's will . . . . (1.1.9)

Here the obvious reference is to a passage from one of Virgil's *Georgics* (2.440–53), which were definitive of the genre. This kind of poetic writing, named from *georgein* = 'to work the soil', correlates well enough with a central narrative agent who is latently Saint George, and who has before taking up Una's quest lived as a farmer. This wood bears with it forms of widely applicable knowledge which generations of human beings have consolidated in arboriculture. It suits Redcross and his companions temporarily as a place to escape bad weather and source of pleasurable instruction (they advance into it 'Led with delight'). But it provides no security for them in their quest; in exploring it they lose the straightforward path and find themselves wandering 'too and fro in waies vnknowne' (stanza 10). In providing this new experience the wood of georgic poetry has mutated into a romance location projecting disorientation and possible threat. It is now, as we have seen, characterized as a 'labyrinth', in which Redcross soon dismounts on finding 'a hollow caue / Amid the thickest woods' (11). Una's new assessment of their situation suggests that it would have been better not to have entered this wood in the first place. This perception goes with further meta-narrative hesitation over genre: within the framework of epic possibly and in the pragmatic view taken by the dwarf certainly it is a peril to be avoided (see 13); Redcross on the other hand, implicitly seeing it as an adventure in a romance knight's self-proof, opts to enter the cave (see 14). The questers' loss of certain direction here, topological with generic connotation, is given narrative immediacy in the parallel experience of the reader, who is in no better position to anticipate or construe these developments than they are.

This episode seems to have been placed at the beginning of *The Faerie Queene* in order to provide cues to reading which will be of relevance throughout. This symbolic poem gets under way as a narrative exploration of common (group experiential) ground, defined in this first instance by two well-established genres, georgic and romance, and perhaps allusively a third, epic (here one thinks, for example, of Odysseus's encounters with monsters where his primary concern is survival). But we can see that this definition works discrepantly, that a genre can morph without warning into another, and that genres simultaneously evoked can pull in different interpretative directions. The figurative labyrinth in which Redcross and his companions wander is in effect that of intertextuality, multiplicity of reference necessarily set in play by any text that engages with its culture's discursive commonplaces, collective experience in textual and figured embodiment. But to confront what is labyrinthine in this intertextuality in the way that the poem does is to recognize that it is the accidental deposit of a multifarious, uncentred collective history. Dealings with it as one finds it have no cognitive security: encountered in its contingency, it is not necessarily useful or good or pertinent to know; moreover, the knowledge-claims which it presents may themselves be specious. *The Faerie Queene* draws the reader into exploration of common ideational ground as the culture has it, on a developing understanding that this ground is dangerous, an understanding which first takes form in the experience of radical disorientation. But to promote such an understanding is also to suggest that controls can be placed on intertextual play and slippage, that it may be possible to find an interpretative *way*, that one need not be indefinitely troubled by the more appalling denizens of the collective mind. At the upshot of Redcross's fight with the serpentine dragon Error she serially explodes, in spewing up poisonous vomit consisting of stinking raw meat and 'bookes and papers' as well as eyeless frogs and toads, followed by 'Deformed monsters (. . .) blacke as inke' (20, 22) which issue from her prolific womb; these burst in their turn as they insatiably drink their mother's blood (see 25–6). The dragon's foul environment is that of a physically loathsome adversary, including in Boschian manner detritus produced by the contemporary culture of print. If the physical progress of the poem's central figures is through the inherently treacherous and perilous terrain of received cultural knowledge, their progress as probing and experiment causes it to make itself known and sometimes, as here, to define itself in a suitably repugnant form.

*   *   *

Book Two produces, however, in the Castle of Alma sequence (see 2.9.1–2.12.1) both a recapturing and a reshaping of received cultural knowledge. In respect of the first it invites the reader to take stock of long-standing traditions of symbolic corporeal representation.[27] This castle-body is a mirror-like apparatus presented as a means of assembling and organizing attributively *collective* knowledge. It draws together, by 'reflecting', what announces itself as shared experience, offering it in a kind of summation to the individual beholder. Setting up an image of the body as a knowledge-mirror projects the principle – more or less an anthropological universal, as Vico recognized (see the following chapter) – that bodily form and process possess a priori validity as a means of organizing and displaying cultural data. The collectivist mirror-body is also loosely integrative of knowledge: it is a medium for the simultaneous, partially co-ordinated presentation of thoughts about the human. Spenser's Castle of Alma stands in continuity with preceding allegorical representations, most obviously the Castle of Anima in Langland.[28] Like collectivist symbolic writing in general, the episode creatively explores dissonances and correspondences between the discrepant systems of understanding with which it simultaneously engages; for example, this castle, which is solidly constructed like a piece of architecture, also shakes apprehensively – so expressing its likeness to a sentient body – when surprised by a sudden noise (see 9.11).

It will be useful to identify the predominant knowledge schemes, co-ordinated and integrated in some degree by bodily reference, which the episode *qua* 'mirror' recalls. Lady Alma's governance of the castle as chatelaine connotes the proper functioning of the human rational soul which, as a later book has it, 'doth rule the earthly masse [i.e. the body, its inferior], / And all the service of the bodie frame' (4.9.2) in the manner which Plato and Aristotle prescribe; but the internal divisions of the castle, progressively explored by its visitors in the narrated action, also reference those of the soul itself, traditionally divided into vegetable (presiding over nourishment and growth), sensitive (the arena of feelings) and intellectual (interrelating judgement, imagination and memory). The Alma narrative defines a major point of crossing between otherwise divergent strands of discourse. Very conspicuously, it sets in play conceptions of the moral life in a broadly classical understanding, where temperance is a finding of balance or reconciliation between extremes, but also in a broadly Christian understanding, as projected in metaphors of unremitting struggle and the search for salvation. It also invokes a transcendent Pythagorean–Platonic mathematics, which is taken to underlie the organization of the real, including that of the cosmos at every level, and which comes to the fore in the well-known *conundra* of the 'mathematical stanza' (9.22); what is stated here has clear, iconic internal structure as a conjoining of the circle, the triangle and the square, but its bearing on bodily form as such and on its surrounding symbolic scene remains indefinitely open to speculative enquiry.[29]

The whole episode's metaphoric conception is, moreover, sustained in part by the notion of the body politic. More will be said of this shortly, but we may note for the time being the episode's manifest concern with the hierarchical distribution of social functions, and with propriety of behaviour in ordinary social interaction, as in warfare. The era's consideration of the *polis* as a body itself mediates tensions between classical thought on optimal structures of rule[30] and the Pauline account of the spontaneous integration of a Christian spiritual community. The castle carries, as was noted earlier, the double connotative weighting of a nervously responsive living organism and a construction that is robust and enduring (see also 9.21,45); in the second respect it is a piece of well-designed architecture, made following medieval practice and as Vitruvian theory recommends in bodily concordant proportions. The image of a properly constructed castle submitted to siege by forces bent on its destruction sits well with the medieval narrative scheme of the *psychomachia*, or struggle within and for the human soul.[31] Finally the episode has contemporary national-cultural and geographic reference, again unstable in character: in so far as the castle is under attack, it seems to be in Spenser's Ireland (assailants rise against Arthur and his squire, who have not yet gained admittance to the castle, like 'a swarme of Gnats at euentide / Out of the fennes of Allan'; 9.16); the castle's fine 'porch' (its chin) is on the other hand made of exceptionally valuable stone 'far from

Ireland brought' (9.24), and therefore self-locates in the England of the poem's publication.

Symbolic narrative in the Alma sequence thus explores several receptions of the image of the body as portal to knowledge, in a spirit of inclusiveness and without disturbing the forms of reception themselves. But, having identified this strong tendency in Spenser's symbolic account of the body, I intend now to identify another, making for the availability of quite a different kind of reading. I shall turn to features of the body-castle episode which are explicitly *disaligned* from reference to what can already be established or posited as collective knowledge. Reading on this other track requires the pursuit of disambiguation and the attempted construction of univocal meaning in a curbing of intertextual play. What is offered to reading along this track is not a resumé of collective experiences but novel instruction to the individual about self-making as a temperate body-mind.

Declaration that a working model for ethical temperance has been provided does not come after the description of Alma's castle in Canto 9, but after the description of Arthur's struggle with Maleger and his followers in Canto 11, where the image of the castle itself loses narrative significance. Canto 12 begins with the following narratorial declaration:

> Now gins this goodly frame of Temperance
> Fairly to rise, and her adorned hed
> To pricke [mark aimed at] of highest praise forth to aduaunce,
> Formerly grounded, and fast setteled,
> On firme foundation of true bountyhed [goodness, virtue]. (12.1)

Temperance's 'frame' as characterized here is partly modelled on the human body – it has a 'head' – and is also firmly founded like an architectural construction. Nevertheless, correct apprehension of it requires us to take account of Canto 11, with its dispersed, relatively chaotic visual scene, and not only the architecturally centred scene of Canto 9. It will be necessary to re-examine our conception of what I have been terming the body-castle episode since, as Spenser's narrator explains at the start, the human body is symbolically represented here not once but twice. As 'kept in sober government' it is the 'most fair and excellent' of God's works; but as deprived of temperance 'though misrule and passions bace: / It growes a Monster, and incontinent [immediately, with a pun on moral 'incontinence'] / Doth lose his dignity and natiue grace.' In reading the passage we will '[b]ehold (. . .) both one and other in this place' (9.1). The episode's human body is the castle

under Alma's governance with its demurely polite social etiquette: here the
going amusements are restrained flirtation (9.36–44) and reading (Canto 10).
But it is also with equal insistence the throng of rabble-insurgents who have
the castle under siege. I think that I can explain why the poem's instructive
body needs to be shown in two entirely different forms.

Book Two describes the moral education of its central figure Guyon,
represented as young and approaching maturation, and is among other things
a bid to civilize its reader along lines well recognized in the period. Individual
attainment of civility here necessitates some withdrawal of emotional-cum-
intellectual attachment to the universal, collective human body. As was
explained, following Norbert Elias, in the first chapter, the period's raising of
the bar for standards of refinement went with the treatment of ever-growing
areas of 'natural' or commonplace behaviour as unmannerly and indelicate. This
involved inter alia self-distancing from one's own and others' bodily functions,
sanctioning use of such novel items as commodes, handkerchieves and
nightwear. As well as evoking traditional symbolisms, the Alma episode offers
an *anatomy* of newly conceived symbolic structures in a specific articulation.
Here 'anatomy' carries its up-to-date, somewhat Vesalian meaning of a precise,
painstaking examination and exposition of bodily forms or processes in their
functional interconnectedness; in respect of this procedure the body's most
significant analogues are the thoroughly planned building and the machine.[32]
A good deal of Canto 9 is given to systematic, anatomical description of this
particular well-designed and properly functional bodily system.[33] Conceived
with topological accuracy as an apparatus which connects mouth and anus (its
'two gates'; 9.23), it takes in guests much as it takes in food; its teeth, for example,
are a welcoming corps of disciplined guards (see 9.26). We are informed in some
detail about the efficient workings of its digestive tract, culminating in excretion
(9.27–33), of its emotional life, leading to self-preoccupied impasse (9.33–44),
and of its cognitive equipment, disposed as three persons who occupy adjoining
chambers in the turret (9.44–60). A. C. Hamilton comments, not unreasonably,
that some of the body-castle's features may be modelled on Spenser's personal
appearance (see 9.24n); this is an individually originated account of optimal
bodily form and function, and one that pointedly emphasizes individual
control or management of the individual body: the body becomes a kind of
well-organized machine which one personally controls and operates.

To view the passage in this other way, also sanctioned for reading, is to witness
a foundering of the metaphorics of the unitary body politic. In so far as the
body under consideration is a collective body, this is shown to exist partly as a

formless horde of '[v]ile caitiue wretches, ragged, rude, deformd, / All threatening death' (9.13), connoting political misrule (popular insurgency in a government view) and disease as a form of bodily dissolution. The polar opposite of such disorder and its proposed remedy is the passage's anatomical modelling of the disciplined, systemically interconnected and pragmatically functional body. This is introduced into the poem's discourse as a novel intellectual construction which is to play its part in the ethical forming of the reader. As has been said, one of the poem's purposes as declared in the 'Letter to Raleigh', to 'fashion (represent, mould, create)' optimal human beings in motion whose compelling example will, like that of Cyrus and his army in the *Anabasis*, contribute towards the 'fashioning' of readers who can live optimal lives (see 714–6).[34] Vesalius' *De Humanis Corporis Fabrica* (1543) has as one of its objectives the dissemination of anatomical knowledge to all, including relatively unlearned practitioners of surgery and courtiers intrigued by the book's design.[35] *The Faerie Queene's* exemplary anatomy of the living body is not, on the other hand, *for* all members of the *polis*: those given over to 'misrule' have thereby demonstrated incapacity to comprehend it, and are discovered raging in the body-castle's vicinity.[36] Its meaning as a matter of applicability to individual life, not already assumed to be a given of group experience, is best acquired, along this track of thought, through a labour and *pathos* of individual understanding.

This returns us to a question which was raised earlier: why should the 'frame' of Temperance be said to come into view after the spatially dispersed fighting of Canto 11, and not after the description of an architectural-*cum*-mechanical structure in Canto 9? The answer is, I would suggest, that the significance of the book's modelling of an optimal body is best grasped through reflection on what is primarily a form of *individual* experience, one which the individual thinking/feeling in isolation mainly possesses or undergoes, and is therefore in a suitable position to interpret. Here our vehicle for such reflection is Arthur, who attempts to fight Malegar as leader of the horde which has been besieging the castle. As this episode makes clear, while the collectivist (knowledge-mirroring) symbolic body is supra-individual and unthreatened by mortality, the individually constructed symbolic body carries significance only in the context of individual life; or, to put it more concretely, we come to value it fully only by learning that we, personally, are going to die, and that what it models, however useful or prestigious, can falter in its personal application – we all sometimes become fatigued or fall sick. The episode of Arthur and Malegar is largely untraditional as narrative allegory (one can source its individual components,[37] but not its whole organization), highly paradoxical as narrative action (see especially 11.39–40) and, against the background of the larger poem, distinctively unchivalric in styling since Arthur nearly dies during the combat not at Malegar's hand but when attacked by two haggard, physically feeble women. Named by the narrator Impotence and Impatience, these project individual, isolating forms of experience, ones which it would be emotionally preferable not to have, and which it is hard to put forward as being of value in the public domain: as well as being self-governing machine-like structures we are also, as seen from the standpoint of attempted self-possession, beings whom exercise limited and unreliable powers and, *qua* 'impatient', ones who struggle against acceptance of that condition. Health – classical *salus*, with connotations of salvation and safety – has by this point in the symbolic narrative morphed into a phenomenon which is to be scrutinized and monitored primarily at the individual level, as distinct from the collective one. The poem's construction of Temperance gains its most strongly shaping imaginative force as a consequence of the reader's cathartic acceptance of vulnerability to personal suffering in the forms of weakness and illness, anticipatory reminders of death as the individual body's terminal dissolution.

I have identified three moments in the reading of Spenser's Alma passage: that of accepting the force of traditional symbolic representations centred on the body, shown in an image which is, however and as it transpires, divided and unintegrated because the body politic itself is divided and unintegrated; that of tracing the interconnections of a novel symbolic body, architectural and mechanical in construction, at the individual's disposal; and that of integrating response to this imposing model body with awareness of individual frailty and mortality. I have also suggested that reading of the passage encompasses these moments sequentially, in the order just set out. Some of the compelling force of the first, collectivist symbolizing of the body spills over into those recensions of the body image whose function is to mobilize individual autonomy and individualized self-awareness. We also find, however, that in the Alma episode the commandingly integrated image of the collective body undergoes division, through the expelling of certain shared forms of awareness – primarily, those which reject conceptions of hierarchy as a means of organizing social experience. An image which should make for the unification of attributive collective and attributively individual experience is thus broken in two, the effect of a controlled conceptual explosion.

*   *   *

What announces itself as vulnerability to suffering in Book Two mutates, however, in Book Three into openness to mentality-altering and potentially enlightening experience. Something of the ethical seriousness and difficulty of Book Three's task can be brought out by reference to a passage from Sidney, whose religious, philosophical and political affiliations are similarly aligned to Spenser's. The fifth sonnet from *Astrophil and Stella*, more sombre in manner than the ones which precede it, offers the following argument against submission to love's powers:

> It is most true, what we call Cupid's dart,
> An image is, which for ourselves we carve;
> And, fools, adore in temple of our heart,
> Till that good god make church and churchman starve.[38]

The narrative here concerns the fabrication of an idol, followed by its oddly dedicated worshipping. 'Cupid's dart', a figure for love's power to get through the mind's defences, to wound and inflict pain, is an agent which the ostensible victim invents or constructs. In a sense it is a thing not there, an image laying false ontological claims, producing real effects out of a gratuitous fabrication. And yet is it found to be present as an item in the heart considered as 'temple', in fact present as an object to be adored, functioning within this internal cult as a kind of substitute for the adored but more elusive person who occasioned love in the first place. It is the product of a false interiorization which accompanies a false construction of externality. We find that the ensuing sonnets are full of stories about this Cupid and his irresistible self-imposition, as if from without, on the lover. Love perceived as an invasive, externally imposed and therefore cruel, degrading force is in *The Faerie Queene* as in *Astrophil and Stella* a paradigmatic idol, a thing perceived as being already *there*, while in fact being created subliminally in the perceptual act itself. This manner of false perception, diagnosed by Sidney and Spenser, does however have a tradition behind it. Their thought in respect of this maps and puts to secular application reformist Protestant thought about the deceitfulness of religious images.[39] *The Faerie Queene*'s confrontation with love takes shape in the understanding that it impinges on the individual mind with a kind of givenness, because it has acquired the substantiality of a familiar collective representation, of a phenomenon found recurrently and over the long term in the semiotic activity of the culture.

Book Three is substantially a wary and often alarming survey of *idées reçues* about love. It does not bid for consistency in its representations of sexual love, or in its statements about the nature of sexual love as issued by an often puzzled narrator. The representations, prior to the summative narrative action of the two concluding cantos, are in the nature of a cultural–historical anthology: they show what love seems to be, as a phenomenon of observed behaviour, and behind that what it has been taken to be in the poem's ambient culture, one whose origins are traceable to the ancient world. Among these archaic deposits of cultural history is the quality of illness ascribed to Britomart's initiatory experience of love, occasioned by sighting the image of a knight in the mirror which is Merlin's gift. Here love seems to be an affliction of mind and body which it would clearly be better not to have. The occurrence is narrated with some humorous, knowing implication, and Merlin explains that this love is necessary, because fated (see 3.3.24), but the suffering is vivid nonetheless: since the sighting, Britomart explains to Glauce, 'the hidden hooke (. . .) hath infixed faster hold / Within my bleeding bowels, and so sore / Now rankleth in this same frail fleshly mould / That all myne entrailes flow with poysnous gore, / And th'ulcer groweth daily more and more' (3.3.38–9). The account develops on conceptions, current since the classical era, of intense love as a pathology. Glauce compares Britomart's love to that of Narcissus, but points out that by good fortune the image of a man which she loves 'a bodie hath in powre' (3.2.45).[40] It is in line with this conception that Glauce takes magical–medicinal curative measures, though maladroitly and without success (see 3.2.49–52).[41]

Book Three has, in Florimell and Marinell, lovers who fly from love – with rational motivation in the case of Florimell, who is in immediate context pursued by would-be rapists and others who might well pose the same threat, and more mysteriously in that of Marinell, whose self-positioning on a shoreline suggests fear of crossing a threshold of self-giving or self-commitment.[42] The sea itself functions in the book as a means of examining love as tempest (see 3.4.7–11) and, embodied in the figure of Proteus, 'Shepheard of the seas' (3.8.30), of love's unlimited capacity to generate images which assail and disturb the mind (see 3.8.38–41). The Squire of Dames recounts a *fabliau*, a joking and in this case sexual story which is inflected towards misogyny, to Satyrane's masculine-hearty amusement (see 3.7.53–61). The primarily comic Hellenore-Paridell story culminates in an episode of Chaucerian swyving, in observing which Malbecco, the sexually feeble, jealous and would-be controlling husband, slips inescapably into the role of voyeur (see 3.10.43–52).[43] Paridell's surreptitious courting of Hellenore shows a lover's cunning in the style of Ovid's *Art of Love* (see 3.9.27–52); in its historical profile it contrasts with Malecasta's susceptibility to the appearance of an adventurous knight on the scene, which evokes and mocks romance convention (see 3.1.14–67). Arthur becomes captivated by the image of a fleeing woman, in fact Florimell, who becomes for him in fantasy the Fairy Queen who is the object of his quest (see 3.4.52–61). Book Three's most compelling object of desire is the false Florimell, a demon operating an artificial female body (see 3.8.5–9). Timias' love of the constitutionally non-amorous Belphoebe exaggerates the frustrations traditionally associated with socially high or aspirational 'courtly' love (see 3.5.27–55); Timias has not chosen this role, but finds himself trapped in it. The sibling giants Argante and Ollyphant meanwhile project domineering sexual appetites, issuing in their case as incest, which lie outside normative cultural regulation (see 3.7.37–51, 11.3–6).

There is, then, a kind of compendiousness to Book Three's imaging of love as produced up to the point where Britomart finds Scudamor, Amoret's lover, held by enchantment at the threshold of Busirane's castle where she is held prisoner (see 11.7–13). But the production of this impression of compendiousness is the opposite of producing an argument about love and its nature, and several of the forms of love shown are dealings with what is at some level illusory. The episodes disconcert, and in that do cumulative work: they engage strongly not only with love's prominence in the cultural imagination, but also with its resistance to becoming a stable object for the same. This prepares the way for the concluding episode of enacted imaginative disengagement, which seeks to go as it were behind the book's mainly dismaying images of love in order to examine the workings of the cultural imagination by which they are produced.

The two concluding cantos are diagnostic as well as apotropaic in character. They demonstrate that mere signs can be and have been taken for wonders and, producing some ostensible wonders, turn these expeditiously back into signs. When Britomart has hurled herself at and through the fire barrier which denies entry to Busirane's castle, she finds herself confronting phenomena which have a double aspect: in the first place they consist of extreme, sometime violent, transformations of objects in the field of perception; in the second place, following the course of reflections which Britomart, projecting the vision of the poem, is in a privileged position to make, they are transformations of perceived objects *produced by the operation of perception itself* – it is in the nature of representations occurring within the field of love, which the book offers in compilation, to deceive the eye.[44]

The interior of the castle as Britomart experiences it consists of three adjacent chambers (see 3.11.27–12.42). In the outer chamber she finds highly accomplished tapestries, interwoven with eye-enticing gold and silk, which depict Cupid's power over the Olympian gods; this is expressed in violent love of mortals (mainly) whose most frequent issue is rape, and the mortals' physical destruction. The familiar progenitor for this story-type, as well as prime source for several of the stories is, of course, Ovid's *Metamorphoses*. But absent from the passage's narrations of sexual love's archetypical course is the Ovidian movement between differing perspectives on the action. Their sole concern is with love's overwhelming power, and with this power's inexorable imposition by the gods, whom it also victimizes, on the human beings who become their prey. The effect of love on the gods is often humiliating and degrading. Among mortals, when they experience it for themselves, love produces more extreme havoc, leaving those whom it has afflicted like bodies heaped after a battle (see 11.46). It is in keeping with ecphrastic convention that the narration should evoke what the tapestries represent as if these were living scenes; some of what is shown is said to deceive the eye in this respect – the viewer forgets that this is a representation (see especially the concluding couplet of 11.46). But in following this convention the passage also pays further interim homage to love as an inexorable cosmological–psychological force: here it is seen as the universal animating principle, albeit one which operates randomly and against all recognizable human interests. At one end of the chamber there has been set up a statue of blind Cupid, hailed by inscription as '*the Victor of the Gods*' and worshipped by others whose presence in the chamber now becomes apparent. Britomart has not formally participated in this 'fowle Idolatree' (11.49), but the giving of perceived life to what the tapestries show counts as a parallel if lesser act of mental self-engagement.

Boldness leads her into the second chamber, where the artwork becomes a good deal more abandoned and grotesque. It is also more directly attractive as a brilliant piece of golden artifice:

> Much fayrer, then the former, was that roome,
>> And richlier by many partes arayd:
>> For not with arras made in painefull loome,
>> But with pure gold it was all ouerlayd.
>> Wrought with wilde Antickes, which their follies playd,

> In the rich metal, as they liuing were:
> A thousand monstrous forms therein were made,
> Such as false loue doth oft vpon him weare,
> For loue in thousand monstrous forms doth oft appeare. (11.51)

The walls, meanwhile, are hung with actual military spoils, armour and weaponry which once belonged to 'mightie Conquerours and Captaines strong' (52). Britomart, herself by choice a warrior (see 3.3.57), now sees with the possibility of self-appraisal a mentality of captivation. When night arrives, announced by fearful cosmic manifestations (a storm, an earthquake, a cloud of smoke and sulphur), there issues into the room an elaborate masque or pageant, a processional performance led in celebratory manner by musicians and singers. Briefly, its symbolic persons represent the course of a love affair as a series of psychological conditions, beginning with Fansy and his companion Desyre, followed by pairings of Doubt and Daunger (resistance to a lover's entreaties) and Feare and Hope, and culminating in forms of experience which seem to constitute a warning against love, come too late: Reproch, Repentaunce, Shame bonded together, Chaunge, Disloyalty, Riotise and Dread, among others. One notes that all of these states can be understood both subjectively and projectively: they are what the lover herself/himself might experience and/or what she/he might want to find, or fear to find, in the one loved.

Disturbance of the subject–object perceptual relation is most fully represented in the pageant's outlandish central tableau, made up of figures who immediately precede Cupid in the procession. Its focus is 'a most faire Dame' who holds, in a silver basin, 'her trembling hart' which has been 'drawne forth' from her body through the still gaping wound in her chest; this is pierced through with a 'deadly dart'. The woman, led by and presumably directed by Despight and Cruelty, 'two grysie villeins', performs an ambiguous and uncompleted gesture which also constitutes her torment: she neither gives this heart, extended before her, to another, nor retains it as her own possession. The Cupid who follows her is by now for perception a living being. Mounted on a 'Lion ravenous', he still not only wears the blindfold which signals the arbitrariness of his actions, but also temporarily removes it in order to savour, for personal satisfaction, the manifold sufferings which he inflicts.

This castle pageant stages with bizarre exuberance one of its period's most familiar conceptions of love: Cupid is a cruel lord, a tyrant, whom human beings succumb to and worship because his violent, relentless assaults on them afford no choice.[45] Acceptance that this *is* a truthful and image of love experience has, though masochistic, a certain cultural normativeness. But this spectacle of 'love' as exhibited to the reader and, in the virtuality of narrative, Britomart, enforces no such compliance; because we and she have had demonstrated the process by which, stage by stage, it acts to recruit subjective assent. In the first chamber the broadly Ovidian scenes of love are tapestries, and Cupid is present as a statue; but the scenes take on virtual life in the psychological response which they elicit, and acts of worship similarly treat him as and convert him into a living force, much as in the cited passage from Sidney. The process of mounting imaginative engagement goes on to produce the monstrous, wildly proliferating golden forms which adorn the second chamber, and then the seeming reality of a performance with live actors which invades it. The episode's directing idea is that fixation too has a history – a cultural history, in fact, to which the individual taking thought and action need not be indefinitely subordinated. There is a systematicity to Book Three's effecting of a process of mental disengagement from powerful collective representations; this is the book's specific *way*, one to which experience of reading the book gives form – as does its central figure's mode of action.

In all her textual appearances, climactically in the Busirane episode, Britomart functions as a counterpart and proxy for the reader as she develops and becomes the bearer of a mode of seeing which the whole text supports. The book's experiential scene, brought to a focus in the awareness which it assigns to her, is one of vigilant seeing, where what one sees becomes an object of fascinated observation but does not at the same time dictate an entirely conditioned response. Much of the narrative's field of perception is taken up by culturally powerful images like that of Cupid the tyrant or chastity as flight (the most obvious templates for the second being provided by Ovid's *Metamorphoses*). They *could* take on the status of compulsions which are to be immediately recognized and accommodated in reception as pure givens of experience, exacting psychic submission; but, militating against such a reception, they are presented under the fiction of romance adventure as unfamiliar practices and customs to be evaluated as one finds them. Faced with the unaccountable and potentially frightening phenomena of Busirane's castle, Britomart develops a pragmatically effective strategy for tracking them to their source. At one point she finds a way of entering the chamber from which the masque where Amoret is exhibited undergoing torture has emerged:

Then when the second watch was almost past,
That brazen dore flew wide open, and in went

Bold *Britomart*, as she had late forecast,
Neither of ydle shows, nor of false charmes aghast. (12.29)

Seeing the devastation wrought by a projective love-god which enthrals minds, and then Amoret's torment as an aspect of 'his' power, Britomart observes the operation of psychological magic without finding herself caught in its field of force. The narrative attributes to her a 'magical' force of her own – projected in the all-vanquishing lance that she carries (see 3.1.7) – which is that of the isolated, group-detached mind, perceiving the world on bases established by its own freed curiosities and choices, unswayed by 'ydle shows' or 'false charmes'. It is the way there for the taking by any affectively solitary, self-directing reader for whom reading can become a freeing of individual thought and choice.

Hobbes and Bunyan: The Subsuming Individual Vision

He that would learn *Theologie*, must first studie *Autologie*. The way to God is by our selves.

Daniel Featly, prefacing The Purple Island[1]

Somewhat shifting the context for discussion of symbolic narrative, I shall begin by returning to the cosmomorphic vision which, in the early modern period, helps to establish its conditions of possibility. Giambattista Vico in *The New Science*, published in three editions between 1725 and 1744, offers some clear-sighted reflections on the decay of cosmomorphism as a cultural mind-set. In Vico's narrative of universal beginnings, primordial human beings, acting without reflection and following the natural bent of the human mind, projected what they immediately encountered in themselves onto the world around them; which is apparent in modern linguistic usage:

It is noteworthy that in all languages the greater part of the expressions relating to inanimate things are formed by metaphor from the human body and its parts and from the human senses and passions. Thus, head for top or beginning; the brow and shoulders of a hill; the eyes of needles and potatoes (. . .). All of which is a consequence of our axiom that man in his ignorance makes himself the rule of the universe, for in the examples cited he has made of himself an entire world. (. . .) [T]his imaginative metaphysics shows that man becomes all things by *not* understanding them (*homo non intelligendo fit omnia*); (. . .) for (. . .) when he does not understand he makes the things out of himself and becomes them by transforming himself into them.[2]

Vico is attempting to account for the spontaneous finding of what one is in the universe and of the universe in what one is which is characteristic of cosmomorphic vision, and which he distinguishes sharply from the effects of systematic enquiry into either. In one of his key stories of origins the gigantic beings who were our forefathers raised their faces to the sky at the first occurrence of lightning and thunder,

> astonished by the great effect whose cause they did not know. (. . .) And because in such a case the nature of the human mind leads it to attribute its own nature to the effect, and because in that state their nature was that of men all in robust bodily strength, who expressed their very violent passions by shouting and grumbling, they pictured to sky to themselves as a great animated body, which in that aspect they called Jove (. . .), who meant to tell them something by the hiss of his bolts and the clap of his thunder. And thus they began to exercise the natural curiosity which is the daughter of ignorance and the mother of knowledge.

The 'vulgar' of his own time, Vico goes on to say, are thinking in the same fashion when, seeing a comet, they 'at once turn curious and anxiously inquire what it means'.[3]

Vico is clear, however, that as an effect of changes in the culture, this fashion of thinking is not available in his own time, certainly to the educated, or even probably to the 'vulgar' in its authentic form:

> But the nature of our civilized minds is so detached from the senses,[4] even in the vulgar, by abstractions corresponding to all the abstract terms our languages abound in, and so refined by the art of writing, and as it were spiritualized (*e quasi spiritualezzata*) by the use of numbers, because even the vulgar know how to count and reckon, that it is naturally beyond our power to form the vast image of such a woman as is called 'Sympathetic Nature' (*la vasta immagine di cotal donna che dicono 'natura simpatetica'*). Men shape the phrase with their lips but have nothing in their minds; for what they have in mind is falsehood, which is nothing; and their imagination no longer avails in giving form to a vast image which is false.[5]

When we moderns attempt to give a symbolic account of 'spiritual things, such as the faculties of the human mind, the passions, virtues, vices, sciences, and arts', writes Vico, 'for the most part the ideas we form of them are so many feminine personifications, to which we refer all the causes, properties, and effects that severally appertain to them.'[6] In this last statement Vico does, I would say, accurately characterize a typical modern understanding of allegory as 'personification', not now taken in the sense of giving a human-like mask (*persona*) to the experience of a human collectivity, but in the sense of putting thought-amenable visual form to a conceptual abstraction (see Coleridge's account of allegory as 'picture language'). This is, needless to say, an understanding which goes with the large-scale cultural attenuation, often outright rejection, of allegorical composition itself, and which still works to impair reading of allegorical texts from the era of the genre's ascendancy. Vico's singling out of the rise of literacy and of applied maths as cultural factors making for the promotion of abstractive ('spiritualized') thinking, resistant to satisfactory visual embodiment, is also historically sound.

In these observations Vico convincingly takes a culture's pulse: the cosmomorphic mind set and one of its focal visions, the 'vast image of such a woman as is called "Sympathetic Nature"', have for many Europeans become impossible to sustain as armatures for the organization of knowledge, and probably even to imagine coherently, by the time in which he is writing. Vico offers a vantage point for retrospection on cultural developments of the preceding two centuries, where what occurs in particular instances of symbolic composition shows that cosmomorphic framing of the world-self relationship undergoes a series of important displacements.

A founding premise of symbolic narrative in the traditions that we have been considering, instanced by *The Faerie Queene*, is that humankind possesses a history which is also written in that of the cosmos, and that the corporeal–spiritual life of the individual is at the same time that universal history's mediation. This is a casting into narrative form, under the auspices of a Christian soteriology, of the analogies between world, group, immediate environment or habitation, and self which are cosmomorphism's elemental intuition. But we have seen that Spenser's Alma episode, selected as an instance of the text's active forming of its reception relationship with the reader, possesses two distinct aspects when consider it as a conveyance of vital knowledge, knowledge which should produce suitable orientation for the individual to and within universal history. Essentially, it offers itself as both *aide-mémoire* and novel instructor, *qua* 'fashioner'. Within well-established gnosiological conventions considered in Chapter 1 and the preceding chapter the body-castle as symbolic 'mirror' recaptures for the individual experience which not only pertains to but also belongs to that individual as a member of the collectivity – here, 'humankind'; considering the symbolic image in its ramifying intertextual relations is in principle making re-acquaintance with what is already given because it is (collectively) known.[7] But the body-castle as anatomized organic form, and as machine explicated in the functional interdependence of its parts – that is, a thing constructed by two culturally novel cognitive procedures – also offers guidance in active self-modelling, the formation by the individual of an optimal mode of personal embodiment. One might say that the presented image as 'mirror' offering access to knowledge *should* not require such supplementation. But, a good deal of the episode is dedicated to the provision of it; and thought of the body also becomes at times a means of *distinguishing* the knowledge which the individual acquires specifically as an individual – for example, through experiencing the personally isolating mental–physical phenomena of sickness – from that of which a group might be considered to be the bearer.

The Alma episode, then, assumes the currency in the culture of perception that 'mirror' knowledge, projected in such familiar collective representations as the body-house or body-castle, is in some respects inadequate to individual requirements. Moreover, it acknowledges the *availability* of this last perception in such a way as to *enforce* it: it is one of several symbolic narratives of the period which seeks to convey the necessity of forming knowledge through individually produced and individually focused acts of understanding. The era's cultural converse of the collectivist mirror-body is the complex individual body, with its many material components, viewed as offering the self's existence as a thing immediately present to the understanding. From the standpoint of our own typical cultural mind-set, this projection of individual selfhood seems odd and paradoxical: imagined 'selfhood' has for us a certain visual inscrutability, and the body's observable components seem a poor or misleading approximation of it;[8] and are not bodies in any case pretty much the same as one other when considered as assemblages of common constituents? Nevertheless, the Alma episode is one of the more influential, though not the only, early modern English giving of symbolic existence to individual life by means of the curiosity-inciting and internally complicated individual body. I would say that the emergence of this new symbolic armature is a partial relegation of the collectivist cognitive paradigm, as bound up with familiar representational practices. It counts as a relegation because every living individual is taken to be intimate, purely by virtue *of* living, with this particular template for understanding of self and world: here is a response to the traditional moral counsel, 'know thyself (*nosce teipsum*)', in a strikingly compelling, modern form.[9] But the relegation is partial because individual bodies are analyzed here, as has been said, down to their constituents on the basis of their fundamental likeness; its procedures 'discover' via what is conceived as self-scrutiny a uniform knowledge held to be of application to all lives.

Among the characteristic products of this new literary tradition are Robert Underwood's *A Newe Anatomie* (1605), not discernibly influenced by Spenser, and Phineas Fletcher's neo-Spenserian *The Purple Island* (1633). It is worth drawing attention to both works' use of a kind of reversible cognitive mapping: in the first, a relatively compact piece in jaunty trimeter, a house and then a civic community serve as means of explaining the internal relations of a body's parts and faculties, while this same internal organization also serves as a means of defining optimal household and civic relations; in Fletcher's poem, setting under way a parallel but more intellectually wide-ranging process, discovery of the body's – read, self's – internal organization and discovery of the unitary history of the world proceed hand in hand. The symbolic designs of these poems announce themselves as means of by-passing traditional collectively oriented symbolic images, with their weight of historical accretion: the living body, so the thought runs, is a vehicle of knowledge ever accessible to and ever renewed in an individual's present experience. Underwood's narrator at the start of his poem takes a raw pleasure in perceiving – following literary convention, within the framework of a dream – the inhabitants of the world as so many houses:

> One caught me vp into the Aire,
> from whence I did descrie
> A *Cittie* large [margin: *the world*], of bignes such
> as it the world had beene:
> A thousand thousand *Houses* there [margin: *The people, or the bodyes of men*],
> a man might well have seene:
> Their fashion, stuffe, and workemanship
> in all points did excel.
> The order of these *Houses* too,
> I marked very well.[10]

One of the odder features of these visionary 'houses' is that they move around at their owners' will.

The poems and other tributes which preface *The Purple Island*, one of which was cited at the head of this chapter, seek to communicate the intellectual excitement of the poem's project as revelatory exploration of 'self' in a novel projection, a-traditional in character because this 'self' is both means and object of enquiry, and because anatomically derived knowledge in the poem's era has the smack of the new. Edward Benlowes, for example, to whom Fletcher has dedicated the poem, contrasts the emptiness of seeking mastery over the world with the value of mastering 'this self-knowing art',[11] itself in metaphor a feat of travel and discovery. I shall, however, juxtapose these intellectual experiments – engaging for contemporaries then largely forgotten as their purposes became opaque – with some more radical attempts to establish collective representations which supersede the ordinary traditions of collective representation. All in their way displacements of the cosmomorphic mentality, two of these initiatives are Bunyan's, while the one with which I shall begin is that of Hobbes.

*   *   *

In the preceding chapter's discussion of the Alma episode I identified three pivotal moments in the reader's encounter with a complex symbolism: that of accepting the force of traditional symbolic representations centred on the body, shown in an image which is, however, divided and unintegrated because the body politic itself is divided and unintegrated; that of tracing the interconnections of a novel symbolic body, architectural and mechanical in construction; and that of integrating response to this imposing model body with awareness of individual frailty and mortality. I have also suggested that reading of the passage encompasses these moments sequentially, in the order just set out. Comparable moments also have great importance in the readerly encounter with Hobbes's *Leviathan*; but the argument of the book is structured in such a way as to fold these moments on to one another, setting them before attention simultaneously and with distinctive impact.

Hobbes has no piety whatsoever towards traditional collective representations, and sees the mentality of ordinary people as a blank sheet apt to be imprinted with such commanding texts or images as the ruling authority chooses:[12]

> The Common-peoples minds, unless they be tainted by dependence on the Potent, or scribbled over with the opinions of their Doctors, are like clean paper, fit to receive whatsoever by Publique Authority shall be imprinted in them. (ch. 30, p. 379)[13]

In this spirit his monstrous anthropomorphic creature, Leviathan, commandingly displayed in the text's frontispiece (see the image opposite), is being put forward as a new, valid collective representation for the ruling authority to relay to its subjects. This symbolic figure stands, I would suggest, in a quasi-parodic and subversive relation to the collective symbolic representations of cultural tradition: those are accepted primarily through habit and custom – and have of late, so runs the underlying thought, been

much contested and, as part of this process, done a lot of damage. But what this impressive and threatening image defines, on the other hand, is well-fitted to *impose* assent. Moreover, the items displayed in boxes in the lower half of the image show how this symbolic figure's power, secular and sacral, is put into practical effect; here a fired cannon, for example, is treated as being equivalent to the thunderbolt of excommunication (the forked objects immediately below symbolize weapons of argument). The image so viewed immediately establishes two focuses of political interest: how is sovereign power implemented, once it has been established, in that series of relays which conserves its triumphant force?; and, the text's more pressing concern, how does it compel the spontaneous and foundational collective acknowledgement which underpins such implementation?

Answering the second question involves paying close attention to the book's rhetorically charged opening statements. In making automata, we are told, human beings give to certain products of engineering 'an artificial life', simulating animals capable of motion in imitation of nature as 'the Art whereby God hath made and governes the World'. But human *techne* can also go beyond this in imitating

> that Rationall and most excellent worke of Nature, *Man*. For by Art is created that great LEVIATHAN, called a COMMON-WEALTH, or STATE, (in latin CIVITAS) which is but an Artificiall Man; though of greater stature and strength than the Naturall, for whose protection and defence it was intended; and in which, the *Soveraignty* is an Artificiall *Soul,* as giving life and motion to the whole body. (Introduction, p. 81)

Aristotle speaks similarly, in the *Poetics*, of *muthos* (plot, story) as the soul which gives life to a tragedy, in so far as we can regard tragic plays as members of an artificial living species which human beings have created. A gigantic fabricated man who supplies protection for a human collectivity evokes ancient stories of Talos, the bronze man who guarded Crete. A figure called 'Leviathan' recalls in name but not in form the Leviathan of Job 40–1 and Isaiah 27.1, variously glossed as a crocodile, a whale, a fish, a snake and a dragon;[14] Leviathan as modern monster and its scriptural counterpart can be taken to be alike only in the challenging sense supplied by the Vulgate citation: '*Non est potestas Super Terram quae Comparetus ei*' – 'There is no power on earth which is to be compared with him.' Later in *Leviathan* the formulations of the quoted passage are recalled when we are told, in the only other reference to the creature Leviathan, how this engineered construction comes to be – or, as simulated 'man', is born. It has to be imagined that all the members of a collectivity at a certain point say to one another, '*I Authorise and give up my Right of Governing my selfe, to this Man, or to this Assembly of men* [i.e. the sovereign power in whatever form], *on this condition, that thou give up thy Right to him, and Authorise all his actions in like manner.*' Once this is done, explains Hobbes,

> the Multitude so united in one Person, is called a COMMON-WEALTH, in latine CIVITAS. This is the generation of that great LEVIATHAN, or rather (to speake more reverently) of that *Mortall God,* to which we owe under the *Immortall God,* our peace and defence. (ch. 17, p. 227)

As the text clearly acknowledges, this is not to be taken as a historical account of a sovereign state's formation. The individuals who compose a given sovereign state, or their forbears, are not to be imagined as having gathered one day to make a verbal contract with one another: that story is provided in order to bring out the political meaning of the contractual principle – which is to say that the problem concerning a collectivity's spontaneous *assenting* to the imposition on themselves of a sovereign power is repeated in the problem concerning a collectivity's spontaneous *construction* of a sovereign power which holds sway over them, as symbolized in both cases by an extremely powerful artificial man or 'Mortall God'. To recapitulate briefly, we have considered *Leviathan*'s putting forward of a new collective representation with political force in the space once occupied by traditional collective representations. And in order to explain what this new representation, 'Leviathan', might be, we have considered the text's account of that constructive act which has produced a mighty artificial man. But the account of the second has to be received as an explanatory fiction, and it has not yet proved possible to say anything revealing about Leviathan's actual construction, its or his engineering, including the fabrication of Leviathan's 'soul', the contractually transferred sovereign power which is said to give this creature 'life and motion'. Here there is an obvious contrast with Spenser's symbolic anatomy of the temperate body. Aristotle's *Poetics*, which is an important intertext for *Leviathan*, likewise offers constructive information about the optimal form of a tragic *muthos*, as well as metaphorically instating it as tragedy's 'soul'.

The resolution of this issue is, however, provided in *Leviathan*'s frontispiece, probably more clearly and certainly more directly than in its written text.[15] Its symbolic anthropomorphic giant represents a human collectivity with a certain grotesque explicitness, since the visible portions of it excepting the head and fingers are composed of a multiplicity of human bodies. These are clothed and, mainly, hatted – that is, wearing their public garb as if at or approaching some form of assembly. Given that Leviathan the creature faces towards us, confronting the reader as if in a mirroring relationship, why are its component bodies, who in some sense represent 'us', facing in the opposite direction? The effect is disconcerting, like that of the Magritte painting ('Réproduction') which shows a man looking at the mirrored image of himself seen from behind, as the spectator already views him. The frontispiece's positioning of the human forms composing Leviathan was evidently not the only possibility that Hobbes envisaged. In a manuscript version prepared under his direction by the same artist for the exiled Charles II, and no doubt designed to win his personal approval, the component forms are heads, unhatted, facing outwards from the image and wearing agitated facial expressions suggestive of excitement or fear.[16] This clearly conveys the awed subordination of the collectivity's individual members to the 'artificiall man' whom they compose, a man who bears the trappings of a monarch and does indeed, as in the printed version, look rather like Charles. The logic of the bodies' positioning in the printed frontispiece has, however, been convincingly identified by Horst Bredekamp: 'the eyes of each one, regardless of position, is directed towards the giant's head *and returns through his eyes back to the viewer*'[17] (my emphasis). In other words, a form of mirroring is indeed taking place: what the reader encounters in meeting the eyes of the gigantic 'artificiall man' is her/his own gaze, which is now to be imagined as belonging to the gazing totality made up of the ensemble of readers and ensemble of political subjects, the assembled throng which the image presents. A place has thus been assigned to the individual as a bearer of volition in the same movement which locates the individual as part of a collectivity living in subjection to the sovereign power, a being whose powers seem to resemble her/his own in a huge magnification. The artificial construction which makes this paradoxical act of (self-) seeing possible is the argument of the book, the force of which is established in this introductory tableau.

At the centre of *Leviathan* considered as an act of persuasion is a moment of uncanny encounter, ingeniously contrived in such a way as to provoke awe and fearful apprehension:[18] in the text's necessary monster, Leviathan, we confront both the implacable character of sovereign power as it bears on the individual subject and the frightful nature of what it has been created to oppose and subdue, human beings' individual disposition towards imposition of self-will. The sovereign state, considered to be the most impressive of human inventions and a virtual 'man' in its own mode of being, is found to exist in the relay of looks that passes continuously between its component human entities considered as disparate individuals and these same human entities, given collective embodiment in the sovereign power, a designated person or assembly. It is not necessary to appeal to a founding contract in order to establish this 'man's' right to exist or principle of existence, much as it is not necessary to make experimental entry to the state of nature (as in the rhetorically brilliant evocation of Chapter 13) in order to establish that life outside this constructed, non-natural legal–political framework is nasty, brutish and short. Such are *Leviathan*'s optical dealings with an issue of political foundation, making for simultaneous individual self-recognition as political agent and political subject. To behold the image of sovereign power in the text's mediation of it is to perceive, immediately, that 'there is no power on earth which is to be compared with him' – *Leviathan* considered as political artefact identifies as foundational constant a continuing subjective condition of fearful apprehension which also goes on discovering its own remedy.

*   *   *

This is the frontispiece of Bunyan's *The Holy War*, published in 1682 when *The Pilgrim's Progress* had gone through six editions and generated a set of illustrations. To turn to Bunyan from Hobbes is, at first sight, to return to the sphere of established collective representations; and at the same time to the thought-world of cosmomorphism, given that the narrative focuses on a human-body-like city, the 'Towne of Mansoul' as in the frontispiece. Here the trajectory of symbolic reading more closely resembles the one that has been defined for the Alma episode than the one that has been defined for *Leviathan*. Nevertheless, the design of *The Holy War* also resembles that of *Leviathan* in that it one of its key purposes is to create and sustain for the reader a moment of definitive recognition, and in that a semiotics of collective representation is brought firmly under authorial control in the interests of fixing a single pattern of response. The frontispiece was probably composed, like that of Hobbes's text, under authorial supervision. It represents what is in important respects an apocalyptic scene, whose focus is the climactic battle of *Revelations* 10 between the great dragon, identified with the Devil, and the host of God's angels. The portion of the terrestrial globe visible beneath the warring parties makes it clear that the fate of the earth is at issue. But the image of a walled town-*cum*-body – the obvious bodily features being 'Heart Castle', 'Eargate' and 'Eyegate' – placed at the image's centre cues a narrative of individually located struggle in the *psychomachia*'s double sense of struggle both within and for the soul: the book will place eschatology within a personal perspective where, as in *The Pilgrim's Progress*, the represented encounters of an individual are offered as possessing universal significance. But while the text's 'Towne of Mansoul', gendered as female along traditional lines (see Alma herself), is by analogy the unitary soul of an individual, its principal narrative concern is the life of the soul as compositely represented by the varied members of a civic corporation; the main actors are agencies of good and evil projected as rival military and occupying forces, and their helpers or enemies among the townsmen whose loyalties they contest. In the frontispiece the most conspicuous figure, larger indeed than the town, the Devil in dragon form, or Emanuel as leader of the opposing army, presents the recognizable image of Bunyan in the person of author.[19] One of the inferences which may be drawn from this placing of weighty visual emphasis on 'Bunyan' is that it will be the responsibility of the author to explain how a story of conflict and deceit with numerous narrative agents bears analogically on the spiritual life of the individual, since received frameworks of understanding will not necessarily do this with clarity and reliability. In the prefatory poem Bunyan states that reading must be guided by his continuously provided marginal glosses on the action: 'Nor do thou go to work without my Key, / (In mysteries men soon do lose their way) (. . .)/ It lies there in the window.' 'The margent' (5)[20] here is the marginally supplied gloss for 'the window', without whose light the narrative allegory would resist interpretation or be interpreted falsely.

As was noted in an earlier chapter, Walter Ong points to the role of the printed book in producing the strong impression that a given text is closed off and separated from other texts, and not locatable within a shared intertextual field; which, in forming the conception and reception of a book with this novel profile, affirms its originality and individuality while conferring the same attributes on its writer.[21] Bunyan aligns himself with the emergent figure of the book author, which harmonizes in his treatment of the role with a familiar Protestant critique of the traditional, priestly conveyance of doctrine. *The Holy War*'s purpose is to establish, on an individual author's initiative, a novel basis on which certain doctrines can be assimilated at the level of experience by the reader who tracks a specific narrative development. The force of this conception depends partly on engagement of the reader's awareness that the attribution to an individual, *qua* author, of distinctive authorizing powers is a cultural practice of comparatively recent invention.[22] The narrated action locally includes an implicit critique of the embodiment of doctrine in customary forms: three 'proper men' called Tradition, Human-wisdom and Mans Invention enlist as Emanuel's soldiers, but following capture in a skirmish they join the diabolic army since, as they explain, they do not 'so much live by Religion, as by the fates of Fortune' (51–2). The shape of the whole narrative establishes convergent paths between a representation of scripturally charted world history, spanning Creation and the Last Days, and the representation of an individual life which spans the fall into sin via temptation, the experience of redemption, and – the text's distinctive concern – entry into a more fortunate though still imperfect condition of life where grace is operative; here, crucially, the traditional security of the body imaged as a defensive enclosure has to be relocated on a new conceptual and pragmatic basis. In the context of a broad awareness of the shape of collective human history, the reader is offered a representative personal history for the truth of which 'Bunyan' stands as guarantor: the prefatory poem includes authorial declaration that 'I myself was in the Town, / Both when 'twas set up, and when pulling down,' and that 'what is here in view / Of mine own knowledge, I dare say is true' (184).[23] The role of the author, constructed between empirical writer, empirical reader and the text which mediates their activities, is to establish conditions of access to a human ethical–spiritual state which is to be shared as an affective condition, and into which the narrative should function to co-opt the reader. In the terms offered by a traditional mapping of mind onto body it is a condition of *heart*; it is this condition of heart which is to govern reception of the symbolic narrative, as distinct from being set forth for knowledge and understanding *by* procedures of narrative symbolism.

The narrative of *The Holy War* has three phases and leads logically towards a newly inflected account of the contemporary Christian believer's condition. As symbolic narrative it also offers a novel anatomy of the living soul, in that the corporate functioning of a town on a contemporary model, with its differentiated officials and volatile, rumour-led collective awareness, is treated as a vehicle for analysis of the soul's individually self-assertive and interacting faculties. Among the marks of the allegory's distinctiveness is that it has relatively little use for the potential body symbolism of an architectural structure, or for representation of the soul as this structure's unitary resident, both falling within the convention of 'mirroring': these commonplaces of collective knowledge are acknowledged but also largely[24] ignored in the interests of developing and exploring new insights. The main schemes of action are the following: (1) Diabolus seduces the inhabitants of Mansoul, a town originally established by King Shaddai and, subverting its institutions, gains unremitting control over the town's life. (2) On hearing of this the King's son, Prince Emanuel, directs and finally leads a prolonged military assault on the town, overcoming the followers of Diabolus and freely bestowing mercy on its inhabitants, beginning with the civic leaders who have expected to be put to death. This arrival of concord, marked by extended celebration, is the text's principal narrative turning point and key moment of recognition in Aristotle's sense, redefining the affective relationship between the inhabitants of the city and their prince; these inhabitants are, vicariously, the reader and the extra-textual Bunyan who, as author, is to be understood as having created a textual phenomenon out of ordinary experience. (3) There is a further lengthy period of grievous internecine struggle between Diabolonians, who remain lurking within and ready to emerge from 'the outsides, and walls' (144) of the town, and those loyal to Emanuel; though the Prince's followers often fail in vigilance or force, his leading soldiers never lose control of Heart Castle, which is 'the strong hold of the town' (204). It is made clear, then, that in the third phase, even though it is emphatically one of uncertainty and confusion, the necessary understanding, power and responsibility for resisting Diabolus have been fully transferred to Mansoul, since the heart of the individual has now undergone experiences which enable it to resist deception and capture; the insight which they provide is what the individual is required continuously to recall as a condition of present spiritual wellbeing. In the striking conception of the frontispiece – where a section of 'Bunyan's' chest corresponding to the heart has been made visually identical with 'Heart Castle' in the town behind him – this insight is figured as a condition of transparent correspondence between the castle-heart of Mansoul, the heart of 'Bunyan', a set of purposes projected in a book, and their counterpart in the text's fashioning of it, the suitably educated heart of the reader: to respond to the text appropriately is to perceive and experience their essential alignment.

The symbolic image of the body as an architectural structure can, in so far as it aligns itself with traditional conventions and practices of collective representation, be received as a reminder of knowledge of the human state whose substance is a vast tissue of individual experiences. But, an anatomizing of the symbolic collective body, of the kind which occurs in Spenser, Underwood, Fletcher, Bunyan and, more abruptly and prescriptively, in Hobbes, implies a re-examination, a supplementation and eventually a replacement of received cultural knowledge in its bearing on the life of the individual. *The Holy War*, which is of these works the most fully conceived as a communication between an individual text and an individual reader, offers a symbolic narrative whose purpose is to mould a style of reception such that it can be received in the proper manner with what should be assured consequences. It is focally as a story of the *heart* that this symbolic narrative bids to avoid the hazards of intertextual connection and vagaries of collective use, with a view to conveying a univocal meaning with individual application which can also in principle be reliably transmitted.

*   *   *

The Holy War defines itself, then, as the ambitious narrative mediation of a recognition individually made by its foregrounded author, the Bunyan of life conflated with the 'Bunyan' whose name stands at the head of the text, vouching for its status as 'authored' communication, and also with the visually represented 'Bunyan', possessed of a certain condition of heart, who dominates the frontispiece. Its methods contrast with those of the symbolic narrative which Bunyan had set in print four years earlier, *The Pilgrim's Progress* being in some respects *The Holy War*'s converse as a narrative which bids to define the conditions of every individual's separate encounter with a universal predicament. The earlier text would, as it transpired, shape conceptions of fictional narrative in such a way as to marginalize – place as culturally *dépassé* – *The Holy War*'s different experimental conjoining of a traditional collectivist symbolism and individualism of promoted outlook.

Seen in one aspect, *The Pilgrim's Progress* is as traditionalist as can be in offering a narrative of the Way which humankind, individually Augustine's *viator*, takes from the earthly to the heavenly city.[25] But in saying this one immediately experiences discomfort in characterizing Bunyan's Christian as 'humankind': no, this is an individual journey made along a Way which is at the same time understood as being there for all. The text's distinctive individualism of orientation emerges quickly in the drawing of comparison with precursor allegories of life as symbolic journey. One of the obvious premises of allegorical invention in texts by Langland and Chaucer (and a matter of strong emphasis in the first three books of *The Faerie Queene*) is that it initiates processes whose tendency is to connect the experiences of the individual with those of a larger human group, that is, the group defined by the writer's circumambient culture, and ultimately those of the fully envisaged human collectivity, *humanum genus.* Such movement towards integration of thought into a summative design is the obverse of dream visions' ostensibly haphazard, serendipitous narrative development. In the foreground we have the figure of the Dreamer, a *persona* of the author considered as a (self-) isolated individual, indeed one isolated ipso facto by the asocial act of writing. The characteristics of the Dreamer also sketch out the task of the poem; that is, of the task lying before its reader or hearer. This figure generically suffers from uncertainty and confusion. He[26] has lost some ability to account for the rationale and continuity of his own experiences; for example, Chaucer's Dreamer in *The Book of the Duchess* is, to partly comic effect, 'a mased thyng, / Alway in poynt to falle a-doun'.[27] In the gradually emerging background, however, we have the more cognitively accomplished figures whom he meets through dreaming, his potential instructors, who are among other things unrecognized aspects of himself and of a shared human state.

The Book of the Duchess, concerned pervasively with the loss of loved ones, finds its dream-focus in the Man in Black. Like the poem's Dreamer, but more explicitly, he is in a condition of mourning. (He is generally considered to be the shadow in the poem for the real John of Gaunt, whose wife's death was a recent memory at the time of composition.) In conversation, the Dreamer and his aristocratic interlocutor circle around, thereby exploring, the extraordinary difficulty – at once intellectual and emotional – of taking the measure of personal loss. Behind this conversation looms what might be the universally applicable instruction of Boethius' Lady Philosophy, which concerns the transience of earthly things and their incapacity to serve as final, abiding objects of attachment. But, in the present lived circumstances, this instruction cannot be *possessed* as applicable knowledge: it merely shades in a personal truth by pointing to a recognizable tendency within mourning, in so far as mourning moves eventually towards some loosening of psychic connection with the person who has left the mourner's world. Over the course of this literary 'dream' the Dreamer's own experience of loss – whatever it was: its nature has been merely hinted at[28] – is gravitationally drawn into the milieu of another, more clearly defined, graver, and more culturally validated experience of loss, and so, along with the latter, into that of the experience of mortality itself as human universal. The upshot of all this is that the undergoing of personal loss can take on a profile of recognizable occurrence – it is part of what is humanly shared, it need not leave the individual walled up in purely private, immobilizing grief; there is a *way* of these things, albeit a way of suffering and difficult emotional discovery.

At the level of its virtual landscaping later medieval allegory typically draws, by stages, the individually experienced – what belongs exclusively to one specific set of spatial and temporal co-ordinates corresponding to one perceptual apparatus – into some degree of perceptible relationship with the collectively known or affirmed. One of its distinguishing and, for the *aficionado*, engaging features is its capacity to deal simultaneously with both the contingent and idiosyncratic, and the attributively universal (see what was said at the start of Chapter 1). The morality play known as *The Castle of Perseverance* represents at once the life of every human being, Humanum Genus, from cradle to grave and beyond, on the assumption that humankind necessarily experiences the psychic pull of covetousness as radical vice, and the life of a representative East Anglian burger who with advancing age becomes myopically absorbed in the accumulation of wealth. *Piers Plowman* begins as its Dreamer, in the *persona* of a clerical vagabond ('dressed as if I were a sheep'[29]), falls asleep beside a spring in the Malvern Hills. The Dreamer in Chaucer's universal drama of loss presents the recognizable image of Chaucer the eccentric government official who has a hobbyist's devotion to old books. In the treatment of time there is a similar mobility of focus between the individually located and what lies within the entire historical span of human experience. Langland's Dreamer witnesses and in some degree participates in the Fall of Man, and also in the inauguration of Antichrist's reign during the Last Days. The action into which 'Chaucer' tumbles through dreaming seems to him to be happening at the court of the Emperor Augustus; Augustus and his world are imaginatively in place, it would appear, because of his connection with Ovid, poet of love and emotional metamorphosis with a passage of whose writing 'Chaucer' has become engaged.

I am suggesting that the literary allegories which, via cultural tradition, underlie and underpin Bunyan's typically appeal, simultaneously and without finally aligning them, to two conceptual supports, that of experience constructed as an individually accessed phenomenon, and that of experience constructed as collective and trans-historical, tending towards the human universal. They draw, in so far as they progress, the second kind of experience into the purview of the first, but never completely. Their larger symbolizations orient the individual towards collective experience but are not directly equivalent to it, since it lies in its projected wholeness outside the scope of individually accomplished acts of consciousness; individual symbols are, as has been said, sites of intertextual ramification. By what discursive moves does the Bunyan of *The Pilgrim's Progress* transform and finally reject this symbolic economy, substituting one of his own? Two markers of independence from tradition in Bunyan's text stand out with special clarity.

(A) It has a generically new and distinctively organized allegorical
      terrain. Although the notion of life as pilgrimage is, as has been said,
      commonplace in itself, the route of this text's symbolic pilgrimage has
      its own, markedly 'authored' linear topography. Narrative places like
      the Slough of Despond or Interpreter's House or Doubting Castle are
      themselves relatively novel inventions. But, more importantly, their
      enchainment takes a new form. The enchainment of narrative places in
      The Faerie Queene is, as in Langland and Chaucer, comparatively loose
      and ill-defined: Britomart encounters Marinell at a seaboard, clearly
      defined as a type of place – also a type familiar from other romances –
      but she has wandered for a long time through undefined spaces before
      she gets to it; Florimell, meanwhile, is seeking her way to it though what
      seems to be a different set of spaces, also lacking specified identity. The
      barely glimpsed background space, lacking topographical specificity,
      against which the adventures of *The Faerie Queene* take form *is* the space
      of collective human experience as it first comes into any individual's view.
      It corresponds to the 'obscure (or dark) wood' (*selva oscura*) where Dante's
      narrator loses his way, finding that he has wandered into the terrain of
      symbolic vision; here most of the ordinary features of life are veiled, but
      at the same time something of what is essential to it begins to make its
      appearance. But compare this with the highly specified and internally co-
      ordinated topography of *The Pilgrim's Progress*. Bunyan's narrative allegory
      presents a close-knit, internally related (often by contiguity, sometimes
      by inter-visibility) and easily remembered organization of places, like
      that provided by the streets or major buildings of a town: from the Hill
      Difficulty the route next takes in the Valley of Humiliation, then the Valley
      of the shadow of Death and so on.[30] The whole topography therefore lends
      itself to unitary mapping[31] in a way that can hardly be said of predecessor
      allegories. Both its places and their *Zusammenhang* are thoroughly
      'authored'. This is a relatively coherent landscaped scene, in which a
      represented pilgrim and the reader at any juncture are determinately
      placed. As Cynthia Wall has argued, the relation of the reader to what

reading brings to light resembles that of an actual traveller to locations on routes defined and co-ordinated by accurate cartographic representation.[32] Effectively, the outcome of collective, temporally accumulated experience has been collective arrival in a charted landscape, which has the consequence that collective experience as such solicits no further individual engagement. One of the primary aims of modern map-making has, after all, been to diminish the force of intertextual relationship, on the principle that any serviceable map should supply the greater part of what is needed for its construal and use.

(B) The text has particularly inventive and far-reaching ways of de-authenticating, attributively collective experience, with the effect that authority is transferred to the immediate experience of and discoveries made by its represented individuals. I shall consider this second characteristic before returning to the first.

Christian is recurrently accosted by know-alls, in his case figures who speak with the pretended authority of accumulated knowledge – knowledge claiming authority on the simple grounds that it *has* accumulated. Behind each one stands an implied society or community, a grouping of people who find it appropriate to think like this, because their shared culture sets the pattern. At an early stage in the journey Christian is of course taken in by Mr Worldly Wiseman, whose smooth teachings (which seem in context to be satirizing those of the Latitudinarian clergy, a major political and social force) succeed in deflecting him from the Way. This very confident giver of advice has a manner of speaking which makes anticipatory nonsense of the whole narrative. He tells Christian,

> thou art like to meet in the way which thou goest, Wearisomness, Painfulness, Hunger, Perils, Nakedness, Sword, Lions, Dragons, Darkness; and in a word death, and what not? These things are certainly true, having been confirmed by many testimonies. (p. 19)[33]

Here the reader faces a clear choice, with predictable outcome: either give up on the narrative itself as meaningless farrago, or reject the claims of this kind of authority, that of what is accepted by many people as being 'certainly true' (p. 19) on the basis of general report and common wisdom. Viewed in a similar light, and as Mr Sagacity explains to the Dreamer in Part Two, long-persistent human attempts to improve the Slough of Despond, apparently well-intentioned, have mainly done the reverse (see p. 177). In Part One, the pilgrims encounter the fair which has flourished (having been established by devils) in the Town of Vanity for some 5,000 years.[34] This is a huge repository of repugnant, in large part, but also normative social practices where the vile and the neutral are thoroughly intermixed:

> Therefore at *this Fair* are all such Merchandize sold, as Houses, Lands, Trades, Places, Honours, Preferments, Titles, Countreys, Kingdoms, Lusts, Pleasures, and Delights of all sorts, as Whores, Bauds, Wives, Husbands, Children, Masters, Servants, Lives, Blood, Bodies, Souls, Silver, Gold, Pearls, Precious Stones, and what not. (p. 86)

Confronted by this real farrago, Christian and Faithful quite properly stop their ears against the crying of its wares. But in approving of this action, the reader implicitly rejects a lot of what is 'of Ancient standing' (p. 85).

The Pilgrim's Progress does not, of course, turn its back on all cultural traditions. While a work announcing its beginnings in a treatment of 'the Way / And Race of Saints in this our Gospel-Day' (p. 3) might seem to belong exclusively to the thought-world of a lately founded separatist group, 'Race' in these lines is, as it turns out, ambiguous, and Bunyan's contemporary saints are given lineage and history. Christian's ancestors are martyrs of the early Church, in a listing largely taken from Foxe (see pp. 242–3). The lions of the Hill Difficulty seem to allude to amphitheatre molestation of early Christians as well as, more obliquely, to modern state-led persecution of Dissenters. Records kept in the Palace Beautiful of worthy acts performed by the Lord's servants include what looks like reference to the Crusades, or perhaps earlier wars against Muslim armies (pilgrims' forbears 'waxed valiant in fight, and turned to fight the Armies of the *Aliens*'; p. 53). *The Pilgrim's Progress* does make considerable use of motifs taken from folktale and chivalric romance, narrative forms of wide cultural diffusion.[35] Nevertheless, the general tendency of Bunyan's text is to reject and actively discredit that diffuse collective experience, widely gathered, trans-historical and pointing to the universal, which is central to the design of precedent literary allegory. It is characteristic of this modern, highly 'authored' text that, between parts One and Two, it should set about constituting and consolidating a novel, independent tradition of its own: the second part is manifestly written about imagined pilgrims and for readers who have already been moved by the narrated acts of Christian and his companions. The errant pilgrims and enemies to pilgrimage of Part One also establish an instructive tradition of sorts, often by leaving in view the traces and signs of their destruction. Tradition happens primarily in *The Pilgrim's Progress*'s own discrete textual spaces.

But, returning to the figured terrain of Bunyan's 'Way', it is now possible to say more about features of its presentation which deliver it over specifically to *individually* effected and confirmed acts of understanding. The text's giving of narrative definition to a successfully made journey contrasts markedly with that of precursor texts. Una's party begins its journey, we may recall, by losing the way – supposing that it was on one – and then contingently falling victim to Archimago in an apparent place of security, after which Una wanders over much of the earth's terrain, and Redcross takes a way which is drastically wrong. In the dream visions of Langland and Chaucer there is considerable preoccupation with *finding* the Way, to a point where the possibility of making discovery through progression – as physically figured and/or in the following of a line of thought – is blocked during long sections of Langland's poem. In *The Pilgrim's Progress*, however, the reader and Bunyan's pilgrims are from an early stage *on* the Way, which corresponds here fairly directly to the linearity of discourse as projected in speech or written language – in fact, *this* written language which is the reader's first visual path – and even wrong ways, like those taken by Christian near the start of his journey and by Ignorance at its very end, are defined within the framework of the text's virtual cartography.

This narrative text as written path opens out not onto what is undefined or on first inspection confused – that is, the experience of open intertextual connectivity – but onto particular supplementary texts deriving from the scriptures which are visible on most of its page-margins; at a *meta*-level of interpretation the scriptures themselves are the integral map of the Way, for which the text's visually defined journey terrain is the thought-amenable approximation[36] – this is made clear when Greatheart the intra-narrative guide pulls from his pocket 'a Map [identified in the margin as *God's Book*] of all ways leading to, or from the Celestial City' (p. 277). The marginal citations of scripture manifestly operate to define, and in so doing circumscribe, intertextual relationship. Though represented pilgrims may and do err, a *right* way is there at every point for the reader's interpretative finding. The particular readerly vigilance which the text solicits is that of one who continuously identifies and follows a path, not a particularly elusive or obstructed one but, nevertheless, the path taken in *this* act of reading, an act which the reader owns personally by accomplishing and having accomplished it. The text thus delivers over to the reader an unscrolling spectacle of the knowable, where the 'noise' of communication correlates with interpretative uncertainties set in play in order to be directly and expeditiously overcome. *The Pilgrim's Progress* offers compelling practical instruction in the writing and reading of what would come to be called novels, offering a means of self-understanding and orientation towards others which is mediated not by symbols marking points of access to an openly extended collective knowledge, nor by registration of the shared-*cum*-individual human bodily state, but by knowledge of a shared world already organized in a lucid and unitary design for appropriation by individual acts of comprehension.

Part C

Introduction

Refiguring Community, Thinking through Festivity

This concluding section will examine two aspects of *Richard II* and *1 Henry IV* considered as a sequence, and of *The Winter's Tale*. I am concerned with these plays as offering material for thought on the dissolution and creation of communities. And I shall consider in particular the role which these dramatic sequences assign to representations and enactments of communal festivity, shared *play*, in the provision. Chapter 6's argument thus gives a prominent place to the Falstaff- and tavern-centred action in *1 Henry IV*, and that of the final chapter to the shearing festival in *The Winter's Tale*. In both of these actions stagings of the festive or playful reaches out to encompass the experience of a theatre audience self-placed in the presence of what occurs: in *1 Henry IV* group play shapes up onstage in the orbit of Falstaff, but more crucially in the relation which Falstaff establishes with those hearing and looking on, 'us', and in the thoughts which this relation cues; in the case of *The Winter's Tale* it is as if the dances and songs of the lengthy pastoral scene are being performed *for us*, and not only the onstage bystanders. What occurs specifically in a theatre thus functions as a medium in which attitudes to play accruing in an assemblage of individuals can be put at issue and become an object of those same individuals' reflective attention.

For the purposes of developing the present argument it will be useful to distinguish between three broad formations or modalities of festivity, as attested by current knowledge and the historical record. They might be viewed as differences of predominant emphasis, cueing different forms of play, more than one of which may come to the fore over the course of a given celebratory period. (1) Festivity can affirm/establish or seek to affirm/establish affective community (*Gemeinschaft*), the felt having in common of particular responses to shared experience, or to experience which can be imagined as shared. Examples of *Gemeinschaft* festivity familiar in the modern United Kingdom are Orange Day parades, oratory-centred political rallies, and the sideline celebrations of team sports supporters. Turning to the historical record, in 1517 London apprentices made celebration of May Day the opportunity for launching a xenophobic riot; it is worth recalling at this point that lynching can be an unimpeachably communitarian activity. At Romans in 1579–80 the festively constituted mock-realms (*reynages*) seem to have become, at least from the standpoint of the social elite as organized in their *reynage*, affectively differentiated and adversary groups. (2) Festivity hosted by a given community or some coming together of communities may cultivate, as distinct from *Gemeinschaft*, experience of human *being-in-common* (Jean-Luc Nancy) which is available in principle to any human beings disposed to participate. (3) The first chapter of this study attempted to characterize a cultural mind-set, often encountered in texts of the medieval-early modern period, which posits or affirms a 'lightness' of differentiation between the humanly constituted and the naturally given. This may provide a mental ambience, a kind of working rationale, for festive activity which throws off the affective bonding of a particular community, at the same time eschewing experience of *being-in-common* which constitutes broader human community, in the interests of pursuing 'wild', asocial, inter-humanly disconnected self-realization. An example which has been considered is Bercilak's hunting in *Sir Gawain and the Green Knight*, significantly paired in that romance's narrative organization with a pursuit of pleasure conducted *à deux* behind closed doors. One of the typical markings of May Day in the early modern period was a pair of lovers' self-removal from their observing community in order to find private solace in some natural zone.

The general characteristics of *Gemeinschaft* festivity (1) are familiar enough from aspects of modern life. Festivity of this kind may not 'work', or 'work' consistently, to produce functional unanimity across an assembled group, but it gives the purpose of doing so clear definition. Festivity as individualistic 'going wild' (3), often locally encountered in early modern celebrations of the coming of summer (but not as we have seen only then), will be considered in due course against the background of *The Winter's Tale*'s complex dealings with matters of 'wildness'. But cultivation of the practical awareness of *being-in-common*, as one meets it in (2), is not only a widespread, even, typifying, feature of medieval-early modern festivity, but also one quite little understood in modern times (where coercive versions of *Gemeinschaft* have set a predominating pattern).

Accordingly, in the remainder of this introductory section I shall seek mainly to explicate festivity of modality (2), referencing the enquiries of Victor Turner and Jean-Luc Nancy.

Turner has identified, in lectures of 1966 which were written up as *The Ritual Process*,[1] a polarization of social behaviour between phases of what he terms 'structure' and 'anti-structure'. Behaviour of the first kind displays pervasive codification – as for example in the assignment of individuals to distinct status groups, living by different rules and norms – whereas behaviour of the second kind displays a loosening or suspension of the prevalent social codes, making for entry to conditions of relative parity between individuals; this second might be facilitated by the adoption of special costume conventions, such as the masking and extravagant dressing up of carnival, which tend to efface that differentiation and setting apart of individuals whose acceptance is part of ordinary, 'structured' life. To embrace conditions of 'anti-structure' is, according to Turner, to accede to the conceptual-practical authority of community in its most basic constitution. His premise is that human societies *are* fundamentally communities, in the sense of being most powerfully imagined as existing between individuals through reciprocal granting of recognition and acceptance, and that social codification arises in and out of underlying recognition that it should serve some defined communitarian interest; for example, assigning to certain individuals the status of warriors and providing them with a warrior's training ought be a means of securing some other, more vulnerable individuals against attack. But codification, as in the example given, also works to set individuals apart from one another and to create non-parities of status (for example, warriors may get given or take for themselves additional food). And therefore, so the argument runs, societies which ordinarily show great respect for 'structure' also tend recurrently to create social conditions of 'anti-structure'; in doing this they bring to consciousness the latent presence in a community of what Martin Buber terms *Zwischenmenschlichkeit* ('between people-ness'),[2] the giving of thought to others on the understanding of their sharing in perceptions and mental conditions which are also those of the self, making of them other 'I's'.[3] Turner thus distinguishes between a 'community' in the ordinary sense, a group existing over time which upholds common norms and institutions, and what he calls '*communitas*', that which comes to exist in a group's accessing of mutualities in shared experience.

Such mutualities can also be viewed as those of Jean-Luc Nancy's *being-in-common*: people entertain perception of them under certain circumstances simply through existing as human, rather than through alignment with a particular affective group, a *Gemeinschaft*.[4] Nancy draws a revealing distinction between 'being-in-common' and 'common being', where the second is what community *qua Gemeinschaft* projects and celebrates as a group's enduring possession, corroborated for example in its myths. Putting together Turner's and Nancy's thinking, one could say that under conditions of 'anti-structure' the codifications of structure are not only suspended, but 'unworked (*désoeuvrés*)'. Realization of the state of *communitas*, marked out for attention as a form of social occurrence by Turner, can promote widening recognition of what it is to exist as a human being who participates in a common human life, whereas givings of definition to community in the ordinary sense assume or seek to create the defining distinctiveness of a particular group's experience. To put it more concretely, *communitas* can quite readily accommodate the stranger, whereas the constitution of affective community, cordoned off from experience of *communitas*, is taken to require individual induction into the mentality of the ambient group. A London theatre audience of c. 1600 might be seen as combining, in an unstable amalgam, orientation towards community and orientation towards *communitas*: it is a coming together of those who tend to share certain kinds of group awareness and knowledge (e.g. because they are culturally European, because they are English, because they live in London at this time . . .); it is a coming together of strangers who may, *qua* play audience, develop through shared responsiveness to what they witness as a group some registration of being-in-common; it is a coming together of the individually isolated who in important respects remain that.

Turner sees the making of recurrent provision for mental accessing of *communitas* as being characteristic of preliterate societies. His exposition of a form of social process, complemented by Nancy's discussion of being-in-common, throws light on much of what is found in medieval to early modern communal festivity, a prominent feature of the later medieval European calendar, generically familiar in the England of c. 1600 though also considerably diminished in an era of Reformation and disciplinary social reform. (As François Laroque has suggested – see the chapter which follows – the tavernish activity in the *Henry IV* plays is in some degree belated festivity, attempting to activate the memory and recapture some of the significance of festivity in its more culturally embedded forms.) Taking account of 'anti-structure's' significance for thought of community – through its bringing to awareness of human capacity to discover mutuality in existence – does, however, direct attention to a misleading move of argument made in Mikhail Bakhtin's highly influential account of carnival, present in the idea that festivity produces a social differentiation of its own. Fundamentally, Bakhtin builds a principle of *Gemeinschaft* into his account of festivity of (what I am calling) type (2), the staple medieval-early modern kind. Collective festivity for Bakhtin gives form and expression to a mentality of 'the common people' – that is, *not* that of people in general – which opposes the mentality of 'official culture', that of the governing classes and governing institutions, such as the Church.[5] *Contra* such an assertion, it seems evident that in numerous medieval to early modern festivities of which we have record the governing classes are enthusiastic participants, variously mounting 'anti-structural' disports of their own, and/or playing roles in those mounted by a larger community, such as that composed by a town where differentiated occupation groups and, frequently, visitors, celebrate together and in parallel.[6] In the account of these matters which I am offering 'anti-structural' activity is not primarily a principled rejection of 'structure': it may offer some alleviation of everyday oppressions, but is more fundamentally an attempt to recapture insights of value to group awareness of any kind – those found by temporarily acknowledging the genuineness of *communitas*-type experience while holding some social-structural imperatives in abeyance.

Anti-structural play in this understanding does not subvert ordinary social structure in the sense of seeking to discredit it and establish the conditions for its replacement;[7] but it does critique the codifications of social structure by facilitating those intuitions of being-in-common which they overlay and suppress. The symbolizations which it typically puts forward displace or estrange the thinking of hierarchy, promoting realignments of vision: they often accrue in the 'low' – that is, corporealizing – treatment of what are ordinarily elevated matters, and the dignifying of what, *qua* bodily, is common to human beings. Being given over to anti-structural play has been no community's abiding condition, but anti-structural play retains value for the mental accessing of *communitas* regardless of the temporal boundaries which structured social process assigns to it.

In the organization of *Richard II – 1 Henry IV*, to be considered sequentially, presentations of 'anti-structure' are nested within those of communities or bids to form or retrieve community, in the sense of abiding organizations of alliance and connection. The discussion of these plays will also be concerned with the imagination of political community as centred on the figure of the sacral monarch, and on the prestige of chivalric achievement. The account of *The Winter's Tale* foregrounds one of the *ur*-conditions of experiencing cultural solidarity, the holding in common of an understanding of 'the way things are', of the vision of an enfolding 'Nature'. I shall argue that group play as represented in the shearing festival, and as contextualized by a more general loss of intuition concerning 'nature', leads in its development *away* from experience of *communitas* as a state of being-in-common. In keeping with the concerns of this study, particular attention will be paid to (not in order of presentation) (1) relations – conceptual, pragmatic, sometimes optically mediated or defined – formed by a represented individual or individuals with a represented group, and also by the spectator or beholder ('us', 'me') with the same group in its potential overflow to include the theatre audience, and (2) with the play – or lack of play – of cosmomorphic mentalities across the phenomena of group formation, such that analogy may be perceived or sought between the bodily life or mentality of the individual, the life of the visibly constituted group, and the life of any larger group of which this group may be considered to be a conceptual model, potentially up to and including humankind and the cosmos.[8] And (1) and (2), above, occurring as represented and enacted in art, will be considered as potential instances of *privatization* in this study's sense – as transferrings of attributively authentic consciousness from what occurs in shared awareness to what occurs in individual reflection.

Taking Sights in *Richard II* – *1 Henry IV*

This chapter gives special attention to modes and methods of seeing – and also, in due course, to changes in cultural conceptions of seeing associated with emergent modernity. *Richard II* incorporates as we know a particularly complex account, based in optical metaphor, of problems that can be involved in perceiving a troubled situation correctly. Richard has left with an army for Ireland and his confidant Bushy attempts to cheer the Queen, who is apprehensive about impending events, by suggesting that the sorrow which she feels is produced by impaired perception of what is there directly in view. Some of the problems which the passage sets interpretation arise from Bushy's use of not one but two optical metaphors of mis-seeing, that of looking through a sharpened glass surface – whose refractive effect directs attention to a similar effect as exerted by tears – which multiply divides the image of the object, but also that of looking at an anamorphic picture (a 'perspective') full on ('rightly') when one can properly appreciate what it shows only by looking obliquely, from the side. The passage's initial shift of thought is from the first of these organizing ideas to the second:

> Each substance of a grief hath twenty shadows [i.e. refractions],
> Which shows like grief itself, but is not so;
> For Sorrow's eyes, glazed with blinding tears,
> Divides one thing entire to many objects,
> Like perspectives, which, rightly gazed upon,
> Show nothing but confusion; eyed awry,
> Distinguish form. So your sweet majesty,
> Looking awry upon your lord's departure,
> Finds shapes of grief more than himself to wail,
> Which, looked on as it is, is naught but shadows
> Of what it is not. Then, thrice-gracious Queen,

More than your lord's departure weep not. More is not seen,
Or if it be, 'tis with false Sorrow's eye,
Which for things true weeps things imaginary. (2.2.14–27)[1]

Anamorphic images like Holbein's representation of a skull in 'The Ambassadors' support, needless to say, two possibilities of seeing. Seen straight on they set a distorted and therefore inauspicious-seeming image of an object in the beholder's vision, which Bushy compares to the fragmented image which comes to view when one looks through tears of sorrow. In putting forward the idea of anamorphosis, Bushy tactfully intimates that a corrective adjustment of seeing is possible: the same object can be re-viewed in a way that favours what is seen – favours justly ('rightly' in the sense of 'correctly') because this is a discerning of its proper, auspicious form. There is, however, a tangle in the passage's metaphorics. Looking 'awry', or from the side (the opposite of 'rightly' in the sense of 'straight on', as from the normal viewing position), would, if we are thinking of an anamorphic image be the correct or un-'confused' way of seeing what is portrayed (see ll. 19–20). But Bushy immediately goes on to say that the Queen misrecognizes the properties of what she sees precisely through looking at it 'awry' – which seems to be a reversion to his first idea that the act of looking itself may be as-if-optically distorted by grief, by analogy with what occurs when one gazes through tears. This extraordinary swerve of language and what surrounds it carry the implication that what is to be seen here does actually support two acts of genuine discernment, one which finds a cause for sorrow, and one which finds the opposite. We happen to know or will know shortly that the Queen's apprehensions are correct – in other words, that the *right* way of viewing Richard's exercise of rule has now become an issue in conflict, which in itself bad news for Richard's party, and that the claims for taking an unfavourable view of it may perhaps be the stronger.

Bushy's complex statement cues the argument of the present chapter. In it I shall examine important actional transitions in the sequence of plays of English history which begins with *Richard II* as transitions in seeing – in what I am calling *takings of sight* – where there may be more than one way of resolving visually presented or conceived material for a discerning act of perception.[2] One takes sights on an object to discern and make use of it correctly, as in the assessment of a star's elevation through the use of an optical instrument for navigational purposes,[3] but also sometimes with the intention of destroying it: the *Oxford English Dictionary* notes the first recorded occurrence in 1588 of 'sight' meant in the sense of 'a device, of the nature of a projection or notch, on a fire-arm or piece of ordinance, etc., to assist in taking aim'. The taking of sight in this sequence of plays with which I am centrally concerned is that performed by Hal at the conclusion of the first tavern scene in *1 Henry IV*; its form is defined by the soliloquy which begins, 'I know you all, and will awhile uphold / The unyoked humour of your idleness.'[4] I shall circle back to Hal's declaration about knowing definitively through seeing via some of these plays' other projections of an act by which a sight is taken.

*   *   *

If one wished to describe as succinctly as possible the special tension which shapes the action of *Richard II*, one would probably say that the play represents the unkinging of a king, the removal of kingly authority, command, visual appurtenances and so on, from someone who *is* nevertheless the king, in the sense that he holds the throne by rightful succession, and has been properly invested with kingship, becoming king in a ritual on which his society confers sacral power. Unkinging a sacral monarch is a highly paradoxical, even perhaps unaccomplishable act – this is an inescapable perception of which Richard in particular, while undergoing the ordeal of political defeat and especially while playing a key role in his own unkinging, communicates strong awareness. Bearing in mind this represented social–cultural reality, I wish to consider certain ways in which the king – at first a figure invested with awe, but then one who loses crucial support and slides towards dethronement – is offered to the beholder's gaze for potential acts of seeing. The visual projection of a kingly Richard, as the play treats it, stands as the – in a later sixteenth-century context – still imaginable focus of a political life drawn into affective cohesion through shared acceptance of a symbol's power; but also as requiring an organization of affect which progressively forfeits psychic authority in and through attempts to enforce it. As a means of characterizing this symbolic presentation it is useful to draw into the argument a portrayal of King Richard enthroned with which Shakespeare and his audiences will almost certainly have been familiar, since it can be assumed to have hung in their time (as it hangs still) on public view in Westminster Abbey.[5] The Westminster portrait underwent heavy-handed 'restoration' in the eighteenth and nineteenth centuries; nevertheless, enough of the original conception and paint survive for us to make out what was shown.[6]

I would suggest, summarily, that it is possible to view this portrayal of the enthroned Richard in two ways. (1) It is the image of a sacral king, where the aura

of kinship pervades the representation – an idea of the auratic being conveyed by the golden field against which Richard and his throne are placed[7] – and where one attribute of the sacral king is a personal face; this is the Richard who is unconditionally the king, where the king who is seen in place rightfully wields a king's authority, projected here in the orb and sceptre which he carries in his hands. But one can also look at the image in another way. (2) This is a person like us who happens to be wearing/ holding /sitting on symbols of kingship. If we wish we can separate perception of the person, Richard, from that of the symbols of royal office which contingently surround him in this representation. I suggest that the reader experiment with flipping between these two perceptual gestalts: here is *the king*; here is someone who bears the trappings of kingship.

What would tilt the spectator towards settling for one of these receptions of the image in preference to the other? The Westminster portrait for any spectator after Richard's time already poses this as an issue: this is the image of a proud king; this is the image of a political loser whom his enemies seized and put to death. And it is posed very extensively by the first two plays of Shakespeare's sequence. Richard's power as staged for us at the beginning of this sequence has the warrant of archaic, but also c. 1600 culturally familiar, cosmomorphic intuition. To this way of thinking there is a kind of identity between monarch and realm, and Richard *is* such a king, there by unchallenged rights of descent and via a ceremony of anointing. His holding of a monarch's power does not require a theoretical justification:[8] it is simply something that he has, much as if his having of it is a natural phenomenon. His power is there as a given reality, rather as the sun is there in the skies – a majestic object which everyone can see and whose force everyone feels. It is noticeable that speakers in *Richard II* and *1 Henry IV* are preoccupied with the idea that the power of the king, including rightfulness in the possession and exercise of that power, ought to be there like a powerful thing in nature, such as the sun, whose presence and effects no one would even think about contesting; King Henry and Hal as well as Richard refer to kingship in its optimal form as a cosmic or cosmos-like phenomenon (see *1 Henry IV* 1.2.187–93, 3.2.46–7).[9] The means that, in Richard's case, and when the intuition is current, in looking at the king one *sees* an individual who is invested with the aura of majesty, much as one *can* see the king of the Westminster portrait as possessing a living integration with symbols of power which are as much his attributes as a personal face (meanwhile the golden background directly manifests majesty, glory, closeness to the divine, to perfection and so on). Sacral kingship, subsisting in important respects *through* such acts of seeing, is part of the world's unnegotiable order – a thing not there to be interfered with or altered or molested. What manifests sacral kingship is thus set apart from ordinary objects in the world which can be touched and manhandled. Up to the point of rebellion in *Richard II* people do what the king says, even when they are far from liking it, as for example when Richard voices a decision about Henry Bolingbroke's banishment which has, we know, been reached out of view in discussion with his council of advisors, and then as if arbitrarily modifies it; such is 'the breath of kings' (1.3.215), both acts project the notion of an unconditioned, personally located authority.

This returns us to the nature of the process by which, in *Richard II*, the aura of the sacral monarch becomes removed for at least some of his onstage beholders, to a point where they *can* molest him, posing still more urgently for the audience the question of how they should perceive this monarch in representation. The pathway of its removal in the play is defined in part by the fact that an actor is playing Richard: as an audience 'taking sight' on this figure we see onstage a person like us, who is also impersonating a king; which also probably helps us to become aware of a potential unglueing of the represented Richard the person like other people from the represented Richard who is the auratic king. But the question remains, even more centrally, that of *how* one sees under circumstances where seeing itself is a problematic act. Anthropological enquiry reminds us that the functioning of any culture's totemizations and taboos occurs through systemic distortions of vision. What totems and tabooed objects have in common is that it is found difficult to see them squarely: they are invested with an awe which dazzles, or conversely they inspire a horror or sense of what is highly problematic in their existence which implies their willed removal from the field of sight; it could occur that one had them, rather like the object of a negative hallucination, within the field of sight still without finding it possible to set them squarely in mental view. In the act by which the subject beholds the monarch in just the same way as any other person presented fully for the seeing, the aura of the sacral is much weakened: unimpeded seeing can be a phenomenon of disenchantment. In so far as theatre offers a representation of a sacral king for unimpeded, scrutinizing seeing, this activity itself probably helps to form a mentality which detaches itself from submission to that figure's aura.[10]

A story about the historical Richard relayed by his political enemies brings out the potential irksomeness, and in doing this the latent vulnerability, of a sacral monarch's taking of a commanding position on seeing. It coheres quite well with the image of Richard presented in the Westminster portrait.

> After this on solemn festivals when by custom [the king] performed kingly rituals (*in diebus solennibus in quibus utebatur de more regalibus*), he would order a throne to be prepared for him in his chamber on which he liked to sit ostentatiously (*se ostendens*) from after dinner until vespers, talking to no one but watching everyone; and when his eye fell on anyone, regardless of rank, that person had to bend his knee towards the king.[11]

The solar king sees all but may not be looked at steadily by those on whom his gaze happens to alight. But what happens when he is nevertheless, as will sometimes happen, there for the steady seeing? The potentially desacralizing effects of being in the common field of vision are central to Henry Bolingbroke's explanation of Richard's loss of regal authority ('The skipping King, he ambled up and down . . .'; 3.2.60 – which seems intended to suggest compulsive self-display) when he is using the idea to belabour Hal. These plays' first bearer of the common gaze is, by implication, the audience itself, placed in the best possible position to scrutinize the actions and demeanour of those onstage, including those of King Richard when at his most politically secure. *Richard II*'s initial stagings of sacral monarchy probably do possess a disenchanting force, and not only because an actor impersonates a king: we are shown the backstage and private Richard as well as the one put on public view, and Richard is all through the first sweep of action a sceptical commentator on public self-staging (see, as addressed to Mowbray and Bolingbroke, who have made resounding protestations of loyalty, 'We thank you both. Yet one but flatters us'; 1.1.25). But placing oneself on public display in these plays is also a phenomenon of unstable valency. Henry Bolingbroke in *Richard II*'s opening action seems to be courting ordinary people, present as members of the crowd ('Off goes his bonnet to an oyster-wench'; 1.4.31), in the king's view with dangerous success – and is thus more Hal-like than one would infer from the plays which follow. When Richard, now dethroned, is paraded through London as the discredited counterpart to the politically glamorous Henry, ordinary citizens respond by throwing 'dust and rubbish' (5.2.6) over his head (see 5.2.30 and *2 Henry IV* 1.3.103–5[12]), an act which again brings out some of the paradoxicality of disenchantment considered as process: Richard is desacralized, therefore physically abused / physical abuse of Richard is itself desacralization. (Meanwhile, to York as he recalls it, this defiling act is a sacrilege whose tendency is to confirm Richard's sacral status; see 5.3.30–6.)

Richard II and *1 Henry IV* are centrally concerned, it transpires, with phenomena of mental self-disengagement which can to a considerable measure be optically conceived. When and how does political or communal vision alter? How does a shift of vision which may be accidentally produced come to be seen as a necessary *correction* of vision? Part of the attempt to resolve these questions adduces active forms of desecration which alter the real aspect of what is seen, as with throwing dirt over someone's head. The opening action of *1 Henry IV* confronts us, inside 50 lines, with the image of defeated soldiers' inventively desecrated bodies, representing a mangling of bodily gestalt which re-instates the soldiers' military humiliation. It is called by the shocked Westmorland a 'beastly shameless transformation' (1.1.44) wrought by triumphant Welshwomen. As will have been known to readers of Holinshed, whose *Chronicles* are being referenced, the women 'cut off [the soldiers'] privities, and put one part thereof into the mouthes of euerie dead man, in such sort that the cullions [testicles in the scrotal sac] hoong downe to their chins; and not so contented, they did cut off their noses and thrust them into their tailes as they laie on the ground mangled and defaced.'[13] When Hal brings off the fatal wounding of Hotspur, the northern contender speaks of having been 'robbed of [his] youth' (5.4.76), a suggestive if ambiguous phrase,[14] but Falstaff more pointedly mangles the body by inflicting 'a new wound in [the] thigh' (5.4.127), where 'thigh' probably stands in for 'groin' or 'genitals'.

Alongside these representations or suggestions of emasculating dismemberment, we find in the play significant flows of ridicule produced by methods of distortion or rearrangement or situationally inappropriate placing – by caricature, effectively[15] –adopted in personal portrayal. For example, in Falstaff's amusingly cartoonish image, Douglas is one who 'runs a-horseback up a hill perpendicular' (2.4.334–5). This is fairly characteristic of the play's treatment of chivalric brotherhood's pretensions. The contents of its thought-world are intelligible to its fellow devotees, but often strained and strange to the wider world; as Worcester says not unreasonably of Hotspur, who has just spoken of 'bright honour' in evident heat of imagination, 'He apprehends a world of figures, / But not the form of what he should attend' (1.3.202, 209–10). Chivalric brotherhood's thoughts as put forward in the play do not make a good fit with ordinary, relatively functional social mentalities; they tip towards the absurd. Its amenability to caricature suggests willed self-limitation and human simplification.[16]

I turn, however, to Falstaff, who as a kind of living caricature is hardly susceptible of being caricatured. Falstaff is in some takings of sight not that engaging a presence;[17] but for audiences, much as for Hal, he is at least *something*, as it were the last focus of a collective mentality left standing. The 'Falstaff effect', clearly an object of keen interest since the plays' own time, is undoubtedly powerful, and has never been very easy to explain; but it must have to do at least in part with the plays' discrediting of other figures who *should* but *fail to* represent the unity and produce the cohesion of a group – most conspicuously Henry Bolingbroke, whose auratic authority as sacral monarch is irredeemably compromised by the manner in which he has seized the throne. Hotspur is a charismatic figure in his way but, as the unfolding of events reveals if it were not already obvious, one whose competitive pursuit of honour brings leads by an exposed logic to political catastrophe. Hotspur's mentality is, as Hal's sharpest indictment suggests, inimical to the ordinary needs of life and probably to personal survival: 'I am not', says the prince in a rare flash of sheer dislike, 'yet of Percy's mind, the Hotspur of the North, he that kills me some six or seven dozen of Scots at a breakfast, washes his hands, and says to his wife, "Fie upon this quiet life! I want work'" (2.4.99–102). Hotspur is eventually betrayed by his kin, and found useful to Hal only as a perceived competitor to be tactically overcome. Falstaff's psychic positioning in the plays is, however, a great deal more secure: he is the play leader of a temporary community, primarily that of the represented tavern-brothel[18] with its shared pleasure-taking and soiled bonhomie, but also in some degree that of the theatre, where he activates the shared mentality of play. And this solidarity-productive play gains in authenticity by making continuous acknowledgement of what is *humanly* shared – even when what is acknowledged as being shared is a profound aptitude for selfishness. Falstaff as rotund, flagrantly bodily man, the symbolic compendium of common appetites which have found satisfaction, does not in fact have to do very much in context to cast himself as the 'plump Jack' whose banishment by Hal would represent a banishment of 'all the world' (2.4.465), of the common-human to which one instinctively links his body-orientated manner of existence. Nor, for that matter, should we be surprised when Hal retorts with 'I do; I will' (2.4.466–8), since the grouping for which 'plump Jack' functions as leader and mascot is an emphatically anti-structural creation, standing to one side of the ordinary political–legal–economic social forms by which the Prince will sooner or later be reclaimed.[19]

François Laroque, investigator of dealings with popular festivities in Shakespeare's plays, writes revealingly of Falstaff's capacity to emblematize festivities as held before the mind serially. Poins at one point identifies him with the autumn feast of Martinmas (11 November), when fattened animals were slaughtered, in asking Bardolph, 'And how doth the Martlemas, your master?' (*2 Henry IV*, 2.2.95–6). Citing this joking language, Laroque comments,

> but the fat knight is a calendar in his own right for the various parts of this body symbolize a whole string of the year's festive traditions. Now a 'Manningtree ox', now a 'wassail candle', Falstaff indeed flaunts the stigmata of his debauchery, which have been etched upon his grotesque physique.[20]

This is accurate and thought-provoking. Falstaff as conspicuous body marked by a history of play and self-indulgence is in being that a kind of repository of wishes to experience, at times, the non-everyday mutuality of shared celebration. 'Plump Jack', claiming world-likeness partly on the basis of being round, evokes the Jack Pudding of festive tradition who signals inveterate seeking of pleasure in the shared satisfaction of appetite.[21] We are made continuously aware of the self-interestedness of Falstaff's personal motivation; but this forms part of his endlessly resourceful performance of 'Falstaff', where a mingling of high and low social themes and registers persistently induces the thinking of group life as potential affirmation of *communitas*.

Hal's solo reflections as delivered at the close of the first Falstaff scene (see *1 Henry IV*, 1.2.185–207) raise, at the same time, the question of the propriety of such thinking. From the speech's assumed vantage point the elevation of play which yields it should already be ethically abhorrent. In attending to the speech, it is hard not to experience a tension between the advancing of a doctrine of social responsibility, that of its era's disciplinary reformism, and the avid seeking of personal advantage. Hal here announces, producing what will necessarily be mixed reactions in spectators and readers, the intention to make use of his low-life, play-disposed associates as a kind of chosen concealment from which he can emerge into serious political life with major, compelling effect. But, as I shall attempt to demonstrate, the effect of this soliloquy in shaping response to the action depends less on Hal's exposition of a plan – in some assessments more attempted self-reassurance than genuine formula for action[22] – than on its status as a *taking of sight*, one which gives the theatre audience, *qua* temporarily formed group, the option of standing both 'inside', as affective participant in, and 'outside', as critical onlooker, the mentality which Falstaffian play produces. I order to explain what I mean, I shall need to circle back to *1 Henry IV* and Hal's soliloquy via consideration of a distinctive profile given by early modern culture to practices of seeing.

*   *   *

Here it will be useful to dwell on a major cultural transition which has figured more briefly in the argument of earlier chapters. By long-standing Western intellectual practice, knowing is given central metaphoric definition as a phenomenon of seeing. The reasons for this underlying disposition of thought do not have to be pursued at present, though Jack Goody argues on interesting evidence that the conceptual framing of knowing as seeing is a typical product of literacy, which produces scannings of information as completely embodied in a reproducible, acoustically dissociated visual form.[23] But it is the case that conceptualization of knowing as seeing was a predominant practice in the literate ancient world. Aristotle's idea of an 'idea' (*eidos*), for instance, is given thoroughgoing visual definition. A locus classicus for Christian thought is Paul's 'For now we see by means of a mirror, enigmatically (*di esoptrou en ainigmati*; Vulgate: *per speculum in aenigmate*);[24] but then [in the defining encounter with

God] face to face' (*1 Cor.* 13.12). Dallas Denery has lately directed scholarly attention to the systematic development in later medieval thought of visual analogy, often based in the era's burgeoning enquiries into optics, as a means of understanding what it is to know.[25] But Denery at the same time distinguishes sharply and revealingly between the development of cognitive theory which places a good deal of reliance on *analogy* with seeing, and the quite novel later medieval – early modern style of thinking, familiar to us for example through the perspectival art pioneered in fourteenth-century Italy, for which *seeing as such* gives privileged access to knowledge. The cultural transition of which I speak is in several of its forms startlingly comprehensive: it is one from tradition-based projections of knowing as seeing, to highly untraditional but increasingly developed projections of seeing as knowing.[26] No thinker prior to the era of this transition would have been likely to postulate that knowing could be intrinsically a phenomenon of sight, not least because the philosophers' highest objects of knowledge – the Platonic Forms, spiritual reality, God – were not *ex definitio* available to natural perception.[27] The technically advanced visual art of the early modern period does, however, count as one of its era's vanguard implementations of the principle that seeing *is* knowing, *tout court*. For seeing-as-knowing, given forceful practical embodiment outside the sphere of visual art, one might also consider Vesalius' compelling visual embodiments of anatomical knowledge, Ramelli's perspicuous drawings of complicated geared machinery, intelligible to the non-engineer, and Ramus' influential tabulations of the forms of logical argument,[28] all of which were disseminated (and would have been very hard to disseminate otherwise than) through the medium of print. Mention was made in the first chapter of the early modern era's many newly devised instruments and methodical procedures, often connected with an emergent applied mathematics, which made for the consolidation of knowledge *in* individual acts of perception. I am, however, concerned at present primarily with developments in visual art, whose procedures evoke those of plays as staged.

One of Bruegel's later paintings, executed c. 1567, is of special relevance to this enquiry as a very considered taking of sights on the festive group. We know of no title conferred on it by the artist, and its common modern titles – 'The Peasants' Dance', 'The Peasants' Kermess' – may be somewhat misleading: its subjects are not necessarily peasants, in the sense of those who work the land, though they might be, and this is not necessarily a Kermess (local-church festival, 'kirk-mass'), though such is possible (a church is visible in the background). It might be called, less tendentiously, 'Festive Dance of Ordinary People'. The notion of 'ordinary people' carries a certain weight here, since part of the painting's angling to the viewer is its producing of recognition that this is *not* a decorous, courtly sort of dance, which was more familiar artistic subject matter. Though dancing is not the only activity in progress, it is the one of which the spectator is made most aware. I wish to pay special attention to the painting's perspectival organization, and to explore the idea that a mentality of taking sights is both its vehicle of production and in some important respects its object of observation.

Let us pause a moment to consider Alberti's laying down of perspectival art's foundational principles in the *De Pictura* of 1435. They articulate the notion of a spectator's taking full control of the act of seeing, and need to be considered against a background of cultural–philosophical assumption that such cannot readily – that is, without some considerable cognitive re-attunement – be put into effect. In the broad classical to medieval philosophical tradition, and as fully articulated by Aristotle, seeing is an aspect of the subject's physical contact with the subject's environment, in effect a form of touching, on the understanding that the production of action at a distance is impossible (or magical).[29] This implies that seeing is a matter of largely involuntary and shared experience, much as the ground presses continuously on everyone's feet unless some individual propels her/himself temporarily to a distance above it.[30] Alberti, on the other hand, speaks very clearly of a subjective empowerment which is to be produced through a particular re-organization of the act of seeing. The master of perspectival representation sets up a chosen framing for the taking of sights on a visual scene, imagined as a now re-examined or reconstituted section of the world. Alberti writes, of going about the business of painting, 'First of all, on the surface on which I am going to paint, I draw a rectangle of whatever size I want, which I regard as an open window (*quod quidem mihi pro aperta finestra est*) through which the subject to be painted is seen.'[31] Charles Taylor comments on this transforming of the imagination of seeing,

> the 'freeing' of the object [i.e. its detachment from given continuity with the world] also carries with it a 'freeing' of the subject, in the form of a greater self-consciousness, a new distance and separation from the object, a sense of standing over against and no longer being entangled by what is depicted [32]

Bruegel's painting deals, in the way which a visual depiction specifically can, with both an experience of inter-human solidarity and solidarity with the world and its processes – the fundamental awareness of festivity, which it at once channels and strengthens – and a 'freed' subjective experience of standing

over against the human and otherwise given environment. Here is a reminder of the painting.

Bruegel's complex image possesses, it should be noted, a particularly dynamic perspectival organization. One feature of this is that its human figures are spread before 'me' as spectator horizontally, which invites me to submit them to a thoughtful scrutiny based partly on visual inter-comparison. It is apparent, for example, that the costume of the woman on the right resembles that of the larger of the girls at bottom left, while her placing in the scene as one being pulled towards a dance also evokes that of the smaller of the two girls. Here is material for reflection: perhaps the woman is to be seen as an older version of the two girls who possesses some of the characteristics of both of them – in which case the visual definition given to these three figures evokes the continuity of this represented community's existence across time, but also a certain repetitiveness in its life. There is a cuteness in the conception which amuses and mentally distances: to the modern eye it suggests Russian dolls. Returning to the whole panorama of figures, I notice a uniformity in their collective behaviour, not much to their credit, which also produces a self-distancing. Modern discussion of the painting has often characterized its intentions as being primarily condemnatory; and, certainly, a good deal of the painting's observation is critically angled. One recalls at this juncture that for Erasmian humanism, a component of Bruegel's intellectual background, there was absolutely no value in the giving of oneself to festive play; Erasmus characterizes as 'Unchristian' the carnival which he witnessed at Siena in 1509.[33] Pursuing their pleasures at a boisterous outdoor gathering, the ordinary people as Bruegel depicts them become in a degree gross and predictable as drink taken in quantity produces its usual effects. Pinned to the tree at the far right and not at all conspicuous is a wood-cut image of the Virgin Mary, with votive flowers. On this evidence and that of the broader cultural context the event which we are witnessing seems likely to mark an ecclesiastical festival, perhaps the Feast of the Assumption (15 August), which has sanctioned the abandonment of work and temporary communal turning to celebration. But the effect of noting this is to lower the perceived tone of the revelry; these celebrations of what seems to be a holy day treat the occasion as an irrelevance, the image of the Virgin receives no attention or acknowledgement, higher aspirations are ignored as an everyday, functional keeping of behaviour within bounds gives way to the serving of basic appetites. This community will probably survive over time, but at a quasi-animal level whose attaining scarcely counts as achievement.

Having said this, however – and I would argue that it does correspond to an available perception of what is shown – one recognizes immediately that there is a good deal in the painting which complicates and problematizes the self-detaching spectatorial response. For one thing, and crucially, the whole organization of the image, as well as constituting a panorama, defines a spectator viewpoint which is extremely close to the action that is being shown. This is a function of the steep recession in figures' sizes: the constructed observing position is placed close up to those in the foreground, as an effect of which figures just a few paces from them are halved in scale. Immediately to 'our' left – and I am speaking now from a virtual position *inside* the scene – a man is playing a very large bagpipe. In the context of bagpipe design, large means loud; from where 'we' are standing the noise would be near-overwhelming, producing in the hearer a kind of acoustic immersion.[34] Perceptual immersion in the scene instils, we find experimentally, heightened understanding of what is there to be experienced. The revellers whom we can see best, because they are closest to us, are not boorishly anonymous rustics or artisans but people of marked facial individuality; most obviously in the case of the near-centrally placed man who is breaking into dance-step, and whose physiognomy is given the sort of painterly attention usually reserved at this time for portrayals of the elite. Mentally positioned 'within' the group, we perceive to some extent with the group's sensorium. Committed dancing to music constitutes something like a universal pulse, a recreation of natural process in humanly amenable form.

There occur the beginnings of self-attunement to genuine festal experience: festivals attract individuals and conserve individuality, while overleaping the barriers that ordinarily enforce human mental separation, so fostering responsiveness to being-in-common. They nurture experiences of solidarity, in keeping with which the small girl is encouraging the still smaller girl to dance. This last tiny person is not, as was noted before, the only one who is being pulled into the common behavioural space of merrymaking: in addition to her and the woman on the right we also notice, in the background to left of centre, a woman whom a man is attempting to drag out of the pub towards the dance. Is she right to resist? The question remains hanging, but Bruegel's composition does seem to be offering for our consideration strongly defined alternatives. We have understood what we are seeing differently by positioning ourselves affectively 'inside' the scene; and a key effect of the composition is precisely to pull or propel us as virtual perceivers towards the scene's visual centre. But resisting the pull is also a represented possibility: to the left of the pub door we notice an individual who is not joining in, but loitering in an attitude of indecision or aimlessness. This alternative is not made particularly attractive, but we know of its availability.

I would claim, further, that the painting is so designed as to prevent the spectator from arriving at a settled and confirmed affective–cognitive standpoint on its presented scene. There is much to encourage and even reward an affective joining in with this festival, set before us through the virtualizing power of an image, as an attainment of individual continuity with other human lives. But entering this space, perhaps a privileged one, is also represented as a thing which may not be readily or steadily accomplishable. Festal experience cannot perhaps be dissociated in practice from the will to be given over entirely *to* festal experience, one not that easily fulfilled; festivals can, paradoxically, be threaded for their participants by awareness of personal separateness. And the ordinary people of the painting are not necessarily adroit in the mental attainment of being-in-common. Attitudes of self-detachment and affective suspension, which I have associated with the taking of a spectatorial position 'outside' this virtual scene, also show a significant tendency to invade it; here Bruegel's art offers itself as an aid to reflection on changing cultural attitudes of its time, manifest in the tendency to embrace and cherish mentalities for which individual self-awareness stands naturally to the fore, while collective or shared self-awareness recedes as an imagined possibility. The painting pointedly displays several instances of the non-overcoming or problematic overcoming of inter-human barriers: the woman at the right does not seem delighted to be

pulled off-balance by her partner as he hastens to join the fun; the man with
the pot in his hand is trying to say something to the piper but, unable to be
heard, or facing the man's performer's obliviousness, succeeds only in blowing
beery fumes in his direction; the snogging couple behind the drinkers eye one
another blankly as if waiting for some transport of bliss which has yet to occur;
the drinking group celebrates the common-human by having an argument;
the drinker who most nearly faces us may be inadvertently striking with
an expressively raised hand the man whose cap has fallen over his eyes; the
woman's flat unwillingness to be dragged through the pub door into the space
of dancing speaks for itself. I am not trying to suggest that premodern festivity
was qualitatively better ('merrier'!) than early modern or modern festivity, but I
am contending that festivity is opened to different understanding when viewed
from what has been defined as an individual's spectator position, and that the
establishment of such a cultural–psychological position is characteristic of the
painting's era – as its very form communicates.

I have argued that, as a consequence of the painting's construction of virtual
space, including its positioning(s) of the spectator, it facilitates the bringing of
quite different *kinds* of scrutiny to its represented human scene. The spectator can
consider this from a standpoint of self-separation, where this will tend to imply
morally inflected condemnation of a form of group behaviour. At the same time
the layout of the image supplies a spectatorial vantage point 'within' the scene
of celebration, from which other affective position one becomes aware of the
play of sympathies, individual to individual and group to environment, which
allows the celebration to cohere as social process. But, still affectively positioned
'within' the scene, the spectator can also register the force of tensions between
individually centred and group awareness: the individual celebrants show in
varying degrees a certain disposition to stand apart from or even resist the flows
of group awareness, being more directly animated by individual concerns. The
painting thus counts as a brilliant demonstration, indeed production through
discovery in the spectator's experience, of the lack of fit between individually
centred self-awareness, when mobilized, and communal arrival at mutuality of
consciousness. This demonstration begins in the giving to a form of individualized
spectatorship, one directly available to the beholder, visual–spatial definition. I
wish to suggest that *1 Henry IV* similarly facilitates diverse takings of sight on
the anti-structural play, improvisation and fantasy of which Falstaff is the central
exponent.

*   *   *

Establishing an individual's spectatorial standpoint on the festive community almost inescapably imports consideration of festivity's utility, or lack of it, with respect to the ordinary needs of social living where an individual works out her/his continuing relations with others, as distinct from its bearing on human relations as such; in other words, it tends to import the paradoxical expectation that anti-structural play should be responsive to social structural requirements. Hal's soliloquy which concludes his first scene of interaction with Falstaff and Poins negotiates this paradox, not entirely convincingly declaring it resolved. We are now in a position to examine the adjustments of seeing which it puts into effect. Hal has just entered into Poins's scheme to trick Falstaff by robbing him incognito of what he has just robbed, finding out what lies he will tell. With Hal I take the execution of this planned trick to be an instance of Falstaff-centred 'holiday' play. Poins exits, on which the prince turns to the audience speaking of his erstwhile companions:

I know you all, and will a while uphold
The unyoked humour of your idleness.
Yet herein will I imitate the sun,
Who doth permit the base contagious clouds
To smother up his beauty from the world,
That, when he please again to be himself,
Being wanted, he may the more be wondered at
By breaking through the foul and ugly mists
Of vapours that did seem to strangle him.
If all the year were playing holidays,
To sport would be as tedious as to work;
But when they seldom come, they wished-for come,
And nothing pleaseth but rare accidents.
So when this loose behaviour I throw off
And pay the debt I never promised,
By how much better than my word I am,
By so much shall I falsify men's hopes;
And, like bright metal on a sullen ground,
My reformation, glittering o'er my fault,
Shall show more goodly and attract more eyes
Than that which hath no foil to set it off.
I'll so offend to make offense a skill,
Redeeming time when men think least I will. (1.2.185–207)

This soliloquy decisively aligns itself with the still relatively novel cultural technologies which reclassify seeing as knowing, beginning as it does with a very forceful marking out of the distanced standpoint from which the spectatorial eye can take the inclusive, panoramic view: 'I know you all, and will a while uphold / The unyoked humour of your idleness.' This arresting statement establishes a foundation for the rest of what Hal asserts, predicts and claims; it is an abrupt suspension of the communally orientated, anti-structural mentality in projecting and sustaining which the prince has just shown himself to be passably adept. Envisaging of the immediate group's thoughts becomes suddenly very marginal to experience; it must be possible, then, for the individual to live amphibiously both 'inside' and 'outside' shared mentalities. As Hal declares and demonstrates this, a new, much larger group mentality comes into thought's scope for which Hal himself as self-staged is to be the central, sight-attracting object, the cynosure. This mentality belongs to 'the world', a generalized human looking on, one of whose manifestations is the ambient political community, from whose abiding concerns anti-structural play by its nature disaligns itself.

The drift of the speech's carefully worked-out solar metaphorics – which recall, as is often pointed out, certain trains of thought in the 'young man' sonnets – is, I would say, not cosmomorphic, because individual, deliberative taking of thought and action shapes reference to cosmic phenomena, not vice versa: we are asked to imagine that the already Hal-like sun allows the 'base contagious clouds' to disfigure his beauty so that he can appear again as himself, at a time personally chosen, with brilliantly gratifying results. (These lines efficiently bring out the difference between modern anthropomorphism of outlook, which they represent, and more traditional placings of human life in relation to cosmic processes which retain a degree of ontological otherness, and are not to be exhaustively understood through individual self-projection.) The substance of the speech is concerned with image management, and with what can be showed for effect to others. Festivity figures as one term in the development of a logical proposition bearing on self-presentation: holidays are valued only 'when they seldom come' (a reductive thought which seems to align itself with post-Reformation thinnings out of the festive calendar); so, forgetting holidays, one should manifest what one wishes to be taken as being in rare impressive acts. Once the idea of debt-redemption has been introduced the calculations concerning image-management seem to become more specifically those of the merchant or shopkeeper, who brings out the glittering allure of goods by setting them against a contrasted background, a 'foil'.

I wish to draw attention primarily, however, to the speech's emphatic, as one might say paid-up, individualism, for which selfhood existing in self-accountable separateness from others is naturally and properly a magnet of concern, and for which projection of the self's reality as that of an onlooker with respect to others arises quite spontaneously; and at the same time to the speech's mobility of reference to groups with which the individual may be situationally involved. In Hal's statement the immediate group around Falstaff, in which we have just seen him embedded, becomes a nexus of people purely seen, therefore utterly and detachedly known. At the same time it registers acute awareness of a generalized social gaze, and of the imagined responses of a political community. Moreover, in the drastic character of its assumed individual detachment it implies the availability of other responses to the shared experience; as Simon Palfrey points out, the initial statement, 'I know you all,' seems to include all present auditors as well as the figures who have just left the stage, in which case members of the audience are being invited to experiment with thoughts of rejecting a kind of experience which they also value, and are to go on valuing in that it is part of what the whole action which they are witnessing provides.[35] *Richard II* and *1 Henry IV*, manifestly political in their concerns, manifestly attuned to the practicalities of performance and spectatorship, elicit fairly continuous reflection on optically defined relations, real and imagined, reciprocal or uni-directional, between individuals and groups. Such reflection is, of course, endemic in stage actions of the period, but I would say that it accrues in these plays to an unusual extent. Henry Bolingbroke as he lectures Hal is right in principle if wrong over the details to make Richard's downfall a matter of altered seeing, and attempts to learn politically from Richard's downfall are one of the sequence's strongest connective motifs.

Shakespeare loses no time in having Hal declare the availability to himself of a set if mind dissociated from Falstaff and condemnatory of him: Hal does this in the first scene in which he appears, repeating the act subsequently; and reformation following riotous youth is, of course, a routinized part of the received Hal narrative. Nevertheless, the plays are not so shaped as to banish the thoughts which Falstaffian play produces, and Hal's initial statement of complete spectatorial disconnection from it implies, as in Bruegel's painting, the availability of an opposed experience, one of immersion going with valid affective participation. Our responses to the action of *1 Henry IV* continue to be shaped to a significant extent by the mentality of play activated by and around Falstaff, which offers its own vantage-point in the plays' representation

of communities formed at several social levels. Probably the law-breaking of
Falstaff and associates evokes ills which more broadly beset the realm of Henry
Bolingbroke. And, as we are reminded frequently enough, Falstaff is ruthless as
well as shameless in the pursuit of his own chosen ends. Nevertheless, Falstaffian
play, much of it embodied in language and so resonating beyond its immediate
context, powerfully mobilizes anti-structural mentalities which are not to be
erased from consciousness by Falstaff's personal condemnation and dismissal.
Falstaff's main function in *1 Henry IV*, enframed as he is by a surrounding action
concerned with failing political cultures, is to sustain that anti-hierarchical
circulation of symbols which recalls what is fundamental to the imagination of
communitas.

A Reconstitution of Community: 'Nature's' Dismantling and Replacement in *The Winter's Tale*

One of the typifying features of a structured community is the possession in common of a certain perception – partly intuitive in character, often quite loosely defined, probably supported by a wider culture – of 'how things are', of how the world works, of what can generally be taken to be the case. We could call this a community's 'nature' in one of the available senses of that word. It is a horizon of the familiarly known in its conditions and tendencies of development, defining a field of the seemingly explicable within which members of the group will ordinarily tend to place phenomena which they observe or of which they are told. It typically encodes principles of hierarchical organization which have a direct bearing on social practice. In the present context I am concerned primarily with notions of 'nature' belonging to normative early modern European cultural perception.

Clear antitheses to early modern 'nature' are the early modern 'supernatural' and 'para-natural', domains to which European culture of our period assigns phenomena which violate its going sense of 'how things (ordinarily) are'. Its attempts to consolidate knowledge of the world often distinguish sharply between the ordinary way of things and the supernatural, the magical, the miraculous, the aberrant, the monstrous and their like. But acceptance of the validity of such a distinction at the same time produces disputes about the placing of particular anomalous phenomena with respect to it; for example, is a major storm which might impair the crop yield to be classified as manifesting the ordinary way of things, or is it a disturbing exception to which one should respond in a different and more alarmed manner, perhaps taking apotropaic measures? As was noted in the discussion of *King Lear*, the era's cosmomorphism of outlook tends to produce evolved reflection on what is and what is not to be counted as 'natural', in the sense of going with the ordinary grain of cosmic process.[1] Within the framework of this outlook the continuous influential interplay between phenomena observable at different levels of cosmic activity – such as those of the celestial motions and the weather, or the condition of the body politic, or the flow of humours in an individual body – is generally assigned to the field of 'nature', but with a paying of vigilant attentiveness to perceived anomalies. It may be considered wise or pious to treat some unusual phenomena as extraordinary, and therefore possessing the force of warnings: Reason in *Piers Plowman* preaches before the king that 'the south-western wind which blew on Saturday evening / Did this manifestly on account of pride, and for no other reason.'[2] Monsters (literally 'showings'), prodigies and portents can become objects of keen interest, since taken to be there to instruct the human group.[3] An earlier chapter considered in its bearing on *King Lear* the intriguing status that was often assigned to eclipses, as phenomena attesting the machine-like regularity of the cosmos but nevertheless, as weird, likely to portend cosmic order's infringement (Gloucester: 'Yet nature finds itself disturbed by the sequent effects').

For purposes of assessing early modern thought of nature it is necessary to become attuned to an outlook for which natural order is normative and not lawlike, as would be basic to the axiology of a later science. The Preface to Newton's *Principia* ('*The Mathematical Principles of Natural Philosophy*') is a rhetorically brilliant adduction of certain *natural laws*, which from now on will, it insists, be acknowledged by all as holding absolute sway. But in a broadly Aristotelian understanding, on the other hand, nature is a somewhat settled order from which deviations quite often occur; which correlates in situ, needless to say, with religious and scientific–philosophical mentalities alert to possible occurrences of what is *not* natural. In the argument that follows I shall pursue two corollaries of the traditional, in its most familiar articulation Aristotelian, enframing of 'nature' for thought which was culturally predominant in the medieval to early modern period.

(A) Its production of a sense of 'the way things (ordinarily) are' takes shape within a consensus view of the natural (see Chapter 1): our constructions of 'nature' are, the *Posterior Analytics* explains, the thoughts of the human collectivity which have been distilled from its 'experience', arising in what has been perceived and undergone by many individuals across long spans of time. And a related cultural tradition-oriented epistemology grounds the premodern to early modern sense of the 'probable' as that which sensible human beings will generally affirm or confirm to be the case. Aristotle and the philosophical tradition contribute strongly in our period to the credentials of a consensus view of 'nature' which bonds at the level of thought and intuitive response those seeking to understand what is there to be perceived.

(B) Its 'nature' has boundaries around it which are not those of the world as such, since they derive pragmatically from the experience of a human group which has in the interests of securing its welfare formed a particular kind of practical relation with the world; which is to say, in the case of Europeans, that from the establishment of farming up to early modern times they flourished or failed to flourish primarily as agriculturalists, stock-rearers, artisans, and traders – people defining a home region, usually organized in territorially demarcated political units, and aware of 'nature' in the ways to which living specifically in this fashion gives rise. Viewing 'nature' from the standpoint of these concerns of life implies possession of a mental world map which has a centre, a periphery and an area of the less known or positively unknown. What one takes to be 'natural' arises in a shared experience affirming the existence and value of a centre, and no doubt shaped by social–political structures which have been shaped in turn by practical relations formed with some piece or pieces of terrain. The pre-Socratic natural philosopher Thales (born c. 625 BCE) is said to have thanked Fortune for three things, 'That I am a man and not a beast; secondly that I am male and not female; thirdly, that I am Greek and not a barbarian.'[4] This implies a set of mental concentric circles in which animals are placed furthest to the outside ('most unlike me and what I know'), then women, then barbarians, whose life approximates somewhat more closely to an acceptable condition. Such a view of 'nature' obviously sanctions forms of social organization in which the power of women is subordinated to that of men. It is also worth noting at this point that the Aristotelian physical world is a model of given self-organizing hierarchy: its constituent elements spontaneously distribute themselves in the vertical descending sequence of fire, air, water, earth, as if knowing their assigned places.

Early modern thought of 'nature' typically posits, then, a central region surrounded by an increasingly 'beyond' which combines relative unfamiliarity, relative unintelligibility and, given the culture's masculinist cast, association with the feminine. One of its names is 'the wild', supported in the first place by a different structure of thought from the supernatural, including the magical and portentous.[5] But these *others* of norm-following early modern 'nature' can, as we quickly become aware on reviewing the early modern evidence, enter quite readily for thought into overlap and complicity, as in conceptualization of the 'monstrous' or the 'marvellous'. This happens fairly pervasively in early modern narratives of travel outside familiar zones, of which the narrative of *The Tempest* is a particularly succinct and inclusive version.

The Winter's Tale, with which this chapter is from now on concerned, launches itself as dramatic action and narrative thought by establishing a profound crisis in the conceptualization of 'nature'[6] which is also a crisis in sharing of awareness by a human group. To consider these issues in reverse order – Leontes at the start of the play takes, of course, a view of what is occurring around him which is maximally *individualist*, in the sense of being maximally alienated from the view taken by everyone else in his represented community. To those around him he looks utterly foolish or stark mad. But, to him, his individually accomplished observations and reflections – rational in character, consistent in what they establish – lead to only one conclusion. The action, then, drastically pits a gnosiology centred on individually conducted enquiry against a traditional or customary one considered to be grounded in group experience, for which understanding as informed by the 'probable' (older sense) is generally to be trusted. But Leontes' decisive rejection of his ambient group's 'probable', dictated by perceptions of which he knows himself to be the only possessor, is also the taking of an axe to that shared, mainly intuitive, understanding of nature which yields collective registration of 'nature', in responsiveness to which individuals share significant forms of awareness. A princely family which has already produced the male heir who should preside over the community in its next temporal formation, one of those collective imagings of 'nature' to which early modern culture generally pays homage, here morphs before the astonished onlooker into the agency of its own destruction. The first large sweep of action in *The Winter's Tale* ends in an epiphany of 'wildness' as the honest-minded counsellor ordered to abandon an infant on a distant shore is dismembered and eaten by a bear, while the ship and crew which have conveyed him are 'flapdragoned' (3.3.96)[7] – casually swallowed up – by a stormy sea. I wish to pay close attention to the play's conceptual dealings with nature – 'what is' – whose general tendency is to dismantle that felt-as-coherent conception of 'nature' which the play's cultural tradition has ordinarily supported, to the play's associated traversals of an imagined and enacted 'wildness', and finally to its reconstitution of a human group whose members can knowingly share in a form of awareness.

*   *   *

To recapitulate a little, the received thought of Shakespeare's era distinguishes fairly consistently between *nature* as a 'way things happen' which, being relatively orderly, is open to conceptualization and can often be put to human use – its development as a cultural representation projects the practical concerns of a society economically centred on farming and stock-rearing – and a *wild*, including the 'savage', which is experienced as disordered, resistant to understanding and largely devoid of utility.[8] Scriptural thought, for example, distinguishes extensively between a terrain which is benignly fertile and a sterile wilderness deprived of God's blessing, not a version of the natural but its antithesis. Human 'wildness' or 'savageness' is as typically conceived in the medieval to early modern era an asocial mode of being, implying non-entry to or self-removal from relations of felt affinity, care and obligation. It is considered to issue in individual isolation and solipsism (see Aristotle's well-known assessment of those who live outside a *polis*),[9] attitudes of ferocity and rapacity, and special exposedness to misfortune, given the absence of the protection which the solidarity of a society ordinarily confers on the individual. Montaigne, choosing to write favourably about indigenous Americans in his essay 'On the Cannibals', treats their appearance of 'wildness' as misleading: characterizing them as possessing a great deal of 'natural' potential, he explains that, similarly, we find a 'lively and vigorous' incidence in some wild-growing fruits of 'genuine and most useful *natural* virtues and properties (*vive et vigoureuses . . . les vrayes et plus utiles et naturelles vertus et proprietez*).'[10]

A further term needs to be introduced into the discussion. In *The Winter Tale*'s pastoral scene Perdita and Polixenes engage, as we know, in a brief but arresting debate about the relationship between nature and artifice ('art'), evoking a familiar tradition of classical to early modern thought.[11] For Aristotelian philosophy, centrally concerned with the issue, processes of natural growth and development (*physis*) and artificial fabrication (*techne*) stand in a mutually explicating relationship with one another.[12] Natural growth exhibits a purposiveness resembling that of *techne*: an acorn in growth has the indwelling purpose of becoming a tree, while the practitioner of a craft applies from outside the purpose of making a table from a piece of wood, but the purposiveness recognizably present in both processes of change is of the same kind. And *techne* for its part imitates the creativeness of nature in its bringing of new things or states into being. Mainstream classical thought makes art an inferior counterpart to nature, inferior on the principle that, in Cicero's formulation, nature's works exhibit a steady inventiveness (*sollertia*) 'which no work of artifice or craftsman can rival or reproduce',[13] but also a counterpart in that the activities of both are considered to be end-directed in the same way, therefore taking a similar form. This, I would say, is the familiar conceptual apparatus: artifice and nature contribute vitally to one another's understanding, which is why they are so often discussed together; nature's works and workings are reliably superior to, while resembling, those of human fabrication. The general tendency of *The Winter's Tale* is, however, to destabilize and discredit this conceptual apparatus, eventually substituting another. I shall identify some of the phases of the dismantling before moving on to the substitution.

Natural process as represented in the play tends towards the *wild*, in its composite sense of the ferocious and humanly inimical, and of the humanly inexplicable, unpredictable and therefore limitlessly threatening. In reaching an appraisal of the represented ferocity, it is instructive to compare *The Winter's Tale* with the pastoral Book Six of *The Faerie Queene*, also containing a shepherdess of concealed noble birth, and similarly concerned with human leanings towards wildness and ferocity. Spenser's poem gives prominence to a Salvage or feral Man, again of unrecognized noble origin, who lacks language and conforms in other respects to the cultural type of the forest-dwelling wild man,[14] but whose behaviour shows forms of spontaneous civility. An incipiently non-wild wild creature, he is the book's conceptual antithesis to the members of the Salvage Nation who, in a paradigmatic act of wildness, prepare to dismember and eat a female victim as a consequence of being attracted to her body (see 6.8.35–51).[15] In its examination of the nature of courtesy, Spenser's book is generally concerned with the possibility of establishing basic, foundational forms of social life under potential conditions of wild incivility. These basic forms are set in place, where they accrue, by elemental, presumably naturally occurring, feelings of affinity between human beings. In the thought of the poem bears in particular project the idea of a wildness and bereftness of affinity which it may, and may not, be possible to overcome.[16] Maureen Quilligan calls attention to Spenser's serial punning on the word 'bear', as denoting the animal, 'carry an object or person', and 'give birth to a child', which comes to a head when the wife of one Sir Bruin, discovered lamenting the barrenness for which her husband holds her to blame, is made a gift of the infant boy whom Sir

Calepine is carrying, having just rescued him from the bear who is about to eat him (see 4.17–40).[17] 'Bear' in its several meanings thus functions as a linguistic and conceptual switch-point between, on the one hand, a wildness which is associated with ferocity, isolation and exposure to the terrible contingency of things and, on the other, practices making for inter-human responsiveness and mutuality of outlook which can countervail these perils and misfortunes.

Book Six's proffered solution to the incidence of human wildness and the parallel wildness of experienced misfortune is the postulate that they can be corrected or redressed by establishing a fresh alignment with the way of nature. The answer is offered with a certain sense of paradox: civility in its elemental forms, such as those shown in Calidore's graceful dealings with chance acquaintances, is also a first flowering of human beings' natural disposedness towards discovery of affinity. 'Courtesy' as this pastoral narrative presents it, in separation from the imagined life of courts, is – like behaviour formed in suitable response to the era's art- and nature-reconciling gardens[18] – movement towards the forming of an optimal relationship between the humanly disposed and intentional on the one hand and the naturally given on the other, through the releasing of nature's valued powers in what is also a humanly shaped environment. But compare this with what occurs in *The Winter's Tale*.

(A) In the play wildness is integral to the human state as represented, not the effect of some local failing or twist of fortune which are there to be overcome. As Stephen Orgel notes, the male sexuality represented in the play's pastoral scenes tends markedly towards ferocity and violence.[19] Florizel regales us with an enthusiastic account of the gods' sexual violations of mortals (see 4.4.25–31),[20] and hails Perdita initially as Flora, who in Ovid's *Fasti* (5.212) becomes the goddess of flowers on being raped by the West Wind. In distributing flowers Perdita finds herself, in vision, playing Persephone's role at the moment of being seized by the god who is abducting her, when she dropped the flowers that she was carrying in terror. Outside the pastoral action, wildness is flagged up as a significant concept in the naming as well as the behaviour of two of the play's principal dramatic agents. Leontes of Sicilia is, as the recent Arden editor notes, one of several related paternal names in Shakespeare which suggest 'hot, insular savagery', referencing volcanic Sicily and the lion's familiar connotations.[21] The name 'Autolycus' is also that of Odysseus' maternal grandfather, famous for thieving and deceit, and may be translated as 'The Wolf Himself' or

'Lone Wolf'. Human entry to destructive conditions of wildness is, as has been said, conspicuously represented at the play's narrative tipping point in the image of the Sicilian ship's destruction in a storm and its complement, that of Antigonus' death as inflicted by a bear which hunters have contingently disturbed. *The Winter's Tale* is, among other things, the story of a lion, a bear and a wolf.

(B) Wildness in Spenser's text has, as has been said, a progressive enframing. Natural process here is – as it is for mainstream classical thought, Aristotelian, Stoic or Epicurean – susceptible of rational description and partly convertible to human advantage. But *The Winter's Tale's* examination of wildness lacks any kind of comparable progressivism, and its represented nature, unamenable to conceptualization (see C, below), contains conversely seeds of wildness whose tendency is to grow and flourish. Leontes feels that he has discovered, in male uncertainty over the paternal relation, a universal and communal life-disruptive *natural* fact.

It is also worth considering in this context the development of the play's shearing festival. The festival's nearest approach to an instatement of nature as orderly is the 'dance of Shepherds and Shepherdesses' (4.4.167SD) in which Florizel as disguised and the elaborately dressed Perdita participate. Pastorally equivalent to the focal dance of a courtly masque, this is a relatively decorous quasi-symbolic acting out of the sexual relationship in a social setting. But it is succeeded by the more anarchic, predominantly comic performance of Autolycus in the guise of a pedlar selling ballads, where absurd wonders are admired as truths, concluding as the pedlar performs a flirtatious song with two of the feistier shepherdesses. This is followed in its turn, before Polixenes breaks up proceedings, by a dance of 'three carters, three shepherds, three neatherds, three swineherds that have made themselves all men of hair', also called 'saultiers' or acrobatic leapers, overlapping phonologically with 'satyrs' (329–32). Modern editors have suggested that this last stands in some relation to the satyrs' dance from the near-contemporary court masque of *Oberon*,[22] commissioned from Inigo Jones and Ben Jonson and primarily an exaltation of Prince Henry. It seems likely that the same music was used for both. But home-made hairy outfits concealing unskilled country people point to a rougher and more boisterous performance than that given by the court masque's suave, neoclassically styled satyrs.[23] And, a fortiori, the progress of the play's festival celebrations reverses that of any normative courtly performance, including

Oberon,[24] in moving from a version of masque, the dance of courtship, to a version of antimasque, the cavorting of hairy males. The play's country people are, we might say, getting further *into* wildness as the day advances. Group celebration here does not promote the experience of mutuality but, on the contrary, facilitates individual enactment of what one is individually disposed to be, in a putting in abeyance of self-recognition as sharing a common existence.

I am drawing attention to a progression in the action of *The Winter's Tale* which in effect formally inverts that of *The Faerie Queene*, Book Six. The general tendency is towards the releasing into the human scene of what makes for wildness, involving greater individual participation in it. Paulina's management of the penitent Leontes is, as we discover more fully when the action returns to Sicily, a confirming of his disposition towards 'insular savagery', one that compels him to seek remedy for it through deeper entry into such a state. The first proposal which she has offered rhetorically is that of cultivating solitude and bodily mortification in a wildly desolate place ('A thousand knees, / Ten thousand years together, naked, fasting, / Upon a barren mountain'; 3.2.207–9). The actual form of penitence which Leontes adopts is a haunting of graves, prefigured in Mamilius's 'There was a man (. . .) / Dwelt by a churchyard' (2.1.29–30). His task, we find, is to explore more deeply the state of existential isolation to which ferocity has led him.

(C)   As well as putting into effect A and B, as above, the play also foregrounds
      difficulties which are to be confronted in the orderly *conceptualization*
      of nature. These are set out with some clarity in a compressed statement
      made near the beginning of the play. Camillo, looking back on the intense,
      long-sustained friendship of Leontes and Polixenes, offers the following
      recollection and prediction:

> They were trained together in their childhoods, and there rooted betwixt them
> then such an affection as cannot choose but branch now. (1.1.22–4)

'Trained' covers 'educated', 'followed in the same retinue or train', and 'were led to grow in the same direction/in the same time/at the same place like trellised plants', and 'branch' picks up the horticultural metaphor – so far, so relatively straightforward. But the reference of 'branch' is difficult to pin down, making for a bifurcation of possible meanings. Understood positively, going with what we assume to be the speaker's intention, the statement points to further flourishing, involving some physical multiplication, of a deeply rooted friendship. If we are dealing with a multiplication, the suggestion may be that Leontes' young son will also be a factor in the same enlarging, consolidating growth. But 'cannot choose but branch now' implies a significant development and alteration that is about to occur, and one that is not necessarily welcome; and natural branching is moreover, clearly enough, a form of division – which other cluster of suggestions will take over possession of the statement in the context of the action which ensues. The problem of anticipated natural growth which Camillo's statement earmarks is that it genuinely contains both these contrary potentialities, for the self-enlargement of a unitary organic body and for its splitting by self-separation (as in modern biology's cellular mitosis), another familiar form of natural growth. Whatever one predicates of nature runs the risk of over-confidently excluding some possibility which happens to have escaped attention, making it the more disruptive when it occurs.

Here it is also worth considering Paulina's valiant, carefully managed attempt to present the infant Perdita to her father as attesting and channelling 'great Nature['s]' powers, so producing parental acknowledgement and reconciliation. Confident in her plan and, presumably, in her vision of nature's benignity, she brushes aside the gaoler's doubts about releasing the child with these majestic words:

> You need not fear it, sir.
> This child was prisoner to the womb, and is
> By law and process of great Nature thence
> Freed and enfranchised, not a party to
> The anger of the king, nor guilty of –
> If any be – the trespass of the queen. (2.2.56–62)

Paulina is singling the infant Perdita out for special attention as a *natural* being, exhibiting and forming part of ordinary process in the world which includes parents' affective bonding their own children. When Perdita has been carried before Leontes she is characterized by Paulina – perhaps implausibly for what looks like a small bundle of cloth – as having been shaped by 'thou, good goddess Nature' (2.3.102) in the king's exact physical likeness, so providing proof of fatherhood. But the perception of father–daughter affinity does not transfer to Leontes, and reference to nature probably reminds him mainly of cuckoldry ('Shall I live on, to see this bastard kneel / And call me father?'; 2.3.153–4). With the failure of her persuasive performance Paulina exits leaving the infant child – that is, for the audience, the bundle of cloth – lying vulnerably and unpromisingly on the floor. Invocation of the goddess

Nature's way has done nothing to bring Perdita into social existence as the king's acknowledged daughter, and here a human attempt to give the concept of nature constructive force has gone badly awry. It might be considered, in context, less cognitively risky to take the pessimistic view, seeing human entry into unconstrained conditions of nature as being humanly destructive. Antigonus does this just before going to his death: abandoning the baby Perdita to her fate, he calls her a 'blossom' (3.3.45), about to become one of nature's ordinary if regrettable casualties. But this reading of 'nature' also turns out, however, to be ill-founded: nature's way remains unavailable to any ready understanding.

This is a suitable point at which to turn to the brief, charged quasi-philosophical debate of Perdita and Polixenes which takes place against the background of the shearing festival. The debate's philosophically unorthodox tendency is to unpick the mutually explicatory relationship of nature and artifice, with the effect that natural process is left unexplained and technical procedure is left unaccountable and undirected. Polixenes' claim (mischievous, of course, in its situational context) is that any artifice brought to bear on nature is nothing other than 'an art / That Nature makes' (4.4.91–2). Conceptions of nature in this view set no constraints on what *techne* is to be welcomed in accomplishing, since this will still be received as a thing of nature's making – the implication seems to be that human beings are, in practice, entirely relaxed in their drawing of the distinction. But Perdita, taking up the already subversive idea, caps it with her account of a *techne* which is, if seen in its true aspect, *entirely emancipated* from nature, and so, for example, capable of turning a living body into that body's mere simulacrum for others' perception: suppose, she says, that I used cosmetics, 'painting', to project an image of beauty, and that these cosmetics alone, as distinct from the body to which they are applied, produced in Florizel the 'Desire (. . .) to breed with me' (101–3); in which case I, *qua* living body, would function merely as the surface bearing the paint. What *techne* produces may in this view have an autonomous pseudo-'life' quite distinct from that of life in its natural occurrence. The crowning insight which emerges from this compressed debate is that human inventiveness, being unruly and *sui generis*, throws no light at all on that of nature, and supplants it when given the opportunity.

I have drawn attention to the play's manner of causing nature's ordinary way to include 'wildness', and at the same time of blocking nature's conceptualization. Perdita's and Polixenes' discussion of the artifice–nature relationship seems to bring this second tendency to a climax, producing the image of a *techne* which entirely alienates human activity from nature, thereby, in a philosophically traditional view, removing the basis on which it (and for that matter, nature) might be understood and evaluated. But, what if it *were* possible to take a positive view of *techne*'s newly identified a-natural powers?[25]

The Winter's Tale offers, I would say, three conspicuous images of a humanly constructed skilful practice, a *techne*, which is fully emancipated from the usually envisaged constraints of *being like* 'nature'; in that it does not assist or further natural processes (as was commonly said of farming or medicine), or take them as its model (as was commonly said of craft production). All are presented by or in connection with Autolycus. He is the play's intriguing re-invention of the traditional figure of the Wild Man, turning him into one who flourishes through craftiness in a human setting while retaining an asocial 'animality' of outlook. *Techne* in the thought of the play can flourish with a wildness of its own; and the play's own *techne* will in due course produce the marvellous. The images of a gratuitously inventive *techne* which Autolycus introduces into the action, though as suspect from the standpoint of a conventional social outlook as he is, become auspicious in the setting of the play's exposition of a 'nature', pervading what human beings take to be civilization, which tips inherently and with unfortunate effect towards wildness while remaining at the same time humanly unintelligible. They eventually point to the possibility that *techne* can remedy deficiencies in the human state arising from 'nature's' practical–conceptual loss.

(i) Autolycus lives in improvised metamorphosis, finding his principle of being in the opportunities provided by contingent circumstances and encounters. He has no fixed mode of being, but exists as what his trickery can make of him. He is in the pragmatically useful position to mingle with all social ranks, sorts and occupational groups. This wanderer, rogue and shape-shifter produces the action's resolution by connecting the life and concerns of shepherds with those of the court. His lack of or repudiation of a 'naturally' assigned social position converts with creative power.

(ii) Autolycus is a comic version of Hermes, the conductor of souls, the psychopomp; the Autolycus of Greek legend being, of course, the son of Hermes, with whom the Autolycus of this play also claims affinity (see 4.3.24). As such, he conducts the spectator psychically towards *The Winter's Tale*'s culminating action, which climaxes in the (perceived) animation of Hermione-as-statue. This is, within the play's structure of conceptualization, the triumph of a *techne* which, in this case marvellous rather than wild, functions independently of nature understood as *phusis*, natural process and development as ordinarily understood. The Sicilian courtiers stress what is non-probable and radically novel in the action of multiple discovery which has just taken place offstage: 'they [Leontes and Camillo] looked as they had heard of a world ransomed, or one destroyed'; 'Who was most marble there changed colour. Some swooned, all sorrowed. If all the world could have seen't, the woe had been universal' (5.2.14–15; 87–90). These remarks, apocalyptic in tenor, rhyme with Time's choric evocation of possible forms of life which stand outside *phusis* as commonly experienced.

(iii) Autolycus as peddler of ballads narrating freakish wonders projects the image of a rising, wild-flourishing, publishing culture, interlinked with stage performance, with which the first audiences of *The Winter's Tale* are (to Ben Jonson's professed disgust)[26] de facto involved, and in which, as Roger Chartier puts it, 'different media and multiple practices almost always mingled in complex ways'.[27] Lori Newcomb observes that it is, for early seventeenth-century literate consciousness, exemplified with special force by the unusually wide social circulation of Greene's *Pandosto*,[28] our play's main narrative source. In the perspective of the play this textual culture's multiform prolificness figures, it would seem, as a seething chaos out of which novelty will spontaneously emerge. The reality projected by Autolycus' ballads is, needless to say, an anarchy from the standpoint of established common sense and 'the probable'. To sell his printed sheets he tells willing hearers of a usurer's wife who gave birth to 20 money bags, and of the fish, previously a woman who refused her lover, who hung above the water singing 'against the hard hearts of maids' (see 4.4.259–85). Although modern commentators generally decline to make the inference, these ballad marvels, inherently bizarre and imaginatively stretched, may nevertheless be taken to allude obliquely to serious actions in the surrounding play: discovered with the baby Perdita are the bags of gold which secure her finders' welfare along with her own; the penitent Leontes is a being transformed in retribution for his cruel rejection of one who loves him. Dorcas's wish to have the fish story's truth confirmed (see 4.4.282) anticipates the Sicilian courtiers' similar wish concerning the revelations of the play's final scenes. Autolycus' penitent singing fish which hangs far above the water, one of a prolific publishing culture's representative *impossibilia* taken for actualities, thus appears to count as a draft for the 'nature' – defying wonders with which the play concludes.

I have characterized the play's shearing festival as developing not towards recognition and affirmation of human being-in-common, but towards willed participation in a condition of wildness which consists in the search for individualizing self-fulfilment. Autolycus' selling of printed ballads from a pack of the same forms part of this development, and encourages reflection on the workings of a publishing marketplace. Central to the allure of such a marketplace is that it should offer items which differentiate their purchasers, items to suit and intensify individual dispositions of mind. Hearing of the penitent fish, Dorcas – drawing attention to what is paradoxical in the project of self-realization through consumerism – seems to think that the story speaks personally to her ('Is it true too, think you?'; 4.4.282), while Mopsa, for her part, opts for something more cheerful (see line 288). The ballad-promoter's effects on his audience are described twice, first with a sense of awed regard by the serving man who announces his arrival, then contemptuously from Autolycus' standpoint. According to the servant,

> He sings several tunes faster than you can tell money. He utters them as he had eaten ballads, and all men's ears grew to his tunes. (. . .) He hath songs for man or woman of all sizes. No milliner can so fit his customers with gloves. (ll. 185–94)

The passage speaks both of the crowd compulsion which a practice of market selling can induce, and of an absolute satisfaction at the same time experienced as being offered to her/him personally by every individual present. Reinforcing these impressions in a different style, Autolycus comments with a certain wonder on the power of one dupe in the audience to recruit others:

> My clown (. . .) grew so in love with the wenches' song [i.e. the novel song performed by him, Dorcas and Mopsa] that he would not stir his pettitoes till he had both tune and words, which so drew the rest of the herd to me that all their other senses stuck in ears. (ll. 609–14)

The *lure*, then, is that of individual satisfaction; the actuality, in Autolycus' caustic account, is that of highly undiscriminating 'herd' behaviour, a forfeiting of such advantages of self-differentiation as wildness might offer.

The Winter's Tale presents, then, something of a conundrum to its audience in suggesting at least the possibility of finding resemblance between the content of Autolycus' peddled ballads and the content of its own action. Newcomb points out that the play is composed in an era when elite and non-elite readers are jointly exploring and accessing what a rapidly expanding culture of print puts on offer, but when elite readers also feel impelled at times to distance their own reading experience from that of their social inferiors. In an Overburian characterization of 1615, for example, the scatterbrained chamber-maid is described as liking to 'read[ ] *Greenes* works over and over.'[29] Nevertheless, Shakespeare's play does not seek to disguise its narrative debt to the very widely read *Pandosto*. Flagging up the implausibilities of discovery and recovery with which *The Winter's Tale* ends, Sicilian courtiers refer twice to the contrivances of 'an old tale' (see 5.2.27–9, 5.3.115–7). Like recalling of its title, this might be taken to distance the play generically from ballads purporting to deal in remarkable actualities of recent occurrence. But in witnessing the play's last sweep of action one might well wonder where, at the level of narrative event, the distinction might be found. I would suggest that *The Winter's Tale*, in several respects a dismantling of 'nature', does not and cannot bid to differentiate its narrative procedures fundamentally from those of ballads and romances in common reading. But it does induce in theatre onlookers a distinctive intellectual registration of what they themselves are doing in granting representational reality to what the concluding action places before them.

Paulina introduces the last scenes' crowning exhibit, the statue Hermione, in conjunction with the 'many singularities', as Leontes calls them, which she keeps in a 'gallery' ('Your gallery / Have we passed through, not without much content / In many singularities'; 5.3.10, 12) dedicated to that purpose – it is interesting to speculate on what other 'singularities' audiences might have imagined the gallery as housing. Paulina is, then, the maintainer of something that resembles a *Kunstkammer* or *Wunderkammer* ('cabinet of artifice', 'cabinet of curiosities') in the era's philosophical–scientific style, often set up in European courts or other private ownership, and highly regarded as an instrument of intellectual enquiry – though modern study has been slow to catch up with their underlying conceptions;[30] they have often been viewed as merely bizarre and aberrant.[31] The compilers and organizers of early modern *Kunstkammern* had as their main theoretical concern metamorphic transitions between the natural and the artificial; and so in practice drew together natural objects displaying characteristics of artifice, and artificial fabrications evoking natural form or process. In the later seventeenth century, Ferdinando Cosmi called his recently assembled *museo* a repository of '*machinamenta* [machinations, complex or cunning feats] of artifice and nature'[32] – that is, of works of nature reminiscent of *techne*'s products, and of works of *techne*, including automata, endowed with natural-seeming movement. Sculptures made out of stone had a special place in the *Kunstkammern*, not simply as displaying craft or artistry but as nature/artifice-bridging, metamorphic objects, presenting the transition between naturally occurring rock, seen as possessing living form in latency, and an object shaped *as if* by nature in resemblance to a thing alive, the mimetic, eye-commanding sculpture. *Techne* in the *Kunstkammer* setting is characteristically progressive and transformative: it often brings genuinely new and valued things into an existence which could not have occurred without its intervention in ordinary processes of nature.

Trompe l'oeil art, especially painted, often figures in the *Kunstkammer*[33] for, it seems, two basic reasons: (1) Because it has a prominent place in Pliny's *Natural History* (given major English circulation when translated in 1601); this was later European culture's source for the story of Zeuxis and Parrhasius, which does the underlying intellectual work for *trompe l'oeil* art.[34] And, on its larger scale, Pliny's work was the most important template for the organization of a typical *Kunstkammer* as an exhibition of *artificialia* alongside *naturalia*, often in a separate but adjoining space, foregrounding the humanly conceived transformatory procedures by which *artificialia* are produced; this strategy of Pliny for the investigation of natural phenomena was developed by the contrivers of the *Kunstkammern*.[35] (2) Moreover, considered in itself, *trompe l'oeil* art is a kind of artificial animation, like that found also exemplified by other means in the *Kunstkammern*, and one in which the viewer is called on to participate; a typical painting of this kind offers a representation in two dimensions which can be taken for a three-dimensional object which one could handle, or space into which one could move. Witnessing *The Winter's Tale* climactic sequence, the audience is called on to 'flip' its perceptual *Gestalt* in this same way, as decisively as in the well-known shift that one can make in looking at a drawing of the duck-rabbit. It sees (represented) a statue which looks very much like a living human being; admiring what is life-like in it, one admires the sculptor's art, finding further proof that this *is* a very accomplished piece of artifice – in the spin given to this first presentation, the more life-like it looks, the more certainly is it a piece of good sculpture; but subsequently, again under Paulina's direction, and non-consonantly, the audience sees not a statue but a living person – 'artifice' has self-transformed conceptually into 'nature', the life-resemblant into the living.

Let us consider a couple of examples of *trompe l'oeil* art. The first (not reproduced here), from the later seventeenth century, Van den Vaardt's violin painted so as to encourage the supposition that we are seeing a real violin hanging from a door,[36] is perhaps what we more usually classify as *trompe l'oeil* art because it does tend initially to deceive the eye; it is in a second evaluation

that we perceive this as a representational image. To make this more like what occurs in *The Winter's Tale*, we would have to imagine being introduced to an image like this *as* a cleverly made two-dimensional representation, and processing it as that, but then realizing that it was a real musical instrument. Perhaps this is one of the characteristic effects of modern animated film in spectatorial perception: we find that what can be sketchy and schematic in graphic character communicates nevertheless the fullness of a 'world'. What happens when we look at Daniel Mijtens' portrait (c. 1616) of Thomas Howard, the Earl of Arundel?,[37] shown above. The seated Earl holds a pointer as if expounding to us what we take to be painting positioned behind him. But, on reflection, this may well not be a painted surface positioned at the rear of the three-dimensional space, containing the Earl, which the larger painting represents, but a further three-dimensional space which opens up behind him, revealing part of his famous gallery with its content of sculptures.[38] In other words, we are being encouraged to re-envisage what at first looked like a flat surface as an architectural space which people can enter and within which they can move around; the sculptures seen in the gallery are there, similarly, to evoke living form in motion, supposing that we make such spectatorial investment in them. The Earl positioned with his pointer stands, meanwhile, as master of the nature–artifice threshold, while the spectator feels compelled to acknowledge the non-determinacy of its represented placing.[39]

Paulina's setting of the Hermione statue in motion is, in effect, a feat of automation, and artifice's triumphant reconfiguring of the raw materials provided by human beings' actions and feelings. This is not a discovery of good properties in ostensibly wild things, in the manner of Montaigne, or of some seeds of civility in the wild-growing, in that of Spenser, but a forming of the organized and humanly satisfactory out of the positively inchoate. It is a 'machination', an application of *techne* which supersedes and supplants nature; since we as onlookers, placed in the same conceptual position as the onstage onlookers, are plainly not being invited to *book it into* natural explanation – that is not part of our *Gestalt* switching; it may come later, or perhaps not at all.[40] The crucial point of resemblance to the Mijtens painting is that we encounter a disturbance of the action's conceptual enframing as uniform representation, and overcome this disturbance by flipping over the organization of our perceptions. The uncanniness of the play's climactic scene is not that of the represented miraculous, but that of a re-defined spectator–action relationship, such that one grasps the scene conceptually by, in effect, entering it, by being drawn unexpectedly into a form of willed participation. The effect of witnessing what occurs is that the spectator's own actions and feelings become automated and quasi-involuntary, like Perdita's when she finds herself kneeling to ask the statue Hermione's blessing (see 5.3.42–6). Summoned to 'awake [its] faith', the audience becomes incorporated into a moving, in both senses, artificial tableau of recognition, reconciliation and human renewal, producing what immediately claims the status of a thing unequivocally *there* for shared perception and response.

What occurs here is the highly controlled creation, through artifice, of a compelling group awareness, one in which the consciousness of the individual spectator suddenly and startlingly fuses with that of the spectators onstage as well as that of the surrounding theatre audience. *The Winter's Tale* thus recruits those who have assembled to witness its action into a psychically aligned community imbued with heightened awareness of being one. The means of putting this recruitment into effect is emphatically technical, removing community-formation decisively from the sphere of traditionally conceived 'nature': it is not Aristotle's community to which an individual 'naturally' belongs, nor is it held together by shared assumptions about the ordinarily occurring or 'natural', which the action of *The Winter's Tale* pointedly flouts. Its technically produced supra-individual group awareness is, I would suggest, being put forward as the group's own object of fascinated reflection, and accessing of a mentality of being-in-common, in a vindication of art by emphatically artificial means.

Notes

Introduction

1 The most common Chinese word for 'self' is 自(*zi*), which means more fundamentally 'nose' (the form of the character suggests the eyes目, *mù*, with the nose projecting). Japanese adopted the Chinese character for 'nose' and 'self', sounded as *ji*. In modern usage, however, there has emerged a new word for 'nose', 鼻(Chinese *bí*, Japanese *hana*), diminishing自's specific reference to the nose and face. I am grateful to Chie Manns for explaining this development to me, and to Xu Jiaqian and Hitomi Masuhara for commenting on the contemporary Chinese and Japanese incidence of indicating 'me' by pointing towards the face.

2 Daniella Gobetti (1992), *Private and Public: Individuals, Households, and Body Politic in Locke and Hutcheson*. London and New York: Routledge, p. 161.

3 For critiques of the idea that practices of distinguishing between private and public spheres of experience are of Western or modern inception, see Martin Hollis (1985), 'Of Masks and Men', and Mark Elvin (1985), 'Between the Earth and Heaven: Conceptions of the Self in China', in Michael Carrithers, Steven Collins and Steven Lukes (eds), *The Category of the Person: Anthropology, Philosophy, History*. Cambridge: Cambridge University Press, pp. 156–89 and 217–33.

4 Contemporary Western ambient culture preserves the vestiges of a distribution of 'mind' between head (reason, calculation), heart (responsiveness, stirrings of emotion) and bowels (emotional disposition), the last referenced in such expressions as 'He's gutless' and 'I don't have the stomach for it.' Hippocrates (fourth-century BCE) allocated the components of the soul to the head, heart and liver.

5 Ariosto's amusing symbolization of the hero Orlando's madness is the locating of his wits on the Moon. Later in this account I shall consider early modern European modellings of interaction, implying the presence or possibility of influential connection, between individual 'minds', and between an individual 'mind' and its environment, often conceived as the cosmos. The individual 'mind' with which I am concerned as a cultural representation is granted a relative autonomy, while being connectible in various respects to parts of its environment.

6 Terry Eagleton, at times associated with this group by commentators, is concerned a good deal more directly with historical process. I do not wish to denigrate cultural materialism as such, but have reservations about the British cultural materialists' ways of seeking to embody it in critical practice, in spite of the value of some of their perceptions. Their approach to literary study resembles that of New Historicism, especially in so far as the two critical movements have arrived at similar receptions of Althusser and Foucault.

7 Catherine Belsey (1988), *John Milton: Language, Gender, Power.* Oxford: Blackwell, p. 85.

8 Francis Barker (1984), *The Tremulous Private Body: Essays on Subjection.* London: Methuen, p. 31.

9 Trans. S. G. O. Middlemore (1960) [1860], *The Civilization of the Renaissance in Italy.* London: Phaidon, p. 81.

10 Catherine Belsey (1985), *The Subject of Tragedy: Identity and Difference in Renaissance Drama.* London: Methuen, p. 33.

11 Lee Patterson (1990), 'On the Margin: Postmodernism, Ironic History, and Medieval Studies', *Speculum*, 65, pp. 87–108 (p. 96). I share Patterson's view that the British cultural materialist analysis of the rise of the bourgeois subject would gain from paying closer attention to Marx – who, especially, considered a self-misleading subjective individualism, which implies the perceiving of oneself as an entirely free individual at the same time as working under conditions where control of one's own labour has been alienated, to be a characteristic phenomenon of his own times, standing in no direct connection with the economic-political transformations of early modernity.

12 Patterson, 'On the Margin', p. 99.

13 See especially Patterson (1991), *Chaucer and the Subject of History.* Madison: University of Wisconsin Press, and, for a concise statement about medieval conceptions of selfhood, 'On the Margin', pp. 99–101.

14 See Brian Stock (2010), *Augustine's Inner Dialogue: The Philosophical Soliloquy in Late Antiquity.* Cambridge: Cambridge University Press.

15 David Aers (1992), 'A Whisper in the Ear of Early Modernists; or, Reflections on Literary Critics Writing the "History of the Subject"', in David Aers (ed.), *Culture and History 1350–1600.* New York and London: Harvester Wheatsheaf, pp. 177–202 (p. 187).

16 Barker, *The Tremulous Private Body*, p. 36.

17 See Aers, 'A Whisper in the Ear', p. 186.

18 Assisted in doing this, needless to say, by the ordinary constitution of English literary studies, such that their scope does not extend beyond the Renaissance, and by the obscurantism – also termed professionalism – which often characterizes the study of medieval literature.

19 See Erica Longfellow (2006), 'Public, Private, and the Household in Early Seventeenth-Century England', *Journal of British Studies*, 45, 313–34 (333).

20 David Cressy (1994), 'Response: Private Lives, Public Performance, and Rites of Passage', in Betty S. Travitsky and Adele F. Seeff (eds), *Attending to Women in Early Modern England*. Cranbury, New Jersey: Associated University Presses, pp. 187–97, p. 187.

21 Longfellow, 'Public, Private, and the Household', p. 319, see p. 315. And see *Oxford English Dictionary*, s.v. 'privacy', definition 1 (the earlier uses of 'privacy' which the dictionary places under this heading seem not to fit the definition).

22 See Sigmund Freud [1923], 'The Ego and the Id and Other Works', in J. Strachey (ed.), *The Standard Edition of the Complete Psychological Works of Sigmund Freud*, Vol. 19; Marcel Mauss, trans. Ian Cunnison (1969) [1923], *The Gift: Forms and Functions of Exchange in Archaic Societies*. London: Cohen and West; Edmund Husserl (1956) [1924], 'Das reine Subjectivität und Intersubjective Bewusstsein', in Rudolf Boehm (ed.), Kant und die Idee der Transcendentalphilosophie: Erste Philosophie (1923/24), Husserliana, Vol. 7. The Hague: Martinus Nijhoff, pp. 248–55. Reflection on the intersubjective relation does, of course, pre-date the twentieth century, though Husserlian phenomenology in particular brings it to explicitness. It may be identified as one of the main threads of enquiry in Hegel's Phenomenology of Spirit.

23 Acceptance of an account of the intersubjective relation which goes with the grain of these psychoanalytic, anthropological and phenomenological enquiries militates against Stephen Greenblatt's assessment of early modern culture as entertaining the 'disconcerting recognition (. . .) that our identity may not originate in (. . .) the fixity, the certainty, of our own body', since all postulate that, in any cultural setting, the forming of 'I' flows from the experience of individual bodily situatedness, as yielding perceptions of personal uniqueness and of given relation to others. Greenblatt's statement occurs in (1986), 'Psychoanalysis and Renaissance Culture', in Patricia Parker and David Quint (eds), *Literary Theory/Renaissance Texts*. Baltimore: John Hopkins Press, pp. 210–24 (p. 218).

24 I am not attempting to treat 'the society or culture to which the individual actor belongs as the source of [that actor's] agency'; see the critique of conflations of individuality and ideological individualism in Nigel Rapport and Joanna Overing (2000), *Social and Cultural Anthropology: The Key Points*. London and New York: Routledge, pp. 178–95 (p. 179). Conceptions of intersubjectivity imply, on the contrary, that experience of existence as an individual subject structurally includes experience of the individual subject's relation to others.

25 Lawrence Stone (1977), *The Family, Sex and Marriage: England 1500–1800*. London: Weidenfield and Nicholson, p. 253.

26 See Alan Stewart (1995), 'The Early Modern Closet Discovered', *Representations*, 50, 76–100, and Lena Cowen Orlin (1998), 'Gertrude's Closet', *Shakespeare-Jahrbuch*, 134, 44–67, which is partly a critique of Stewart.

27 See Cecile Jagodzinski (1999), *Privacy and Print: Reading and Writing in Seventeenth-Century England*. Charlottesville: University of Virginia Press, esp. pp. 1–6.

28 Reference is to William Shakespeare (1968) [1609], *Shake-Speares Sonnets*. London: G. Eld; Facsimile. Ilkley: Scolar Press.

29 See Sonnet 137's extremely troubled dealings with the recognition that what appears to be a very personal and special experience of love, in metaphor the possession of 'a severall plot', a piece of land for private use, is also 'the wide worlds common place', as bound up with apprehensions concerning the loved one's sexual common-ness.

30 Here it is worth recalling the early modern importance of the commonplace book, by no means equivalent in function to a modern diary. It is generically a collection of valued texts and statements which an individual has privately compiled, but whose primary use is as material for conversation or correspondence with others. See especially David R. Parker (1998), *The Commonplace Book in Tudor London: An Examination of BL MSS Egerton 1995, Harley 2252, Lansdowne 762, and Oxford Balliol College MS 345*. Lanham: University Press of America.

31 See Margaret Spufford (1981), *Small Books and Pleasant Histories: Popular Fiction and Its Readership in Seventeenth-Century England*. Athens, Georgia: University of Georgia Press, pp. 45–82. Spufford contends that print often led 'not to the introversion of the literate, and their remoteness from the non-literate, but, on the contrary [fed] into the oral tradition'; p. 68. See also Keith Thomas (1986), 'Literacy in Early Modern England', in Gerd Baumann (ed.), *The Written Word: Literacy in Transition*. Oxford: Clarendon Press, pp. 97–131.

32 I would distinguish such literary constructs generically from neo-Petrarchan sonnets, such as Shakespeare's, which place writer and reader already on the 'private' side of the public–private experiential division.

33 References are to C. A. Patrides (ed.) (1985), *The Complete English Poems of John Donne*. London: Dent. 'The Canonization' is on pp. 57–9.

34 Stanton J. Linden (1996), *Darke Hieroglyphicks: Alchemy in English Literature from Chaucer to the Restoration*. Lexington: University of Kentucky Press, p. 175.

35 If I may add a somewhat technical observation: The final stanza specifically references Plato's World Soul, as in the *Timaeus*, producer of absolute, simultaneous interconnection between everything that is, as being present to the lovers' consciousness, in epitome; which is as near as one could get to explaining how this consciousness could be genuinely all-inclusive. See also the following note. More will be said about the World Soul in Chapter 1.

36 In the first printed edition the lovers, in their devotees' prayer, 'did the whole worlds soule contract, and drove / Into the glasses of your eyes', a phrasing followed in most modern editions. Gary Stringer informs me, however, that the manuscript tradition strongly supports authorial 'extract' for 'contract', which partly shifts the metaphoric field of reference.

37 *Poems of John Donne*, p. 54.

Chapter 1

1 See V. A. Kolve (1972), '*Everyman* and the Parable of the Talents', in Jerome Taylor and Alan H. Nelson (eds), *Medieval English Drama: Essays Critical and Contextual*. Chicago: Chicago University Press, pp. 316–40.

2 For helpful general comments on the coincidence of individuality and universality in these plays' definition of their characters, see Natalie Crohn Schmitt (1978), 'The Idea of a Person in Medieval Morality Plays', *Comparative Drama*, 12, pp. 23–34. And for the broader issue of medieval discursive representation of selfhood see A. C. Spearing's discussion of labile movement in medieval poetry between different speaking positions, none of them rigorously conceived as that of one individual consciousness though including numerous markings of subjectivity; (2005), *Textual Subjectivity: The Encoding of Subjectivity in Medieval Narratives and Lyrics*. Oxford: Oxford University Press, esp. pp. 1–36.

3 For an overview of ancient and classical conceptions of a cosmic 'breath', as in Stoic *pneuma*, see M. R. Wright (1995), *Cosmology in Antiquity*. London: Routledge, pp. 61–3.

4 Our word 'emotion' derives from Latin '*emovere*', meaning 'to move out', 'to stir up', 'to move the mind (in the way that such effects of *pneuma* do)'.

5 See Joseph R. Roach (1985), *The Player's Passion*. Newark: University of Delaware Press, p. 27. The most pertinent section of Quintilian's *Institutes* describes the functioning of *phantasiae*, Latin *visiones*, 'by which the images of absent things are presented to the mind in such a way that we seem actually to see them with our eyes and have them physically present to us,' to sway the emotions of the actor or orator and, *via* her/his projection of them, those of the audience; ed. and trans. Donald A. Russell (2001), *The Orator's Education: Books 6 to 8*. Cambridge, MA: Harvard University Press (Loeb), 6.2.26–31, pp. 58–61. Roach, pp. 23–9, considers these directives in the context of mainstream classical conceptions of the relationship between soul and body. For ancient theorization of all-pervasive *pneuma* see M. R. Wright (1995), *Cosmology in Antiquity*. London: Routledge, pp. 113–25.

6 See E. Ruth Harvey (1975), *The Inward Wits: Psychological Theory in the Middle Ages and the Renaissance*. London: Warburg Institute, pp. 50–3; Andrew Gowland (2006), 'The Problem of Early Modern Melancholy', *Past and Present*, 191, 77–120 (90–3); and Dag Nicolaus Hasse (2007), 'Arabic Philosophy and Averroism', in James Hankins (ed.), *The Cambridge Companion to Renaissance Philosophy*. Cambridge: Cambridge University Press, pp. 113–36 (pp. 121–5).

7 John Jeffries Martin (2006), *Myths of Renaissance Individualism*. Basingstoke: Macmillan Palgrave, p. 110. The reference is to Benedict, Saint, Abbot of Monte Cassino, ed. Rudolphus Hanslick (1977), *Benedicti Regula* (2nd edn). Vienna: Hoelder-Pichler-Temsky (Corpus Scriptorum Ecclesiasticorum Latinorum), sect. 18. The remainder of this paragraph is indebted to Martin's account of medieval–early modern ideals of *harmonia*, and of the notions of 'sincerity' which eventually displaced them, pp. 109–13.

8 See Alanus de Insulis, ed. Marie-Thérèse d'Alverny (1965), *Textes Inédits*. Paris: Plon, p. 156.

9 Marsilio Ficino, trans. Members of the Language Department of the School of Economic Science, London, with a preface by Paul Oskar Kristeller (1975–94). *Letters*, 5 vols. London: Shepheard-Walwyn, 1 (77); 5 (21).

10 H. Rackham (ed. and trans.) (1961), *De Natura Deorum, Academica*, 2,7. London: Heinemann (Loeb), p. 142.

11 F. E. Robbins (ed. and trans.) (1940), *Tetrabiblos*. Cambridge, MA: Harvard University Press (Loeb), 1.2, pp. 4–7.

12 Brian B. Copenhaver (2007), 'How to Do Magic, and Why: Philosophical Prescriptions', in James Hankins (ed.), *The Cambridge Companion to Renaissance Philosophy*. Cambridge: Cambridge University Press, pp. 137–69 (p. 157).

13 Giambattista Della Porta, ed. Derek J. Price (1957), *Natural Magick* [reproducing the English version of 1658]. New York: Basic Books, Book 1, ch. 6, p. 7; ch. 9, p. 13.

14 The reference is to Virgil's account of the *mens divina*, whose operation has been discerned in the organized life of bees, in *Georgics* 4, ll. 219–27; Virgil, trans. H. R. Fairclough and G. P. Gooch (1999), *Eclogues, Georgics, Aeneid 1–6*. Cambridge, MA: Harvard University Press (Loeb), p. 234.

15 See Martin Heidegger, trans. William Lovitt (1987), 'The Age of the World Picture', in *The Question Concerning Technology*. New York: Harper and Row, pp. 22–51.

16 See John M. Rist, ed. (1978), *The Stoics*. Berkeley: University of California Press, pp. 34–70 and Michael Lapidge (1979), 'Lucan's Imagery of Cosmic Dissolution', *Hermes*, 107, 344–70.

17 Stephen Mackenna (trans.), (1991), *The Enneads*. London: Penguin, 2.3.7, p. 81.

18 Michel Foucault comments that, for this manner of thinking, 'no path [making for recognition of influential connection] has been determined in advance,

no distance laid down, no linkage prescribed. Sympathy plays in a free state across the vastnesses of the world. It can traverse the wisest spaces in an instant: from the planet to the man which it rules, it falls from afar like a thunderbolt; and on the other hand, it can be born in one single contact'; (1966), *Les Mots et les Choses*. Paris: Gallimard, p. 38 (my translation).

19   See Maurice Leenhardt, trans. Basia Miller Gulati with preface by Vincent Crapanzano (1979) [1947], *Do Kamo*. Chicago: University of Chicago Press, p. xxiv. Leenhardt, whose main fieldwork was carried out in New Caledonia, pioneered a phenomenological anthropology which is valued in contemporary enquiry. Located in New Caledonia as a missionary for some 20 years, he was able to observe the unfolding effects on the local culture of Western influence, including that of his own activities.

20   For a particularly vivid account of this sort of posited relationship between individual and cosmos, see Madeleine Pelner Cosman (1978). 'Machaut's Musical Medical World', *Annals of the New York Academy of Sciences*, 314, 1–36.

21   Peter Brown (1988), *The Body and Society: Men, Women, and Sexual Renunciation in Early Christianity*. New York: Columbia University Press, p. 17.

22   See William Harvey (1660), *Exercitationes Anatomicae, de Motu Cordis & Sanguinis Circulation*. London: R. Daniel, ch. 8, pp. 58–9. The *De Motu* was first published in 1628.

23   See Mary Feeney (trans.), (1981), *The Carnival at Romans: A People's Uprising at Romans 1579–1580*. Harmondsworth: Penguin.

24   The reference in this instance to the formation of a textual genre, the novel, but the formula has equal bearing on particular signifying acts.

25   Julia Kristeva, trans. Margaret Waller (1984), *Revolution in Poetic Language*. New York: Columbia University Press, p. 59.

26   See the short essay of that name, dated 1903, in (1961), *Essays and Introductions*. London: Macmillan, pp. 215–16.

27   Walter J. Ong (1982), *Orality and Literacy: The Technologizing of the Word*. London: Methuen, p. 133.

28   For a survey of the tradition, see James J. Murphy and Richard A. Katula (1995), *A Synoptic History of Classical Rhetoric* (2nd edn). Davis, CA: Hermagoras Press.

29   Ernst Robert Curtius, trans. Willard R. Trask (1953), *European Literature of the Latin Middle Ages*. London: Routledge and Kegan Paul, p. 70.

30   For Curtius' rather differently angled account of the *locus amoenus* or 'pleasance', see *European Literature and the Latin Middle Ages*, pp. 195–200.

31   For the very substantial body of texts offering explicit self-comparison with mirrors, see Herbert Grabes, trans. Gordon Collier (1982), *The Mutable Glass: Mirror-Imagery in Titles and Texts of the Middle Ages and English Renaissance*. Cambridge: Cambridge University Press.

32   Jonathan Barnes (ed.), (1984), *The Complete Works of Aristotle: The Revised Oxford Translation* (2 vols.). Princeton, NJ: Princeton University Press, 1.31.

33   For the shift from early modern to modern, mathematizing constructions of the 'probable', see Ian Hacking (1975). *The Emergence of Probability*. Cambridge: Cambridge University Press.

34   See Matthias Schramm (1963), 'Aristotelianism: Basis and Obstacle to Scientific Progress in the Middle Ages', *History of Science*, 2, 91–113 (esp. 104–5), and Peter Dear (1995). *Discipline and Experience: The Mathematical Way in the Scientific Revolution,* Chicago: University of Chicago Press, pp. 21–4.

35   I wish to hold at a certain distance the celebrated Bakhtinian account of carnival, which has tended to over-direct modern interpretation of the historical evidence. Bakhtin is discussed in the Introduction to Part C.

36   For an a-Bakhtinian account of such play, see Nick Davis (1997), ' "His Majesty Shall Have Tribute of Me": The King Game in England', in Alan J. Fletcher and Wim Hüsken (eds), *Between Folk and Liturgy*. Amsterdam: Rodopi, pp. 97–108.

37   See Malory, *Works*, p. 649.

38   What follows draws on the discussion of the poem in Nick Davis (1999), *Stories of Chaos: Reason and Its Displacement in Early Modern English Narrative*. Aldershot: Ashgate, pp. 39–73, 189.

39   At the beginning of the deer hunt, for example, the female deer are scrupulously separated from the males, for which it is close season ('fermysoun'); see J. R. R. Tolkien and E. V. Gordon (eds), revised Norman Davis (1967), *Sir Gawain and the Green Knight*. Oxford: Clarendon Press, ll. 1154–9.

40   See *Sir Gawain and the Green Knight*, ll. 759–62: 'He rode in his prayere, / And cryed for his misdede, / He sayned hym in sythes sere [crossed himself many times], / And sayde "Cros Kryst me spede!"'

41   Mary Thomas Crane notes the frequency with privacy in the early modern period is conceived as movement into an exterior, outdoor space – one where, in view of a house and household's typical organization, the individual was less likely to be under surveillance. See Mary Thomas Crane (2009). 'Illicit Privacy and Outdoor Spaces in Early Modern England', *Journal for Early Modern Cultural Studies*, 9, 4–22.

42   The many chimneys which Gawain notes on approaching the unfamiliar castle – see ll. 798–9 – indicate that it has many rooms or recesses, making for, by the standards of the day, a particularly ready availability of 'interior' privacy.

43   See *Sir Gawain and the Green Knight*, ll. 2354–5: 'Trwe mon trwe restore,/ Than thar mon drede no wathe', a fairly gnomic pronouncement which translates, roughly, as 'A true man should give back to a true man – then one need fear no danger.'

44   See *Sir Gawain and the Green Knight*, ll. 1876–84. I can see no good reason for reading the passage ironically, drawing the inference that Gawain makes a faulty

confession: cheating in a recreational game is not a Christian sin, though it may be a social solecism.

45 See Norbert Elias [1939, subsequently revised], ed. Eric Dunning, Johan Goudsblom and Stephen Mennell, trans. Edmund Jephcott (2000), *The Civilizing Process: Sociogenetic and Psychogenetic Investigations*. Oxford: Blackwell Press.

46 One might single out Shakespeare's *Measure for Measure* as offering abundant material for reflection on the difficulties of policing the public sphere, and on the dangers of attempting to set up a full practical-conceptual cordoning between private and public domains of life.

47 See Elias, *The Civilizing Process*, p. 71.

48 See Oxford English Dictionary, s.v. 'foist'.

49 Keith Thomas (2010), 'Bodily Control and Social Unease: The Fart in Seventeenth-Century England', in Angela McShane and Garthine Walker (eds), *The Extraordinary and the Everyday in Early Modern England*. Basingstoke: Palgrave Macmillan, pp. 9–30 (pp. 16, 17, 19). The quoted phrase is the title of an imaginary work from Gargantua and Pantagruel's library of St Victor. Verses on 'The Great Parliament Fart' produced by the MP for Ludlow in 1607 circulated in variant versions, printed and handwritten, throughout the seventeenth century.

50 For a brief account of the last two developments in this broader cultural context, see Davis (1999), *Stories of Chaos*, pp. 122–7.

51 The spiritual interconnectedness of individuals had, conversely, been much foregrounded in the two religious practices which received the fiercest criticism in the Protestant Reformation's first phases, the sale of indulgences and the setting up of chantries.

52 See especially Delumeau (1983), *Le Péché et la Peur: la Culpabilisation en Occident (XIII–XVIII siècles)*. Paris; trans. Eric Nicholson (1991), as *Sin and Fear: The Emergence of a Western Guilt Culture 13th–18th Centuries*. New York: St. Martin's Press.

53 See Charles Taylor (2007), *A Secular Age*. Cambridge, MA: The Belknap Press of Harvard University Press.

54 See Peter Burke (1994), *Popular Culture in Early Modern Europe* (revised edn). Aldershot: Scolar Press, pp. 207–43.

55 See *Oxford English Dictionary*, s.v. 'Culture', III.5.a,b.

56 James A. Snead (1981), 'On Repetition in Black Culture', *Black American Literary Forum*, 15, 146–54 (147).

57 See Taylor, *A Secular Age*, p. 159.

58 Cecile Jagodzinski (1999), *Privacy and Print: Reading and Writing in Seventeenth-Century England*. Charlottesville: University Press of Virginia. Jagodzinski contends, piquantly deploying a Burckhardtian language, that private reading

played a leading causal role in 'the awakening of a new subjectivity and a consciousness of the self as a person separate from the community'; p. 1.

59 See James Simpson (2007), *Burning to Read: English Fundamentalism and Its Reformation Opponents*. Cambridge, MA: Belknap Press of Harvard University.

Part A: Introduction

1 Here one might consider, for example, the fairly wide spectrum of differences over astrology and natural prognostication which is covered by the thinking of the early Protestant reformers. To single out two key instances, Melanchthon is broadly an enthusiast of prognosticative thinking while Luther, though deploying it for certain purposes, remains suspicious of the larger project.

2 For an English instance of this, see Henry Howard, Earl of Northampton (1583), *A Defensative against the Poyson of Supposed Prophecies*. London: John Charlwood. Howard's book runs through many of the familiar intellectual objections to astrology, and has the general purpose of suppressing prognostication that undermines government.

3 See, for example, Michel de Montaigne, trans. M. A. Screech (1987), *The Complete Essays*. London: Penguin, pp. 604–5: people often claim to understand the grand workings of the universe when they don't even understand themselves. Among the proverbs assembled by George Herbert is 'Astrologie is true, but the Astrologers cannot find it'; ed. F. E. Hutchinson (1941), *Works*. Oxford: Clarendon Press, p. 342.

4 With historical hindsight we can say that installation of a non-cosmomorphic scientific outlook did not occur by any smooth procedure; for example, one effect of the 'mechanical philosophy's' continuing prestige in early eighteenth-century continental Europe was widespread rejection of Newtonian gravity as a natural force because its operation is *ex hypothesei* occult (i.e. not to be explained by the collisions of particles, though this was sometimes attempted). The 'mechanical philosophy' is intellectually conservative in one respect, since it reinstates in its own fashion the traditional Aristotelian antipathy to the principle of action at a distance.

5 As Stanton J. Linden explains, alchemy is centrally concerned with the artful acceleration of *natural* processes, such as those by which ore in the earth becomes gradually sublimated and transformed – some said, as influenced by the pervasive Aristotelian quintessence; see (1996), *Darke Heiroglyphicks: Alchemy in English Literature from Chaucer to the Restoration*. Lexington: University Press of Kentucky, opening chapter. Alchemy thus rests on felt intellectual security concerning what natural process is.

6 Donne, *Variorum*, Vol. 6, pp. 7–17. For Donne's poems references are to the *Variorum* edition or, where the relevant volume is not available, to C. A. Patrides, (ed.), (1985), *The Complete English Poems of John Donne*. London: Dent, based on the printed text of 1633 and showing important variant manuscript readings.

Chapter 2

1 For 'fondling' here some manuscript texts have 'changeling'; 'fondling', if accepted, seems to include both 'foundling' and 'one who fondles' – who fondles the speaker, presumably, in the word's modern sense.

2 Berlin develops the idea from a maxim attributed to Archilocus. To be truer to the maxim and Berlin's extended formulation of it, they illuminate but do not completely fit this speaker's predicament: he seems to be ambiguously a fox (who knows many things) secretly drawn to becoming a hedgehog, and a hedgehog perplexedly attracted by the fox's mentality.

3 In the Overburian account of 'a fantastic Innes of Court man', 'his very essence he placeth in his outside'; W. J. Paylor (ed.), (1936), *The Overburian Characters*. Oxford: Blackwell, p. 45.

4 An instance of complexional melancholia is provided by the central figure in Dürer's *Melencolia I*, whose face is somewhat dark. (Dürer's composition is discussed later in this section.) I am assuming the framework of Hippocratic-Galenic humoural theory, generally accepted, though with many differences of interpretation, in early modern medical practice.

5 For an excellent overview of the period's understandings of the condition, see Andrew Gowland (2006a), 'The Problem of Early Modern Melancholy', *Past and Present*, 191, pp. 77–120, and (2006b), *The Worlds of Renaissance Melancholy: Robert Burton in Context*. Cambridge: Cambridge University Press.

6 See John Livingstone Lowes (1914), 'The Loveres Maladye of Hereos', *Modern Philology*, 11, 491–546, and Michal Altbauer-Rudnik (2006), 'Love, Madness and Social Order: Love Melancholy in France and England in the Late Sixteenth and Early Seventeenth Centuries', *Gesnerus*, 63, 33–45. As Lowes explains, the word 'hereos' seems to have been used from about the tenth century as a Graeco-Latin equivalent to Arabic 'al-išk', meaning 'ardent and excessive love'; taken up in the European medical tradition, it is *formally* related to 'eros', non-aspirated, while being semantically distinct. Robert Burton found it puzzling, and decided that *amor hereos* must be love as experienced by heroes. By tradition the most reliable therapy for *amor hereos* was large-scale, indiscriminate coitus, but later medical practitioners tended to resist this approach.

7   Robert Burton, of course, gives a substantial section of *The Anatomy of Melancholy* to discussion of it. In the book's frontispiece a love-melancholic (labelled 'Inamorato') who looks like a caricatural version of the Lothian Donne is shown in the frame at the middle left.

8   Adapted from *Psalms* 18.28, 'Deus meus illumine tenebras meas', which occurs in the third collect for Evensong; see Jonathan F. S. Post (2006), 'Donne's Life: A Sketch', in Achsah Guibbory, (ed.), *The Cambridge Companion to John Donne.* Cambridge: Cambridge University Press, pp. 1–22 (p. 6). The shift to the plural form in the portrait inscription is interesting, but I remain uncertain of its purpose.

9   Marsilio Ficino, trans. Sears Reynolds Jayne (1985), *Commentary on Plato's Symposium on Love.* Dallas: Spring Publications, p. 168.

10 Jacques Ferrand, ed. and trans. Donald A. Beecher and Massimo Ciavollella (1990), *A Treatise on Lovesickness.* Syracuse: Syracuse University Press, pp. 4–5.

11 Tarnya Cooper (2012), 'John Donne Nearly Finished', dated 16 May 2012, accessed 4 July 2012. www.npg.org.uk/research/conservation/john-donne-and-his-picture.php.

12 I make the indentification in (2013a) 'Melancholic Individuality and the Lothian Portrait of Donne', *ANQ*, 26, 5–12.

13 John Donne, ed. John Sparrow (1923), *Devotions upon Emergent Occasions.* Cambridge: Cambridge University Press, Meditation 12, pp. 67–9.

14 T. S. Eliot (1934), *Selected Essays* (2nd edn). London: Faber and Faber, p. 287.

15 Michael Macdonald draws attention to a passage in Lyly which brings out the status association of claims laid to melancholia (see also the following note), as well as the growing social tendency to override it: when a barber in *Midas* complains that he is 'melancholy as a cat', he is told,' Melancholy? Marry, gup, is melancholy a word for a barber's mouth? Thou shouldst say heavy, dull and doltish: melancholy is the crest of courtiers' arms, and now every base companion, being in his muble fubles, says he is melancholy'; Macdonald (1981), *Mystical Bedlam: Madness, Anxiety, and Healing in Seventeenth-Century England.* Cambridge: Cambridge University Press, p. 151.

16 We may note also that in some ideological contexts of the period it is reprehensible to account for a condition of the soul in predominantly naturalistic and medical terms; see D. A. Beecher (1989), 'Erotic Love and the Inquisition: Jacques Ferrand and the Tribunal of Toulouse, 1620', *The Sixteenth Century Journal*, 20, 41–53. Conversely, for the voguishness of melancholia among the period's courtly elites see Brian Nance (2001), *Turquet de Mayerne as Baroque Physician: The Art of Medical Portraiture.* Amsterdam: Rodopi, esp. pp. 134–6.

17 The comparison is not gratuitous, since the era's newly made acquaintance with tobacco probably affected its conception of physiologically produced and absorbed influential vapours, and vice versa. James I's *A Counterblaste to Tobacco* (1604) is largely a rejection of the curative and sanative effects which some attribute

to tobacco smoke. In James's view it is a 'stinking suffumigation' – that is, a foul vapour which can penetrate the body – likely to upset the balance of the humours; King James VI and I, ed. Neil Rhodes, Jennifer Richards and Joseph Marshall (2003), *Selected Writings*. Aldershot: Ashgate, p. 283.

18 Raymond Klibansky, Erwin Panofsky and Fritz Saxl (1964), *Saturn and Melancholy*. London: Nelson, pp. 18–24.

19 See Noel L. Brann (2002), *The Debate over the Origin of Genius During the Italian Renaissance*. Leiden: Brill.

20 See Klibansky et al., *Saturn and Melancholy*, pp. 95–6.

21 Stuart Clark comments, in this connection, 'Despite the temptation to assume otherwise, modern sadness and depression are not (. . .) melancholia's synonyms, nor modern melancholy its equivalent'; (2007), *Vanities of the Eye: Vision in Early Modern European Culture*. Oxford: Oxford University Press, pp. 50–1.

22 William Shakespeare, ed. Keir Elam (2008), *Twelfth Night*. London: Arden Shakespeare.

23 Jacques Du Bosc (1639), *The Compleat Woman [L'honneste femme]*. London: Thomas Harper and Richard Hodgkinson, pp. 40–1.

24 For examination of this composition and its influence on other artists, see Klibansky et al., *Saturn and Melancholy*, pp. 283–393. The discussion that follows is also influenced by Bałus, Wojciech (1994), 'Dürer's "Melencolia I": Melancholy and the Undecidable', *Artibus et Historiae*, 15, 9–12. It is instructive to compare Dürer's depiction of melancholia with a less artistically accomplished one from the mid-sixteenth century where it is evidently recalled, the engraving by Franz Isaac Brun which shows both a mathematically inclined symbolic female figure and who is also sullen or doltish, reminding us that early modern accounts of melancholy were extremely varied in their interpretative weighting. Brun's image is reproduced in Clark (2007), *Vanities of the Eye*. Plate 5.

25 Thomas C. Faulkner, Nicholas K. Kiesling and Rhonda L. Blair (eds) (1989–2000), *The Anatomy of Melancholy* (6 vols.). Oxford: Clarendon Press, 1.3, Memb.1.Subs.2, Vol. 3, p. 391.

26 In a poem addressed to Maria Tesselschade, written to accompany Constantin Huygens' translation of poems by Donne; Joost van den Vondel, ed. R. N. Roland Holst et al. (1927–37), *Werken* (10 vols.). Amsterdam: Goedkoope Lectuur, Vol. 3, p. 415. I am grateful to Nadine Akkerman and Richard Todd for helping me to locate this reference. Vondel is himself portrayed as a melancholic in a portrait of c. 1645 by Philips Koninck, now in the Collegium Maius collection, Krakow.

27 This seems to set an absorbing intellectual problem: can one tell whether or not it is a *regular* polyhedron?

28 In the account of Bałus, 'Dürer's "Melencolia I"', the representations of the composition destabilize one another, existing for the interpreter in a state of undecidability.

29   *Melencolia I* is sometimes grouped with two other highly achieved engravings
     produced by Dürer at about the same time, *The Knight, Death and the Devil* and
     Saint Jerome in His Study, but the individual images or scenes of this notional group
     seem not to be thematically related.

30   Seneca, ed. and trans. John G. Fitch (2002), *Hercules, Trojan Women, Phoenician
     Women, Medea, Phaedra*. Cambridge, MA: Harvard University Press (Loeb),
     pp. 496–7 (l. 607).

31   With apologies to the reader with basic mathematical knowledge – a circle cannot
     be transformed by ordinary ('Euclidean') geometrical construction into a square of
     equal area, or vice versa.

32   See Katherine Eisamen Maus (1995), *Inwardness and Theater in the English
     Renaissance*. Chicago: University of Chicago Press, p. 4: 'For Hamlet, the internal
     experience of his own grief "passes show" in two senses. It is beyond scrutiny,
     concealed where other people cannot perceive it. And it *surpasses* the visible –
     its validity is unimpeachable. The exterior, by contrast, is partial, misleading,
     falsifiable, unsubstantial.' My point, related to Maus's, is that in placing certain
     thoughts and feelings as internal and non-public Hamlet defines them as being, if
     not exactly unimpeachable, constitutively *different* from what can be seen by and
     made manifest in the exterior world.

33   There is a similarly intense registration of personal interior separateness and
     disjunction in Richard II's response to Bolingbroke's dismissive comment that, in
     destroying the mirror in which he has viewed his reflection, he has been motivated
     by the 'shadow (darkness) of [his] sorrow' to destroy the 'shadow' (reflection) of his
     face: 'Say that again! / The shadow of my sorrow? Ha, let's see. / 'Tis very true, my
     grief lies all within; / And these external manners of laments / Are merely shadows
     to the unseen grief / That swells with silence in the tortures soul. / There lies the
     substance' (4.1.293–9); William Shakespeare, ed. Charles R. Forker (2002), *King
     Richard II*. London: Arden Shakespeare.

34   Achsah Guibbory (2006), 'Erotic Poetry', in Achsah Guibbory (ed.), *The Cambridge
     Companion to John Donne*. Cambridge: Cambridge University Press, pp. 133–47
     (p. 140).

35   See also Victor Harris (1950), *All Coherence Gone: A Study in the Seventeenth
     Century Controversy over Disorder and Decay in the Universe*. London: Cass.

36   This poem and the *Anniversaries* are cited as they appear in the Donne *Variorum*,
     Vol. 6.

37   The Aristotelian elements spontaneously organize themselves, of course, in the
     ascending–descending order of fire, air, water and earth.

38   For an unusual instance of this see the opening 14 lines of 'Obsequyes upon the
     Lord Harrington', which lean towards the style of Jonson.

39   A particularly determined skewing of microcosm–macrocosm analogy occurs in
     the fourth Meditation from the *Devotions Upon Emergent Occasions*.

40   John Dryden, ed. James Kinsley and George Parfitt (1970), *Selected Criticism*. Clarendon Press: Oxford, p. 211.

41   I wish to suggest that this poem does with a special explicitness things which are characteristic of Donne's poetry.

42   Not many Europeans c. 1611 accepted Copernicus' account of a sun-centred planetary system with mobile rotating Earth, generally seen as an affront to common sense and valid intellectual tradition, and the treatment of it in 'The First Anniversary' should not, I think, be taken as rhetorically implying that they did or should have done. In the poem's perspective Copernicanism is a particularly alluring projection of the melancholic vision, touched appropriately by madness.

43   Jacques as melancholic has a function in his society as one who secretes and relays melancholic thoughts, valued as defining a distinctive viewpoint on the world.

Chapter 3

1   Caryl Churchill's translation, (1998), *Plays: 3*. London: Nick Hern Books, p. 335.

2   See further below, however, for the place of *miraculous* eclipses on Christian tradition.

3   Except, that is, for mine. See Nick Davis (2013b), 'The Heavens and *King Lear*', in Nicholas Campion and Darrelyn Gunzburg (eds), *Heavenly Discourses*. Lampeter: Sophia Press (forthcoming). The present section draws material and part of its argument from this paper. For a first account of the eclipse action of *King Lear* see my *Stories of Chaos*, esp. pp. 150–1.

4   For a spirited critical defence of Seneca and underlining of his positive influence on early modern European drama, see Dana Gioia (1993), 'Seneca and European Tragedy', *New Criterion*, 12, 16–26. See Frederick Kiefer (1978), 'Seneca's Influence on Elizabethan Tragedy: An Annotated Bibliography', *Research Opportunities in Renaissance Drama*, 21, 17–34, for studies since 1875 whose general tendency has been to deny Seneca's deep or extensive influence. Thomas G. Rosenmeyer (1989), *Senecan Drama and Stoic Cosmology*. Berkeley: University of California Press, on the other hand, representing a tendency which has developed lately in classical studies, offers committed exposition of the plays. He also refers to features of their reception in Tudor-Jacobean drama. Rosenmayer's account of Senecan drama's dealings with cosmology has a considerable bearing on *King Lear*, as will be acknowledged.

5   Cited Gioia, 'Seneca and European Tragedy', p. 16.

6   It is noticeable that in contemporary classical studies the Neronian writers, principally Seneca, Lucan and Petronius, are receiving a great deal more critical attention.

7   References are to René Weis (ed.), (1993), *King Lear: A Parallel Text Edition*.
    London: Longman, which places alongside one another the Quarto text of
    1608 and the Folio text of 1623. Unless otherwise stated citation is of the
    Quarto.

8   Compare Henry Vaughan's 'The Rain-bow', where the comet is 'the sad world's ill-
    boding book'. The *locus classicus* for discussion of comets as prognostications was
    Pliny's *Natural History*, Book 2, chs. 22 and 23.

9   Henry Howard, Earl of Northampton (1620) [1583], *A Defensative against the
    Poyson of Supposed Prophecies*. London: H. Iaggard, ch. 16, fo. 77a.

10 Nor was a comet necessarily malign in its influence or significance, though this
    was the view more commonly taken; Pliny notes as unusual and striking Augustus'
    treatment of a comet as auspicious.

11 Such a conclusion would be fairly characteristic of the era's 'moderate'
    epistemological attitude to astrology: astrological causation is to be taken seriously,
    but partly because awareness of it can help to prevent what is threatened from
    occurring.

12 Nicholas Culpeper (1652), *Catastrophe Magnatum or, The Fall of Monarchie*.
    London: T. Vere and Nath. Brooke, p. 75.

13 Keith Thomas (1971), *Religion and the Decline of Magic*. London: Weidenfield and
    Nicholson, p. 106. I am generally indebted to Thomas's account.

14 In the medieval to early period it was sometimes noted that particular comets
    showed a tendency to reappear, but the phenomenon of periodicity in some
    comets' appearance was not satisfactorily defined until the eighteenth century.

15 Lunar eclipses occur, of course, with some frequency, whereas solar eclipses to be
    observed from any given Earth location are much rarer. The present century's first
    major eclipse of the sun visible from a part of the United Kingdom will occur in
    2090. The seventeenth century was unusual in having several.

16 Lynn Thorndike (ed.), (1949), *The Sphere of Sacrobosco and its Commentators*.
    Chicago: University of Chicago Press, pp. 117, 142; translation modified. For
    Julian of Norwich the observation attributed to Dionysius serves to bring out
    the universal and rationally incomprehensible force of the Passion; see Marion
    Glasscoe, ed. (1986), *A Revelation of Love*. Exeter: Exeter University Press, ch. 18,
    p. 21.

17 Deborah Houlding (ed.), (2006), *The Centiloquium of Hermes Trismegistus*, section
    53. Accessed 20 July 2012. www.skyscript.co.uk/centiloquium2.html. This text
    circulated in Western Europe from the thirteenth century, when it was translated
    out of Arabic.

18 Ficino famously speculated on the possibility that the great Hermes was identical
    with Moses. In 1614 Isaac Casaubon argued on linguistic grounds that the more
    philosophically substantial of the Hermetic writings had to be dated c. AD 300.

This diminished the authority of the writings, but Casaubon's argument was also disputed; or, the writings could still be viewed as late linguistic renderings of ancient originals.

19 E. A. J. Honigmann (ed.), (1996), *Othello*. London: Arden Shakespeare. Note will be taken later of a reference to a double eclipse in *Tamburlaine 2*.

20 Book 2, ch. 82.

21 The general, Stoic tendency of Pliny's study is to assert the rational explicability of natural phenomena.

22 The fourth choral song from the ninth *Paean*.

23 References are to John G. Fitch (ed.), (2004), *Oedipus, Agamemnon, Thyestes, Hercules on Oeta, Octavia*. Cambridge, MA: Harvard University Press (Loeb). Shakespeare would have been able to read *Thyestes* in the reasonably faithful translation of Jasper Heywood, though he is also likely to have read Seneca in Latin while at school.

24 See Katharina Volk (2006), 'Cosmic Disruption in Seneca's *Thyestes*: Two Ways of Looking at an Eclipse', in K. Volk and Gareth D. Williams (eds), *Seeing Seneca Whole: Perspectives on Philosophy, Poetry, and Politics*. Leiden: Brill, pp. 183–200.

25 Seneca, ed. John J. Fitch (2002), *Hercules, Trojan Women, Phoenician Women, Medea, Phaedra*. Cambridge, MA: Harvard University Press (Loeb), p. 432 (l. 1027).

26 Volk, 'Cosmic Disruption', p. 195.

27 Caryl Churchill (2003), *Plays: 3*. London: Nick Hern Books, pp. 334–5.

28 This is the title of the concluding chapter in his *Senecan Drama and Stoic Cosmology*. In Rosenmeyer's account, the Senecan tragic hero's characteristic bid to assert control of the universe takes the form of cataloguing its components: as the semi-futility of the gesture reveals, 'it is a universe in which he is both at home and an alien. Cataloguing is his strategy of distancing and familiarization. With his catalogues, the threatened hero declares both his control and, more profoundly, his capitulation before the enormity and the changeableness of that which he cannot master because he is an inseparable part of it and it is part of him. The meteorological and celestial systems spin their cycles through the resistant souls of Hercules and Atreus and Medea'; p. 161 – another way of saying which seems to be that these figures are the bearers of a visibly fragmenting and failing Stoic philosophical vision.

29 For discussion of Cicero's account, which encapsulates Stoic tradition, of what it is to live in accordance with nature, see Nick Davis (2011), 'Desire, Nature, and Automata in the Bower of Bliss', in Wendy Hyman (ed.), *The Automaton in English Renaissance Literature*. Farnham: Ashgate, pp. 163–79 (p. 178, note 40).

30 See David H. Levy (2011), *The Sky in Early Modern English Literature: A Study of Allusions to Celestial Events in Elizabethan and Jacobean Writing*. New York:

Springer Books, p. 29. Levy reproduces, p. 23, the chart of the 1605 eclipse produced by Fred Espenak with the assistance of NASA computers.

31   For unequivocal statement of their significance for dating, see Stanley Wells and Gary Taylor (1987), *William Shakespeare: A Textual Companion*. Oxford: Clarendon Press, p. 128.

32   *A Discoursiue Problem Concerning Prophesies*. London: Iohn Iackson, for Richard Watkins, p. 119.

33   For the background to Harvey's rather tortuous polemic in that decade's controversies over astrological prediction, see Walter W. B. Stone (1953), 'Shakespeare and the sad augurs', *Journal of English and Germanic Philology*, 52, 457–79.

34   During this decade the sun, moon and earth were at that phase of the Saros cycle, identified first by Babylonian astronomers, where eclipses are particularly incident.

35   Himbert de Billy (1604), *Certain Wonderful Predications for Seauen yeeres ensuing*. London: W. Firbrand, pp. 8–11. It is hard to know what to make of Himbert de Billy, whose full self-naming suggests mountebank inventiveness: 'the Lorde of *Billy*, Secretarie to the most illustrious Princess, the Lady Celestine Olalampa, Dutchesse of *Pancosme*'; German *billig* = 'cheap'. For the original, which the English text closely follows, see Himbert de Billy (1602), *Prédictions pour Cinq Années des Choses plus Memorables*. Paris: Nicolas Rousser. The eclipse of 1605 was total in an arc running across northern France, so de Billy has rather more motivation to emphasize its effects. And see the following note, which also helps to explain the difference of tone between de Billy's almanac and an English one covering 1605.

36   The Stationer's Company which issued Dade's almanac enjoyed a state monopoly of almanac production, and in return for this enforced a toning down what might be unsettling in their almanacs' astrological prognostications; see Bernard Capp (1979), *Astrology and the Popular Press*. London: Faber and Faber, p. 29.

37   John Dade (1605), *A Prognostication in Which You May Behold the State of This Yeere of Our Lord God. 1605*. London: Company of Stationers, pp. B3 + 6–7.

38   See 2 *Kings* 22–3, and 2 *Chronicles* 34–5.

39   Robert Pricket (1606), *Times Anotomie. Containing: The poore mans plaint, Brittons trouble, and her triumph. The Popes pride, Romes treasons, and her destruction: Affirming That Gog, and Magog, both shall perish, the church of Christ shall flourish, Judeas race shall be restored, and the manner how this mightie work shall be accomplished*. London: George Eld[er], pp. G iv, v, verso, H i, r. Anne Henry directs attention to *Times Anotomie* in a discussion of the significance of reference to eclipses in *King Lear*, (2007), 'Tragedy and the Sign of the Eclipse', in Sarah Annes Brown and Catherine Silverstone (ed.), *Tragedy in Transition*. Oxford: Blackwell, pp. 78–102 (p. 86).

40   It was felt subsequently that the events of 'Black Monday', which was as things turned out a very ordinary day and one of settled weather, had done a good deal to discredit astrological prognostication; some expected as much before the day arrived. Nevertheless, the character of the events themselves reminds us not to predate the general cultural entrenchment of modern-style scientific scepticism.

41   For the logical strangeness and strainedness of Kent's position, see Davis (1999), *Stories of Chaos*, pp. 146–8.

42   See Charles R. Forker, ed. (2002), *King Richard II*. London: Arden Shakespeare, 3.2.10–11.

43   For an image of the eclipse dragon from the *Astronomicum Caesareum* (1540) of Petrus Apianus, see Peter Whitfield (2001), *Astrology: A History*. London: British Library, p. 153; in this expensively produced edition of Apianus the image of the dragon is designed to rotate against a cosmological chart. The 'dragon' eclipse nodes in their interrelation correspond to Persian-Arabic *al-djawzahar*.

44   Eclipses were considered to be coincident with ascendance of the eclipse dragon's tail or head, which partly motivates Edmund's reference.

45   The eclipse dragon had been referred to in *Tamburlaine 2*: Christopher Marlowe, ed. David Bevington and Eric Rasmussen (1995), *Doctor Faustus and Other Plays*. Oxford: Oxford University Press, 2.4.51–4. Here, one notes, Tamburlaine describes the effects of Zenocrate's illness on him as being equivalent to lunar and solar eclipses. The notion of a cosmic dragon or serpent associated with eclipses must have been recognizable to ordinary playgoers.

46   See further, Davis (1999), *Stories of Chaos*, pp. 141–5, which broaches the issue of eclipses in investigating the play's treatment of its culture's commonplace signifiers and media of practical reasoning, letters and numbers. Anne Henry (2007), 'Tragedy and the Sign of Eclipse', p. 84, notes that in the anonymous play of 1606 *Nobody and Somebody* a king's death, and also loss of regal power generally, are analogically connected with the sun's suffering of eclipse.

47   Reference ranges across the bawdy – especially, the female genitals are a disconcertingly powerful and sometimes generative 'no thing' – and the seriously toned, as in Edgar's 'I Nothing Am' (2.3.21). In more or less the whole of Shakespearean usage reference to 'nothing/ no thing' raises questions verging on the insoluble about the signification of personal identity. The motif becomes, paradoxically enough, a kind of signature in Shakespeare's writing.

48   See Brian Rotman (1999), *Signifying Nothing: The Semiotics of Zero*. Basingstoke: Macmillan, and Davis (1999), *Stories of Chaos*, pp. 143–8.

49   See 'A Song for St. Cecilia's Day, 1687'. For the intellectual background, see Gary Tomlinson (1993), *Music in Renaissance Magic*. Chicago: University of Chicago Press.

50 For instances see Nick Davis (2011), 'Nature, Desire and Automata in the Bower of Bliss'.

51 On this topic see especially Stanley Cavell (1987), *Disowning Knowledge in Six Plays of Shakespeare*. Cambridge: Cambridge University Press.

52 See especially Antonio Péres-Ramos (1988), *Francis Bacon's Idea of Science and the Maker's Knowledge Tradition*. Oxford: Oxford University Press.

Part B: Introduction

1 The visual figuredness which stands out as a feature of premodern and early modern collective representations is, I have suggested, a phenomenon associated with widespread lack of literacy.

2 In important respects the Duessa of Book One *is* the contextually meretricious allure of Catholic religion, by which Redcross in his function of standing for the-English-Church-and-people is all too readily swayed.

Chapter 4

1 See Edmund Spenser, ed. William A. Oram, Einar Bjorvand, Ronald Bond, Thomas H. Cain, Alexander Dunlop and Richard Schell (1989), *The Yale Edition of the Shorter Poems*. New Haven: Yale University Press, p. 422, ll. 209–10; Keats modernizes the spelling. Like other Romantic writers, Keats found Spenser's poetry personally welcoming and, in a manner, accommodating, offering space for free imaginative movement of the kind which this passage celebrates. The 1817 *Poems* also includes the following: 'Spenser, thy brows are arched, open, kind, / And come like a clear sun-rise to my mind; / And always does my heart with pleasure dance / When I think on thy noble countenance, / Where never yet was aught more earthly seen / Than the pure freshness of thy laurels green'; John Keats, ed. Miriam Allott (1970), *The Poems*. London: Longman, p. 35.

2 A caveat to the reader: An influential school of contemporary criticism has it that one should not closely examine the thought and design of Spenser's poetry, since his writing is of modern interest solely as a historical formation and symptom, and that one would have to be very naïve to engage with his poetic art as poetic art, since this would imply that one had been duped by it as distinct from seeing it for what it is. This view can be traced to statements made in the inaugural text of New Historicism in the field of early modern study, Stephen Greenblatt's *Renaissance Self-Fashioning* (1980), where critical discussion of *The Faerie Queene* climaxes in assertion that Spenser's poem entirely subserves ideology (whereas the writing of Marlowe and Shakespeare questions and thwarts it), and that his art is effete

and diversionary ornamentation. A good few contemporary critics still adopt this stance, which makes for the ready dismissal from serious consideration of a major body of writing.

3   *Muiopotmos* is a miniature, but one which creates in its opening sequence a sense of the expansiveness of a world whose contents are there to be explored and sampled, enframed by the fiction as the world of a butterfly.

4   Reference is by book, canto and stanza to Edmund Spenser, ed. A. C. Hamilton (2001), *The Faerie Queene*. London: Longman.

5   And foregrounded especially in John 14.6, 'I am the way, the truth, and the life'. Augustine develops the conception of the faithful person as *viator* ('way-taker'), participating in a pilgrimage that leads from the earthly to the heavenly city.

6   Paul writes 'those who perish (*tois apollumenois*)', which is often translated as 'those on the way to destruction (or perdition)'. In Luther's translation they are 'lost (*verloren*)'. The penultimate sentence of *The Pilgrim's Progress* (Part One) is 'Then I saw that there was a way to hell, even from the Gates of Heaven, as well as from the City of Destruction.'

7   The fable, based loosely on the Judgement of Paris, is in Xenophon's *Memorabilia* (2.1.21–34). See John Dillon and Tania Gergel (eds) (2003), *The Greek Sophists*. London: Penguin Books, pp. 111–6.

8   All of these terms encode a good deal of cultural assumption; selection of 'the reader' distances us from mentalities not strongly affected by literacy. I invite the reader of what follows to mentally interpolate the other terms.

9   Langland probably grew in repute, if anything, during the Reformation, when he was often seen as a kind of Protestant *avant la lettre*, and medieval writers in general were reconsidered as part of a search for suitable ideological precursors. Chaucer's reputation was similarly enhanced during this period by the prominence given to anti-clerical satire in *The Canterbury Tales*.

10   Chaucer's portrayal of the ploughman is sometimes seen as paying homage to Langland's.

11   Ploughing in fourteenth-century England does not carry an aura of socio-cultural conservatism, especially given that the increasingly complex construction of ploughs was an important route of technical advance; the ploughman here has an implied modernity of outlook.

12   References are by passus and line to William Langland, ed. A. V. C. Schmidt (1978), *The Vision of Piers Plowman: A Complete Edition of the B-Text*. London: Dent.

13   Given visual-spatial definition, Piers' 'journey' would consist, one supposes, in walking behind his oxen up and down the small field which he ploughs.

14   This brings us up to the conclusion of Passus 6 in the B-Text. At the start of Passus 7 the idea or possibility of progression is abruptly reinstated as Truth obtains a

pardon, a document remitting punishment for sin, for Piers and those who work alongside him.

15 Gordon Teskey writes suggestively of 'a driving of roots down into the material world – such as we see in the greatest allegorical poets, in Dante, Langland, and Spenser'; (1996), *Allegory and Violence*. Ithaca: Cornell University Press, p. 45.

16 References are to the 'Letter' as printed in Edmund Spenser (2001), ed. A. C. Hamilton, *The Faerie Queene*. Harlow: Longman, pp. 714–8.

17 Though in Aristotle there are not 12 of either; the reference is to the actual and envisaged subdivisions of the poem. As the 'Letter' explains later, Arthur as representing 'magnificence', Aristotle's *megalopsuchia*, is shown in the poem as having brought all the virtues to perfection, while the knights at the centre of individual books are the exponents ('patrons') of a particular virtue.

18 Sir Philip Sidney, ed. Katherine Duncan-Jones (1973), *Miscellaneous Prose*. Oxford: Clarendon Press, p. 79.

19 See *Poetics*, ch. 4, 37.

20 Ed. cit., p. 714, 8n.

21 See *Oxford English Dictionary*, s.v. 'patron'.

22 It seems quite possible that components of the wood itself 'wander' (see Acrasia's island), making this a more paradoxical and entrapping labyrinth.

23 See Nick Davis (2011), 'Nature, Desire and Automata in the Bower of Bliss', in Wendy Beth Hyman, ed., *Automata in Renaissance Literature*. Basingstoke: Ashgate, pp. 163–9.

24 The books seem unlikely to have been composed in this order. It would be interesting to know how far sustained sequential reading of the poem was its reception norm; the 'Letter' seems to assume a reading that works through the books in order as one would read those of a romance narrative, but the poem also develops in such a way as to reward activities of sampling.

25 See Nick Davis (1999), *Stories of Chaos: Reason and Its Displacement in Early Modern English Narrative*. Aldershot: Ashgate, pp. 104–6.

26 Broadly, poetry that deals instructively with agriculture or husbandry, often including praise of rural life.

27 See Leonard Barkan (1975), *Nature's Work of Art: The Human Body as Image of the World*. New Haven: Yale University Press, and Martin Kemp (1998), 'Temples of the Body and Temples of the Cosmos', in Brian Baigrie (ed.), *Picturing Knowledge: Historical and Philosophical Problems Concerning the Use of Art in Science*. Toronto: University of Toronto Press, pp. 40–85.

28 The Castle of Anima episode occurs in Passus 9 of the B-Text of *Piers Plowman*. 'Alma' is, as Walter R. Davis explains, 'both a poetical contraction of (. . .) Latin and Italian *anima*, whose meaning evolved from 'breath' to 'the vital principle' to 'the soul', and the feminine form of Latin *almus* ['that which nourishes'; 'fair, beautiful, gracious'], as in the modern phrase *alma mater*'; 'Alma, Castle of', in A. C.

Hamilton (ed.), (1990), *The Spenser Encyclopaedia*. Toronto: University of Toronto Press, pp. 24–5 (p. 24). A. C. Hamilton points out that 'Alma' can also signify 'a maiden' (from Hebrew *almah*), and that Langland's Anima is also named 'Life'; ed. (2001), *The Faerie Queene*, 2.9.18n.

29 I have argued that the stanza's transcendent mathematics *is*, as presented, inherently incommensurable with surrounding statements in the poem and that, here as elsewhere, Spenser insists on the reciprocal irreducibility of significant symbolic systems; see Davis (1999) 79. No one is going to find this stanza's truth as 'hidden': its truth is on the surface, making for speculative openness.

30 See Paul Archambault (1987), 'The Analogy of the "Body" in Renaissance Political Literature', *Bibliothèque d'Humanisme at Renaissance*, 29, 21–53.

31 The *psychomachia* has its fullest known English realization in the already mentioned morality play known as the *The Castle of Perseverance*. The adventures of its central figure, *Humanum Genus*, span crucial battles fought within the soul, as virtues and vices lock in combat, and over the fate of the human soul, as for example when *Humanum Genus* leaves the safety of the play's symbolic castle under the persuasion of Covetousness. The basic motifs of the *psychomachia* are established in the later fourth-century poem of Prudentius which has been given that name.

32 For the relation to architectural treatises, see Pamela Long (2002), 'Objects of Art / Objects of Nature', in P. Long and P. Findlen (eds), *Merchants and Marvels: Commerce, Science, and Art in Early Modern Europe*. London: Routledge, pp. 63–82 (pp. 74–9), and for positive roles given to machine analogy in the era's moral thinking, see Jessica Wolfe (2004), *Humanism, Machinery, and Renaissance Literature*. Cambridge: Cambridge University Press.

33 Here it is useful to compare the passage with its closest contemporary intertext, the citadel-body of Du Bartas' *Divine Weeks* (First Week, Sixth Day, ll. 401–944; (1979) ed. Susan Snyder, trans. Joshua Sylvester. Oxford: Clarendon Press, pp. 269–95. Du Bartas' account, which more closely resembles the paintings of Arcimboldo, is an ingenious, multi-focused description of organic form as artefact, whereas Spenser's primary concern is with the working interconnectedness of the whole.

34 For the exemplary figure in Spenserian narrative as an automated and automating life-form, see Davis (2011).

35 See the Preface to Vesalius' work, sections xlix–lii, and Pamela Long (2002), 'Objects of Art / Objects of Nature'.

36 This is one of the poem's several non-inclusive definitions of its understanding readership; the teachings of the egalitarian giant in Book Five, for example, are said to be of interest only to 'fooles, women, and boyes', who as represented in the passage turn into a 'lawless multitude' (2.30,52) when Artegall and Talus destroy him.

37 The central combat, for example, directly recalls that of Hercules and Antaeus, of which the best-known narration was probably that of Apollodorus.

38 Sir Philip Sidney, ed. Katherine Duncan-Jones (1989), *The Major Works*. Oxford: Oxford University Press, p. 154.

39 According to Calvin, in a formulation which Sidney seems to be echoing, 'Man's nature, so to speak, is a perpetual factory of idols (. . .) the mind begets an idol; the hand gives it birth'; cited Margaret Aston (1988), *England's Iconoclasts; Volume I: Laws against Images*. Oxford: Clarendon Press, p. 437.

40 When Herodotus begins a chain of narrative with 'Candaules fell in love with his wife (*epasthe tes heoutou gunaikos*)' (1.8), we are being led to expect that some catastrophe will ensue. In Ovid, Narcissus' erotic captivation by his own image has 'novelty as a form of madness (*novitas furoris*)'; *Metamorphoses* 3.350. In Ovid's developmental history of human life this seems to be the harbinger of all loves which become destructive in their force; the emphasis of the episode falls not so much on the illusoriness of the love object as on its power as image and the inescapability of the entrapment. Glauce compares Britomart's love to that of Narcissus, but points out that by good fortune the image of a man which she loves 'a bodie hath in powre' (3.2.45), suggesting ways of escaping the trap.

41 For classical thought on the madness of love and on attempted remedies, see John J. Winkler (1990), *The Constraints of Desire: The Anthropology of Sex and Gender in Ancient Greece*. New York: Routledge, pp. 71–98.

42 Merlin's advice to Britomart on the necessity of accepting her disturbing experience of love as the crossing of a threshold comes at 3.3.21.

43 The episode distinctly evokes *The Merchant's Tale*, where the elderly husband sees his wife enjoying sex with a young lover: 'He swyved thee; I saugh it with myne yen'; Geoffrey Chaucer, ed. Larry D. Benson (1988), *The Riverside Chaucer*. Oxford: Oxford University Press, p. 167, l. 2879.

44 For the cognitive status of vision, often held highly suspect, in the early modern period, see Stuart Clark (2007), *Vanities of the Eye: Vision in Early Modern European Culture*. Oxford: Oxford University Press, and the discussion of these issues in Chapter 6.

45 As Chaucer's narrator says of the Love god in *The Parliament of Fowls*, 'I dar nat seyn, his strokes been so sore, / But "God save swich a lord!" – I can na moore'; Larry D. Benson, ed. (1987), *The Riverside Chaucer*. Oxford: Oxford University Press, p. 385, ll. 13–14.

Chapter 5

1 Giles Fletcher and Phineas Fletcher, ed. Frederick S. Boas (1909), *Poetical Works* (2 vols.). Cambridge: Cambridge University Press, p. 4.

2 Giambattista Vico, trans. Thomas Goddard Bergin and Max Harold Fisch (1968), *The New Science*. Ithaca: Cornell University Press, 2.2.1, section 405; pp. 129–30. Translation modified by reference to Giambattista Vico, ed. Fausto Nicolini (1911–14), *La Scienza Nuova* (3 vols.). Bari: Laterza e Figli, 1, p. 216.

3 *The New Science*. 2.1.1, section 377; pp. 117–18.

4 It is a premise of enquiry for Vico that 'the human mind is naturally inclined by the senses to see itself externally in the body, and only with great difficulty does it come to understand itself by means of reflection'; axiom 63, section 236; p. 78.

5 *The New Science*. 2.1.1, section 378; p. 118.

6 *The New Science*. 2.2.1, section 402; p. 128.

7 See H. Grabes, trans. G. Collier (1982), *The Mutable Glass: Mirror-Imagery in the Titles and Texts of the Middle Ages and English Renaissance*. Cambridge: Cambridge University Press. Grabes' account establishes important cognitive presuppositions of the 'text as mirror to knowledge' metaphor.

8 Visually defined 'horror' in contemporary popular narrative violates a modern taboo in conflating the self's existence with that of a violable, de-integrable body. For the functioning of the body as representation of the early modern self, see Michael C. Schoenfeldt (1999), *Bodies and Selves in Early Modern England: Physiology and Inwardness in Spenser, Shakespeare, Herbert, and Milton*. Cambridge: Cambridge University Press.

9 See Mauro Spicci (2012), '"After an Unwonted Manner": Anatomy and Poetical Organization in Early Modern England', in Matthew Landers and Brian Muñoz (eds), *Anatomy and the Organization of Knowledge, 1500–1850*. London: Pickering and Chatto, pp. 53–69.

10 Robert Underwood (1605), *The Little World* [*internally title: A New Anatomie*]. London: William Jones, ll. 11–24.

11 Giles Fletcher and Phineas (1909), *Poetical Works*, 2, p. 5. As one might expect, 'Featly' (actually Fairclough) and Benlowes were personal friends of Fletcher. The second was a younger man of considerable wealth, 'The Maecenas of the North', who gave financial support to Fletcher and other writers.

12 For the vivid conjunction in Hobbes of sensationalist psychology and a strong interest in crowd control, see Patricia Springborg (2000), 'Hobbes and Historiography: Why the Future, He Says, Does Not Exist', in G. A. J. Rogers and T. Sorell (eds), *Hobbes and History*. London and New York: Routledge, pp. 43–77.

13 References are to Thomas Hobbes, ed. C. B. Macpherson (1968), *Leviathan or, The Matter, Forme and Power of A Common-Wealth Ecclesiasticall and Civill*. Harmondsworth: Penguin Books. Hobbes goes on to declare with unfathomable sarcasm that if ordinary people can be led to accept the officially promulgated doctrine of the Eucharist, 'which is against Reason' (ch. 30, p. 379), they can certainly be led to accept his rational doctrine of the sovereign state.

14   See J. Tralau (2007), 'Leviathan, the Beast of Myth', in Patricia Springborg, (ed.), *The Cambridge Companion to Hobbes's Leviathan*. Cambridge: Cambridge University Press, pp. 61–81 (p. 62).

15   I concur with Horst Bredekamp's view that the frontispiece to the first edition 'constitutes one of the most profound visual renderings of political theory ever produced', and with his high estimation of 'its capacity to address elements of political thought [which are] bizarre or even offensive to the modern reader'; (2007), 'Thomas Hobbes's Visual Strategies', in P. Springborg (ed.), *The Cambridge Companion to Hobbes's Leviathan*, pp. 29–60 (pp. 30, 33). Among Bredekamp's conclusions are that it was designed in Paris by the engraver Abraham Bosse with Hobbes's collaboration; see p. 30.

16   The image is reproduced in Bredekamp, as above, p. 41.

17   Bredekamp, as above, p. 40.

18   Traulau, in 'Leviathan, the Beast of Myth', the comments on the radical 'otherness' and conceptual irreducibility of Leviathan as invented monster with strong mythic overtones.

19   See the image of the sleeping Bunyan, accompanied by one of the book's scenes *qua* dream, which appears as frontispiece to the third edition of *The Pilgrim's Progress*, a text which had already gained a considerable circulation.

20   Reference is to John Bunyan, ed. Roger Sharrock and James F. Forrest (1980), *The Holy War*. Oxford: Clarendon Press; italicization is normalized.

21   Walter J. Ong (1982), *Orality and Literacy: The Technoligizing of the Word*. London: Methuen, pp. 132–5.

22   For an examination of relations between authority and authorship in Bunyan, see Tamsin Spargo (1997), *The Writing of John Bunyan*. Aldershot: Ashgate. The poem headed 'An Advertisement to the Reader', printed at the end of *The Holy War*, addresses the problematic authenticating or deauthenticating relationship between the empirical John Bunyan, John Bunyan the now celebrated author, and whoever might have written *The Pilgrim's Progress* and/or *The Holy War* as texts to which the reader now has access. The poem begins 'Some say the Pilgrims Progress is not mine'; p. 251.

23   One should also consider the text's treatment of narrative time, one of whose periods of demarcation seems to correspond to a phase of Bunyan's own spiritual development as described in *Grace Abounding*; see the comments of the editors, p. xxxii.

24   The traditional, unitary image of the soul is brought to the fore in the representation of the victorious Emanuel's arrival in the town, his privileged treatment of it and the celebrations which ensue; pp. 106–16, 135–50. In a climactic passage, Mansoul steps forward as a distinctly feminine creature: 'Now did Mansoul's cup run over, now did her Conduits run sweet wine, now did she eat the finest of the wheat, and drink milk and hony of the rock! Now she said, how great

is his goodness! For since I found favour in his eyes, how honourable have I been!';
p. 149. This passage, disaligned from the remainder of the text, counts as the very
pointed reprise of a traditional symbolism, marking the soul's special elevation at
this moment.

25 Some of the argument which follows appears in Nick Davis (2010), 'Bunyan with
Mandeville: Allegory, Originality and the Superseding of Collective Experience in
The Pilgrim's Progress', *Bunyan Studies*, 14, 9–33.

26 In dream poems' construction of gender the Dreamer is invariably a puzzled
male.

27 Reference is to *The Riverside Chaucer*, ed. Larry D. Benson 3rd edn. Oxford:
Oxford University Press, 1987, p. 330, ll. 12–13. All references are to this edition.

28 We are told by the Dreamer that 'there is phisicien but one / That may me hele';
The Riverside Chaucer, p. 331, ll. 39–40. In so far as the poem imitates French love
visions, this 'physician' must be the woman whom the Dreamer loves – the amatory
sufferings come with the genre.

29 See William Langland (1978), *The Vision of Piers Plowman: A Complete Edition of
the B-Text*, ed. A. V. C. Schmidt. London: Dent, 1978, Prologue, l. 2.

30 Bunyan may have had some familiarity with the traditional art of memory –
for which, see Frances A. Yates (1966), *The Art of Memory*. Harmondsworth:
Penguin Books – of recognized practical use to the preacher. It recommends the
organization of topics against the background of a sequence of envisaged places
which has been established and interlinked in the rememberer's mind.

31 Cynthia Wall compares Bunyan's projection of topography with that of the detailed
liner road maps in John Ogilby's widely circulated *Britannia*, first published
in 1675; see (2006), *The Prose of Things: Transformations of Description in the
Eighteenth Century*. Chicago: University of Chicago Press, pp. 41–69.

32 See Cynthia Wall (2006), *The Prose of Things: Transformations of Description in the
Eighteenth Century*, pp. 53–69.

33 References are to John Bunyan, ed. W. R. Owens (2003), *The Pilgrim's Progress*.
Oxford: Oxford University Press.

34 This is the longest time-span mentioned in *The Pilgrim's Progress*. It may be
identifying the town, centring on its permanent fair, with the first city founded by
Cain, Genesis 4.17, or perhaps with the city of Iopa which Mandeville describes as
having been founded by Japheth before the Flood, and as being the oldest in the
world; see Sir John Mandeville (1677), *The Voyages and Travels*. London: R. Scott,
T. Basset, J. Wright and R. Chiswel, ch. 7.

35 See Nick Davis (2014), 'Bunyan and Romance', in Michael Davies (ed.), *The Oxford
Handbook to Bunyan*. Oxford: Oxford University Press (forthcoming).

36 Thought of the text as provider of journey-related information can of course be
transposed in such a way as to make it an explanatory supplement to foundational
scriptural discourse.

Part C: Introduction

1 Victor W. Turner (1969), *The Ritual Process: Structure and Anti-structure*. London: Routledge & Kegan Paul.

2 Jean-Luc Nancy writes similarly of 'this strange being-the-one-with-the-other to which we are exposed'; trans. Peter Holland, Lisa Garbus, Michale Holland and Simona Sawhney (1999a), *The Inoperative Community* [*La Communauté Désoeuvrée*]. Minneapolis: University of Minneapolis Press, p. xxxix. These formulations are broadly indebted to Heidegger, whose own philosophical expositions, however, privilege *Dasein* over *Mitsein* for reasons which seem not to be intrinsic to the philosophy itself; see in particular Jean-Luc Nancy (1991b), 'Of Being-in-Common', in Miami Theory Collective, (ed.), *Community at Loose Ends*. Minneapolis: University of Minnesota Press, pp. 1–12.

3 See Martin Buber, trans. Maurice Friedman (2002), *Between Man and Man*. London and New York: Routledge, pp. 240–3.

4 See Nancy (1991a), *The Inoperative Community*, and (1991b), 'Being-in-Common'.

5 See Mikhail Bakhtin, trans. Hélène Iswolski (1984), *Rabelais and His World*. Bloomington: Indiana University Press.

6 See Peter Burke (1994), *Popular Culture in Early Modern Europe* (revised edn). Aldershot: Scolar Press, esp. pp. 23–9.

7 My argument thus differs markedly from that of Stephen Greenblatt's celebrated essay 'Invisible Bullets', which has it that the setting up of the image of an ideal king in the Hal-centred plays 'involves as its positive condition the constant production of its own powerful subversions and the powerful containment of that subversion', an instance of what is produced being 'the noise overheard in the tavern' of *1 Henry IV* which 'seem[s] to signal a subversive alternative to rebellion' until discredited in *2 Henry IV*; (1988), *Shakespearean Negotiations: the Circulation of Social Energy in Renaissance England*. Oxford: Clarendon Press, pp. 21–65 (pp. 41, 47).

8 In fairness to Bakhtin, his poetically compelling examination of carnival has done a good deal to attune contemporary academic study to the special *logics* of cosmomorphism as a form of creative thinking; the problem is that his trackings of these thought processes to claimed conclusions are unduly prescriptive, loaded by a vitalism of philosophical outlook, and largely without evidential support. For the lack of fit between interpretative claims made in *Rabelais and His World* and the text of Rabelais, see Richard M. Berrong (1986), *Rabelais and Bahktin: Popular Culture in Gargantua and Pantagruel*. Lincoln and London: University of Nebraska Press.

Chapter 6

1. Reference is to William Shakespeare, ed. Charles R. Forker (2002), *King Richard II*. London: Arden Shakespeare.
2. Henry S. Turner (2006), *The English Renaissance Stage: Geometry, Poetics, and the Practical Spatial Arts*. Oxford: Oxford University Press, considers the drama of the period extensively in the context of its mathematized arts of observation and construction.
3. Navigational instruments using astronomical data were undergoing technical refinement in this era, as in the instance of the Davis Quadrant of 1594, an improved mariners' backstaff.
4. Reference is to William Shakespeare, ed. David Scott Kastan (2002), *King Henry IV, Part 1*. London: Arden Shakespeare.
5. It seems quite likely that Shakespeare had also seen the more artistically accomplished and very beautiful Wilton Diptych, part of the royal collection, with its portrayal of a younger Richard kneeling before the Virgin Mary and Christ, who are surrounded by angels, while flanked by his patron saints; but of his seeing the Westminster Abbey portrayal we can be considerably more certain. It is also significant, of course, that his audience had some likely familiarity with it.
6. From this point on the book will include a number of paintings in small half-tone reproductions. These are offered as mere reminders of the paintings themselves, which can be accessed in colour reproduction of reasonable quality via the Web.
7. Before overpainting the background consisted of stamped and gilded gesso, a small portion of which is preserved at the painting's top left.
8. A sacral monarch does not rule by virtue of, let us say, claimed 'divine right'. This is a legal–theological explication of the monarch's claim to political sovereignty which was sometimes put forward by early modern rulers. But what I am terming sacral monarchy is not a theoretical construction: if it obtains at all, it is as a thing experienced more simply as being *there*. The idea of sacral monarchy was familiar to early modern Europeans, but as an idea, archaic and largely superseded in political practice though it continued to inform court ritual.
9. Hal's development of this metaphor is, however, more *modern* than Richard's; see further below.
10. See the argument of David Scott Kastan (1986), 'Proud Majesty Made a Subject: Shakespeare and the Spectacle of Rule', *Shakespeare Quarterly*, 37, 459–75. Kastan notes that Elizabeth I 'was always unusually sensitive about being subjected to her subjects' representations [of her]'; 463.
11. Chris Given-Wilson (ed.), (1993), *Chronicles of the Revolution 1397–1400*. Manchester: Manchester University Press, p. 68; translated from Frank Scott

Haydon, ed. (1863), *Eulogium Historiarum sive Temporis* (3 vols.). London: Longman, Vol. 3, p. 378.

12 Reference is to William Shakespeare, ed. René Weis (1997), *Henry IV Part Two*. Oxford: Oxford University Press.

13 Kastan's edition, 1.1.44n, citing Raphael Holinshed (1587), *The Chronicles of England, Scotland, and Ireland* (2nd edn, 3 vols.). London: Henry Denham, Vol. 3, p. 528.

14 In every production that I have seen Hal, on his back and apparently overcome, wounds Hotspur fatally by striking upwards, which implies a sword thrust into the vitals entering by the lower abdomen or groin. This seems an entirely viable staging, which re-emphasizes characteristics which we have come to recognize in the two figures by pitting the valiant, overconfident warrior against the canny opportunist.

15 The sculptor Bernini was to experiment with formal visual caricature, pioneering the form, as in this portrayal of a cardinal.

16 See James Knowles (2003), '*1 Henry IV*' in Richard Dutton and Jean E. Howard, (ed.), *A Companion to Shakespeare's Works, Vol. II: The Histories*. Oxford: Blackwell, pp. 412–31 (pp. 418–9 and 425–6) on Falstaff's especially prominent function in rendering ludicrous the themes of chivalric culture.

17 Argument need not align itself, however, with a 'pro-Falstaff' or 'anti-Falstaff' interpretative position on the plays. I shall suggest that their design strongly encourages discrepant takings of sight on this complex figure.

18 The play's tavern mixes some of the characteristics of the contemporary alehouse and the more socially select tavern, where such things as sack were sold. It is in the nature of an ideal construct. Its functioning as a brothel, not untypical of either, adds to the inclusiveness of the pleasures which it has to offer.

19 C. L. Barber has offered a justly influential critical account of what is carnivalesque in the conception of Falstaff's and his group's activities in (1959), *Shakespeare's Festive Comedy*. Princeton, NJ: Princeton University Press, pp. 192–221. Though I am like others exploring the field indebted to Barber, the emphasis of my own account does not fall on conformity to pre-established 'ritual patterns' (p. 217), but on the synchronous features of social anti-structure in a Turnerian understanding. Moreover, this last does not conceive of carnival primarily as the releasing of a metaphoric pressure-valve, an idea central to Barber's account.

20 François Laroque (2002), 'Popular Festivity', in Alexander Leggatt (ed.), *Cambridge Companion to Shakespearean Comedy*. Cambridge: Cambridge University Press, pp. 64–78 (p. 69).

21 The figure of Carnival in Bruegel's 'Battle of Carnival and Lent' (1559), who seems to be naturally round-bellied, has among his followers a figure whose costume in the region of the belly is grotesquely padded into a half sphere. We may take these body forms as projecting, in context, the pleasures of food consumption. The second seems to be an instance of the body shaped on the pattern of a commonitem of food, evoking the 'Hanswurst' of sixteenth-century German cultures and the 'Jack Pudding' well attested in eighteenth-century English accounts of popular festivity. The Fourth Book of Rabelais has the Sausage People (*les Andouilles*), enemies to Shrovetide, who is an embodiment of Lenten austerity.

22 I do not wish to contest this issue: perhaps some of Hal's motives are to be imagined as being unfathomable, even to himself.

23 See Jack Goody (1977), *The Domestication of the Savage Mind*. Cambridge: Cambridge University Press.

24 The King James translators' resonant but not very accurate 'through a glass darkly' was influenced by Tyndale's 'Nowe we se in a glasse even in a darke speakynge', which preserves the idea of riddling expression.

25 See Dallas G. Denery II (2009), *Seeing and Being in the Later Medieval World: Optics, Theology and Religious Life*. Cambridge: Cambridge University Press, esp. pp. 1–18.

26 This cultural transition provides, I would argue, a crucial context in which to place the evidence for emergent suspicion of the faculty of sight which is marshalled in Clark, Stuart (2007), *Vanities of the Eye: Vision in Early Modern Culture*. Oxford: Oxford University Press. In so far as seeing ceased to be a metaphor for knowing, and became the thing itself, the faculty of sight was required to carry what could well be regarded as an impossible cognitive burden.

27 And for the medieval mystics 'seeings' were either impediments to genuine awareness (the tradition of negative theology, *The Cloud of Unknowing*) or objects of reflection that might perhaps serve to produce it), as oblique, disorientating forms of contact with a higher reality (Hadewijch, Julian of Norwich).

28   For this last, see Walter J. Ong (1958), *Ramus: Method and the Decay of Dialogue*. Cambridge, MA: Harvard University Press.

29   One notices that in early modern natural philosophy even readily observed instances of action at a distance, such as the effects of magnetism, were typically placed in the technical category of magic.

30   This intuition seems to have supported medieval philosophers' notion that sight can *model* experiential contact with what remains pragmatically unseen, as would be the case for spiritual realities.

31   Leon Battista Alberti, ed. and trans. Cecil Grayson (1972), *The Latin Texts of De Pictura and De Statua*. London: Phaidon, pp. 54, 55.

32   Taylor, Charles (1989), *Sources of the Self: The Making of the Modern Identity*. Cambridge, MA: Harvard University Press, p. 202.

33   Erasmus explains that the carnival is Unchristian because it contains 'traces of ancient paganism', and because on occasions like this 'the people over-indulges in licence'; cited Peter Burke (1994), *Popular Culture in Early Modern Europe* (revised edn). Aldershot: Scolar, p. 209. It should be recalled that in the more traditional view playing on a holy day did not of itself count as irreverence or sinful indulgence, but as an entering into relationship with the holy on terms of beneficial familiarity; see Burke, p. 212.

34   By virtue, especially, of a large bagpipe's production of, alongside high-frequency sound, sound of low frequency experienced in the viscera.

35   See Simon Palfrey (2005), *Doing Shakespeare*. London: Arden Shakespeare, pp. 234–7.

Chapter 7

1   See Lorraine Daston (1999), 'Marvelous Facts and Miraculous Evidence in Early Modern Europe', in Peter G. Platt (ed.), *Wonders, Marvels, and Monsters in Early Modern Culture*. Newark: University of Delaware Press, pp. 76–104, and Lorraine Daston and Katharine Park (2001), *Wonders and the Order of Nature 1150–1750*. New York: Zone Books, esp. pp. 173–214 on problems encountered in the conceptualization of monsters.

2   'And the south-westrene wynd on Saturday at even / Was pertliche for pride and for no point ellis'; B-text, Passus 5, ll. 14–15.

3   For sixteenth-century attempts to establish a systematic classification of *monstra*, see Euan Cameron (2010), *Enchanted Europe: Superstition, Reason, and Religion 1250–1750*. Oxford: Oxford University Press, pp. 184–7.

4   See Jonathan Barnes (ed. and trans.), (2001), *Early Greek Philosophy*. London: Penguin Books, p. 15. The saying is cited in its pertinence on understandings of

'nature' by Jeanne Addison Roberts (1991), *The Shakespearean Wild*. Lincoln: University of Nebraska Press, p. 15.

5   See Stephen Wilson's account of relations perceived against a background of conceptual distinction between the house, the fields, and wild places in (1980), *The Magical Universe: Everyday Ritual and Magic in Pre-Modern Europe*. Hambledon and London: London and New York, pp. 3–24.

6   I shall go on using quotation marks when referring to 'nature' in a broadly Aristotelian, pre-Enlightenment understanding.

7   Reference is to William Shakespeare, ed. John Pitcher (2010), *The Winter's Tale*. London: Arden Shakespeare.

8   For ancient and early modern conceptions of wildness, see Hayden White (1972), 'The Forms of Wildness: Archaeology of an Idea', in Edward Dudley and Maximillian E. Novak (eds), *The Wild Man within: An Image in Western Thought from the Renaissance to Romanticism*. Pittsburg: University of Pittsburg Press, pp. 3–38.

9   Aristotle states in the *Politics* that 'he who by nature and not by mere accident is without a state (*polis*), is either a bad man [or 'mean sort', akin to a beast] ar above humanity [a god].' For Aristotle the *polis* exists by nature, and the human aninal is naturally a *zoon politikon*. Nevertheless, there are human beings for whom this natural disposition is in abeyance. Such feral or godlike human beings will, Aristotle observes here, be considered from the standpoint of the *polis* as 'tribeless, lawless, hearthless' and probably bloodthirsty, individuals not to be safely absorbed (1253a 1–7); Aristotle, ed. Jonathan Barnes (1984), The Complete Works: The Revised |Oxford Translation (2 vols). Princeton, NJ: Princeton University Press, 2, pp. 1987–8.

10 Michel de Montaigne, ed. Alexandre Micha (1969), Essais (3 vols.). Paris: Garnier-Flammarion, 1, p. 254, my emphasis.

11 For this tradition, see A. J. Close (1969), 'Commonplace Theories of Art and Nature in Classical Antiquity and in the Renaissance', *Journal of the History of Ideas*, 30, 467–86.

12 See Francis Woolf (2007), 'The Three Pleasures of Mimesis According to Aristotle's *Poetics*', in Bernadette Bensaude-Vincent and William R. Newman (eds), *The Artificial and the Natural*. Cambridge, MA: MIT Press, pp. 51–66 (p. 54). One of Aristotle's prize specimens of *techne* is, of course, the tragic drama of Athens, which the *Poetics* treats as imitating by technical means several of the characteristics of a living organism.

13 *De Natura Deorum* 2.32.

14 For this tradition, see Richard Bernheimer (1952), *Wild Men in the Middle Ages: A Study in Art, Sentiment, and Demonology*. Cambridge, MA: Harvard University Press, and Claude Gaignebet (1986), *A Plus Hault Sens: L'Ésotérisme Spirituel et Charnel de Rabelais* (2 vols.). Paris: Maisonneuve et Larose, 1, pp. 157–72.

15 Here as, for example, in *Titus Andronicus* the image of dismemberment projects the thought that human wildness violates the *social* body as nexus of human connection.

16 For the relationship between the concept of the bear and that of the wild man, see Bernheimer, *Wild Men*, esp. pp. 53–5.

17 See Maureen Quilligan (1979), *The Language of Allegory: Defining the Genre*. Ithaca: Cornell University Press, pp. 48–50.

18 The poem's benign planned garden is the one in the environs of Venus's temple; see 4.10.21–29. For the era's philosophically implicative gardens, see Nick Davis (2011), 'Desire, Nature, and Automata in the Bower of Bliss,' in Wendy Beth Hyman, (ed.), *The Automaton in English Renaissance Literature*. Farnham: Ashgate, pp. 163–79 (pp. 168–9).

19 'The scene invokes myths in which male sexuality is characteristically disguised, violent, compulsive, often bestial, but also an essential part of nature'; William Shakespeare, ed. Stephen Orgel (1996), *The Winter's Tale*. Oxford: Oxford University Press, pp. 45. An important imaginative template here is Ovid's *Metamorphoses*.

20 References are to William Shakespeare, ed. John Pitcher (2010), *The Winter's Tale*. London: Arden Shakespeare.

21 See Pitcher, (ed.) (2010), p. 140. The others are Sicilius Leonatus, the name of the hero's father in *Cymbeline*, and Leonato, that of the Governor of Messina, Sicily, in *Much Ado About Nothing*.

22 See Orgel, (ed.) (1996), 4.4.333n, and Pitcher, (ed.) (2010), p. 70.

23 See Jones's drawings for the costuming of the satyrs, Stephen Orgel and Roy Strong, (ed.) (1973), *Inigo Jones: The Theatre of the Stuart Court* (2 vols.). Sotheby: London, 1, p. 221, and the verbal exchanges between the satyrs, for which Jonson draws on Euripides' surviving satyr-play, *The Cyclops*.

24 In *Oberon*'s transition from antimasque, danced and spoken by satyrs, to masque, danced by courtiers, action which evokes the more unruly and unrestrained side of court life is supplanted by action which stages nature's reformation in a definitive achievement of virtue and order. This is seen as the prince's special accomplishment, and the chaste dances performed by Oberon-Henry and his knights with ladies of the court are offered as a climactic figure of it. The second, masque sequence of the action takes place not in represented daylight but prior to the appearance of the morning star; it is the night vision of a 'new nature'; Ben Jonson, ed. Stephen Orgel (1969), *The Complete Masques*. New Haven: Yale University Press, p. 170, l. 273. This hypernature, inclusive of white bears, has in principle been divinized by the influence of the prince and his associates, and is superior to the nature which daylight reveals.

25 For some of the era's reflections on the a-naturalness of an advanced *techne*, see William Eamon (1983), 'Technology as Magic in the Late Middle Ages and Renaissance', *Janus*, 70, 171–212 and Davis, 2011, pp. 173–9.

26 In the Induction to *Bartholomew Fair* the author's articles of agreement drawn up with the audience famously include 'he is loth to make nature afraid in his plays, like those that beget tales, tempests, and such-like drolleries, to mix his head with other mens heels'; Ben Jonson, ed. Felix E. Schelling (1910), *The Complete Plays* (2 vols.). London: Dent, Vol. 2, p. 182.

27 Robert Chartier, trans. Lydia G. Cochrane (1987), *The Cultural Uses of Print in Early Modern France*. Princeton: Princeton University Press, p. 5. In Chartier's account it is the print-enabled mingling of different media and multiple practices which generates varied constructions of the 'popular'. For the development of what we may term popular print culture – perhaps better, cultures – in England, see Alexandra Halasz (1997), *The Marketplace of Print: Pamphlets and the Public Sphere in Early Modern England*. Cambridge: Cambridge University Press and Matthew Dimmock and Andrew Hadfield (eds) (2009), *Literature and Popular Culture in Early Modern England*. Farnham: Ashgate.

28 See Lori Humphrey Newcomb (1994), '"Social Things": The Production of Popular Culture in the Reception of Robert Greene's *Pandosto*', *ELH*, 61, 753–81 (esp. 756).

29 W. J. Paylor, (ed.) (1936), *The Overburian Characters*. Oxford: Blackwell, p. 43. The passage is cited Newcomb (1994), p. 758.

30 See especially Oliver Impey and Arthur MacGregor (eds) (1985), *The Origins of Museums: The Cabinet of Curiosities in Sixteenth- and Seventeenth-Century Europe*. Oxford: Clarendon Press; Horst Bredekamp, trans. Allison Brown (1995), *The Lure of Antiquity and the Cult of the Machine: The Kunstkammer and the Evolution of Nature, Art and Technology*. Princeton: Marcus Wiener; Daston and Park (2001), pp. 255–301 and Pamela H. Smith (2008), 'Collecting Nature and Art: Artisans and Knowledge in the *Kunstkammer*', in Barbara A. Hanawalt and Lisa J. Kiser, (eds), *Engaging with Nature: Essays on the Natural World in Medieval and Early Modern Europe*. Notre Dame, Indiana: University of Notre Dame Press, pp. 115–35.

31 Rudolf II's establishment of a large-scale *Kunstkammer* in the style of its times is sometimes adduced by modern historians as being in itself sufficient grounds for believing that he was mad.

32 Cited Bredekamp, *The Lure of Antiquity and the Cult of the Machine*, p. 44.

33 There is a representative instance in the Strahov Monastery at Prague. Set up c. 1700 to house, as it still does, the remnants of Rudolph II's once grand *Kunstkammer* collection, an elongated chamber in the monastery has on one of its shorter walls a painted false perspective. I am grateful to Barbara Traister for drawing my attention to this chamber's existence.

34 In the famous story which Pliny recounts, Zeuxis paints grapes so real-seeming
    that birds fly down to peck at them; on being shown which a rival artist, Parrhasius,
    takes Zeuxis to his studio, inviting him to draw aside a curtain which conceals his
    own masterpiece. On attempting to do this Zeuxis discovers that the supposed
    curtain is a painting, and owns that Parrhasius has won the contest.

35 See Hans-Olof Boström (1985), 'Philip Hainhofer and Gustavus Adolphus's
    Kunstschrank in Uppsala', in Impey and MacGregor, *The Origins of Museums*,
    pp. 90–101 (p. 95), and Bredekamp, *The Lure of Antiquity and the Cult of the
    Machine*, p. 68.

36 It is displayed at Chatsworth House, Derbyshire.

37 Reproduced in Orgel, (ed.), *The Winter's Tale*, p. 54; Orgel draws attention, p. 55,
    to the scale and socio-cultural importance of the Earl and Countess of Arundel's
    art collection, but does not set the painting and the collection in the context of the
    period's *Kunstkammern*.

38 Bredekamp comments, 'Using a pointer. [the Earl] brings the gallery close to the
    viewer, though at the same time shifting it into the realm of pictorial imagery, since
    he appears to be seated near not a room but a painting on the wall'; in Bredekamp's
    assessment the sculptures in the gallery, or painting of it, have been 'transmuted
    into ideal images by reflecting aspects of Roman palace architecture'; Bredekamp,
    pp. 18, 19.

39 The portrait of the Earl has its contrastive counterpart in a portrait of the Countess.
    She holds no pointer and sits in an antechamber which is more physically
    continuous with the gallery behind, where portraits instead of statues are displayed.
    This representation of her is thus of the same kind as that of the painted figures
    glimpsed in her portrait.

40 Scott F. Crider helpfully lists the seven imperfectly consonant pieces of information
    of which explanation would have to take account: Paulina's announcement of
    Hermione's death (3.2.170–241); Antigonus' vision of Hermione's ghost (3.3.115–
    45); Paulina's insistence that Leontes remarry when 'your first queen's again in
    breath' (5.1.76–84); the Steward's account of the statue (5.2.91–8); Rogero's account
    of Paulina's frequent visits to the chapel (5.2.102–5); Hermione's explanation for
    what has occurred (5.3.125–8); Leontes' statement that he saw Hermione dead
    (5.3.139–41); (1999), 'Weeping in the Upper World: The Orphic Frame in 5.3 of
    The Winter's Tale and the Archive of Poetry', *Studies in the Literary Imagination*,
    32, 153–72 (p. 161). Part of Crider's broader argument is that we cannot possibly
    know that we are *not* dealing with a generically mythic narrative in which a statue
    might come to life. Scott Maisano further underlines the problem of stabilizing
    an understanding of what is to be taken as having occurred in pointing out that
    the visionary figure of Hermione described by Antigonus evokes the hydraulic
    automata of the period; (2007), 'Infinite Gesture: Automata and the Emotions in

Descartes and Shakespeare', in Jessica Rifkin (ed.), *Genesis Redux: Essays in the History and Philosophy of Artificial Life*. Chicago: University of Chicago Press, pp. 63–84 (pp. 75–6). Stephen Orgel comments, crisply, 'Leontes is our guarantee that the two deaths are real: if Mamilius is dead, so is Hermione; and, by the same token, if Leontes is being deceived by Paulina about the reality of death, so are we being deceived by Shakespeare. What this means is not that at the play's conclusion, Hermione really is a statue that comes to life (we have the word of Hermione herself that this is not the case), but that Shakespearian drama does not create a consistent world'; (ed.), *The Winter's Tale*, p. 36.

Bibliography

Aers, David (1992), 'A Whisper in the Ear of Early Modernists; or, Reflections on Literary Critics Writing the "History of the Subject"', in David Aers (ed.), *Culture and History 1350–1600*. New York and London: Harvester Wheatsheaf, pp. 177–202.

Alanus de Insulis, ed. Marie-Thérèse d'Alverny (1965), *Textes Inédits*. Paris: Plon.

Alberti, Leon Battista, ed. and trans. Cecil Grayson (1972), *The Latin Texts of De Pictura and De Statua*. London: Phaidon.

Altbauer-Rudnik, Michal (2006), 'Love, Madness and Social Order: Love Melancholy in France and England in the Late Sixteenth and Early Seventeenth Centuries', *Gesnerus*, 63, 33–45.

Archambault, Paul (1987), 'The Analogy of the "Body" in Renaissance Political Literature', *Bibliothèque d'Humanisme at Renaissance*, 29, 21–53.

Aristotle, ed. Jonathan Barnes (1984), *The Complete Works: The Revised Oxford Translation* (2 vols). Princeton, NJ: Princeton University Press.

Aston, Margaret (1988), *England's Iconoclasts; Volume I: Laws against Images*. Oxford: Clarendon Press.

Bakhtin, Mikhail, trans. Hélène Iswolski (1984), *Rabelais and His World*. Bloomington: Indiana University Press.

Bałus, Wojciech (1994), 'Dürer's "Melencolia I": Melancholy and the Undecidable', *Artibus et Historiae*, 15, 9–12.

Barber, C. L. (1959), *Shakespeare's Festive Comedy*. Princeton, NJ: Princeton University Press.

Barkan, Leonard (1975), *Nature's Work of Art: The Human Body as Image of the World*. New Haven: Yale University Press.

Barker, Francis (1984), *The Tremulous Private Body: Essays on Subjection*. London: Methuen.

Barnes, Jonathan (ed. and trans.) (2001), *Early Greek Philosophy*. London: Penguin Books.

Beecher, D. A. (1989), 'Erotic Love and the Inquisition: Jacques Ferrand and the Tribunal of Toulouse, 1620', *The Sixteenth Century Journal*, 20, 41–53.

Belsey, Catherine (1985), *The Subject of Tragedy: Identity and Difference in Renaissance Drama*. London: Methuen.

— (1988), *John Milton: Language, Gender, Power*. Oxford: Blackwell.

Benedict, Saint, Abbot of Monte Cassino, ed. Rudolphus Hanslick (1977), *Benedicti Regula* (2nd edn). Vienna: Hoelder-Pichler-Temsky (Corpus Scriptorum Ecclesiasticorum Latinorum).

Bernheimer, Richard (1952), *Wild Men in the Middle Ages: A Study in Art, Sentiment, and Demonology*. Cambridge, MA: Harvard University Press.

Berrong, Richard M. (1986), *Rabelais and Bahktin: Popular Culture in Gargantua and Pantagruel*. Lincoln and London: University of Nebraska Press.

Billy, Himbert de (1602), *Prédictions pour Cinq Années des Choses plus Memorables*. Paris: Nicolas Rousser.

— (1604), *Certain Wonderful Predications for Seauen Yeeres Ensuing*. London: W. Firbrand.

Boström, Hans-Olof (1985), 'Philip Hainhofer and Gustavus Adolphus's *Kunstschrank* in Uppsala', in Oliver Impey and Arthur MacGregor (eds), *The Origins of Museums: The Cabinet of Curiosities in Sixteenth- and Seventeenth-Century Europe*. Oxford: Clarendon Press, pp. 90–101.

Brann, Noel L. (2002), *The Debate over the Origin of Genius During the Italian Renaissance*. Leiden: Brill.

Bredekamp, Horst, trans. Allison Brown (1995), *The Lure of Antiquity and the Cult of the Machine: The Kunstkammer and the Evolution of Nature, Art and Technology*. Princeton: Marcus Wiener.

Bredekamp, Horst (2007), 'Thomas Hobbes's Visual Strategies', in P. Springborg (ed.), *The Cambridge Companion to Hobbes's Leviathan*. Cambridge: Cambridge University Press, pp. 29–60.

Brown, Peter (1988), *The Body and Society: Men, Women, and Sexual Renunciation in Early Christianity*. New York: Columbia University Press.

Buber, Martin, trans. Maurice Friedman (2002), *Between Man and Man*. London and New York: Routledge.

Bunyan, John, ed. Roger Sharrock and James F. Forrest (1980), *The Holy War*. Oxford: Clarendon Press.

Bunyan, John, ed. W. R. Owens (2003), *The Pilgrim's Progress*. Oxford: Oxford University Press.

Burckhardt, Jacob, trans. S. G. O. Middlemore (1960) [1860], *The Civilization of the Renaissance in Italy*. London: Phaidon.

Burke, Peter (1994), *Popular Culture in Early Modern Europe* (revised edn). Aldershot: Scolar Press, pp. 207–43.

Burton, Robert, ed. Thomas C. Faulkner, Nicholas K. Kiesling and Rhonda L. Blair (1989–2000), *The Anatomy of Melancholy* (6 vols). Oxford: Clarendon Press.

Cameron, Euan (2010), *Enchanted Europe: Superstition, Reason and Religion 1250–1750*. Oxford: Oxford University Press.

Capp, Bernard (1979), *Astrology and the Popular Press*. London: Faber and Faber.

Cavell, Stanley (1987), *Disowning Knowledge in Six Plays of Shakespeare*. Cambridge: Cambridge University Press.

Chartier, Robert, trans. Lydia G. Cochrane (1987), *The Cultural Uses of Print in Early Modern France*. Princeton: Princeton University Press.

Chaucer, Geoffrey, ed. Larry D. Benson (1988), *The Riverside Chaucer*. Oxford: Oxford University Press.

Churchill, Caryl (1998), *Plays: 3*. London: Nick Hern Books.

Cicero, ed. and trans. H. Rackham (1961), *De Natura Deorum, Academica*. London: Heinemann (Loeb).

Clark, Stuart (2007), *Vanities of the Eye: Vision in Early Modern European Culture*. Oxford: Oxford University Press.

Close, A. J. (1969), 'Commonplace Theories of Art and Nature in Classical Antiquity and in the Renaissance', *Journal of the History of Ideas*, 30, 467–86.

Cooper, Tarnya (2012), 'John Donne Nearly Finished'. *National Portrait Gallery*, 16 May. Accessed 4 July, www.npg.org.uk/research/conservation/john-donne-and-his-picture.php.

Copenhaver, Brian B. (2007), 'How to Do Magic, and Why: Philosophical Prescriptions', in James Hankins (ed.), *The Cambridge Companion to Renaissance Philosophy*. Cambridge: Cambridge University Press, pp. 137–69.

Cosman, Madeleine Pelner (1978), 'Machaut's Musical Medical World', *Annals of the New York Academy of Sciences*, 314, 1–36.

Crane, Mary Thomas (2009), 'Illicit Privacy and Outdoor Spaces in Early Modern England', *Journal for Early Modern Cultural Studies*, 9, 4–22.

Cressy, David (1994), 'Response: Private Lives, Public Performance and Rites of Passage', in Betty S. Travitsky and Adele F. Seeff (eds), *Attending to Women in Early Modern England*. Cranbury, NJ: Associated University Presses, pp. 187–97.

Crider, Scott F. (1999), 'Weeping in the Upper World: The Orphic Frame in 5.3 of *The Winter's Tale* and the Archive of Poetry', *Studies in the Literary Imagination*, 32, 153–72.

Culpeper, Nicholas (1652), *Catastrophe Magnatum or, The Fall of Monarchie*. London: T. Vere and Nath. Brooke.

Curtius, Ernst Robert, trans. Willard R. Trask (1953), *European Literature of the Latin Middle Ages*. London: Routledge and Kegan Paul.

Dade, John (1605), *A Prognostication in Which You May Behold the State of This Yeere of Our Lord God*. London: Company of Stationers.

Daston, Lorraine (1999), 'Marvelous Facts and Miraculous Evidence in Early Modern Europe', in Peter G. Platt (ed.), *Wonders, Marvels, and Monsters in Early Modern Culture*. Newark: University of Delaware Press, pp. 76–104.

Daston, Lorraine and Park, Katharine (2001), *Wonders and the Order of Nature 1150 – 1750*. New York: Zone Books.

Davis, Nick (1997), '"His Majesty Shall Have Tribute of Me": The King Game in England', in Alan J. Fletcher and Wim Hüsken (eds), *Between Folk and Liturgy*. Amsterdam: Rodopi, pp. 97–108.

— (1999), *Stories of Chaos: Reason and Its Displacement in Early Modern English Narrative*. Aldershot: Ashgate.

— (2010), 'Bunyan with Mandeville: Allegory, Originality and the Superseding of Collective Experience in *The Pilgrim's Progress*', *Bunyan Studies*, 14, 9–33.

— (2011), 'Desire, Nature, and Automata in the Bower of Bliss', in Wendy Hyman (ed.), *The Automaton in English Renaissance Literature*. Farnham: Ashgate, pp. 163–79.

— (2013a), 'Melancholic Individuality and the Lothian Portrait of Donne', *ANQ*, 26, 5–12.

— (2013b), 'The Heavens and *King Lear*', in Nicholas Campion and Darrelyn Gunzburg (eds), *Heavenly Discourses*. Lampeter: Sophia Press (forthcoming).

— (forthcoming), 'Bunyan and Romance', in Michael Davies, (ed.), *The Oxford Handbook to Bunyan*. Oxford: Oxford University Press.

Dear, Peter (1995), *Discipline and Experience: The Mathematical Way in the Scientific Revolution*. Chicago: University of Chicago Press.

Della Porta, Giambattista, ed. Derek J. Price (1957), *Natural Magick [reproducing the English version of 1658]*. New York: Basic Books.

Delumeau, Jean, trans. Eric Nicholson (1991), *Sin and Fear: The Emergence of a Western Guilt Culture 13th –18th Centuries*. New York: St. Martin's Press.

Denery, Dallas G. II (2009), *Seeing and Being in the Later Medieval World: Optics, Theology and Religious Life*. Cambridge: Cambridge University Press.

Dillon, John and Gergel, Tania (eds) (2003), *The Greek Sophists*. London: Penguin Books.

Dimmock, Matthew and Hadfield, Andrew (eds) (2009), *Literature and Popular Culture in Early Modern England*. Farnham: Ashgate.

Donne, John, ed. C. A. Patrides (1985), *The Complete English Poems*. London: Dent.

Donne, John, ed. John Sparrow (1923), *Devotions upon Emergent Occasions*. Cambridge: Cambridge University Press.

Donne, John, general editor Gary A. Stringer (1995–), *The Variorum Edition of the Poems*. Bloomington: Indiana University Press.

Dryden, John, ed. James Kinsley and George Parfitt (1970), *Selected Criticism*. Clarendon Press: Oxford.

Du Bartas, Guillaume de Saluste, ed. Susan Snyder, trans. Joshua Sylvester (1979), *The Divine Weeks and Works*. Oxford: Clarendon Press.

Du Bosc, Jacques (1639), *The Compleat Woman [L'honneste femme]*. London: Thomas Harper and Richard Hodgkinson.

Eamon, William (1983), 'Technology as Magic in the Late Middle Ages and Renaissance', *Janus*, 70, 171–212.

Elias, Norbert, ed. Eric Dunning, Johan Goudsblom and Stephen Mennell, trans. Edmund Jephcott (2000) [1939], *The Civilizing Process: Sociogenetic and Psychogenetic Investigations*. Oxford: Blackwell Press.

Eliot, T. S. (1934), *Selected Essays* (2nd edn). London: Faber and Faber.

Elvin, Mark (1985), 'Between the Earth and Heaven: Conceptions of the Self in China', in Michael Carrithers, Steven Collins and Steven Lukes (eds), *The Category of the Person: Anthropology, Philosophy, History*. Cambridge: Cambridge University Press, pp. 156–89.

Ferrand, Jacques, ed. and trans. Donald A. Beecher and Massimo Ciavollella (1990), *A Treatise on Lovesickness*. Syracuse: Syracuse University Press.

Ficino, Marsilio, trans. Sears Reynolds Jayne (1985), *Commentary on Plato's Symposium on Love*. Dallas: Spring Publications.

Ficino, Marsilio, trans. Members of the Language Department of the School of Economic Science, London, with a preface by Paul Oskar Kristeller (1975–94). *Letters*, 5 vols. London: Shepheard-Walwyn, 1 (77); 5 (21).

Fletcher, Giles and Fletcher, Phineas, ed. Frederick S. Boas (1909), *Poetical Works* (2 vols). Cambridge: Cambridge University Press.

Foucault, Michel (1966), *Les Mots et les Choses*. Paris: Gallimard.

Freud, Sigmund (1953–74) [1923], 'The Ego and the Id and Other Works', in J. Strachey (ed.), *The Standard Edition of the Complete Psychological Works of Sigmund Freud* (24 vols). London: Hogarth Press, 19.

Gaignebet, Claude (1986), *A Plus Hault Sens: L'Ésotérisme Spirituel et Charnel de Rabelais* (2 vols). Paris: Maisonneuve et Larose.

Given-Wilson, Chris (ed.), (1993), *Chronicles of the Revolution 1397–1400*. Manchester: Manchester University Press.

Gobetti, Daniella (1992), *Private and Public: Individuals, Households, and Body Politic in Locke and Hutcheson*. London and New York: Routledge.

Gioia, Dana (1993), 'Seneca and European Tragedy', *New Criterion*, 12, 16–26.

Goody, Jack (1977), *The Domestication of the Savage Mind*. Cambridge: Cambridge University Press.

Gowland, Andrew (2006a), 'The Problem of Early Modern Melancholy', *Past and Present*, 191, 77–120.

— (2006b), *The Worlds of Renaissance Melancholy: Robert Burton in Context*. Cambridge: Cambridge University Press.

Grabes, Herbert, trans. Gordon Collier (1982), *The Mutable Glass: Mirror-Imagery in Titles and Texts of the Middle Ages and English Renaissance*. Cambridge: Cambridge University Press.

Greenblatt, Stephen (1980), *Renaissance Self-Fashioning from More to Shakespeare*. Chicago: Chicago University Press.

— (1986), 'Psychoanalysis and Renaissance Culture', in Patricia Parker and David Quint (eds), *Literary Theory/Renaissance Texts*. Baltimore: John Hopkins Press, pp. 210–24.

— (1988), *Shakespearean Negotiations: The Circulation of Social Energy in Renaissance England*. Oxford: Clarendon Press.

Guibbory, Achsah (2006), 'Erotic Poetry' in Achsah Guibbory (ed.), *The Cambridge Companion to John Donne*. Cambridge: Cambridge University Press, pp. 137–47.

Hacking, Ian (1975), *The Emergence of Probability*. Cambridge: Cambridge University Press.

Halasz, Alexandra (1997), *The Marketplace of Print: Pamphlets and the Public Sphere in Early Modern England*. Cambridge: Cambridge University Press.

Hamilton, A. C. (ed.) (1990), *The Spenser Encyclopaedia*. Toronto: University of Toronto Press.

Harris, Victor (1950), *All Coherence Gone: A Study in the Seventeenth Century Controversy over Disorder and Decay in the Universe*. London: Cass.

Harvey, William (1660) [1628], *Exercitationes Anatomicae, De Motu Cordis & Sanguinis Circulation*. London: R. Daniel.

Hasse, Dag Nicolaus (2007), 'Arabic Philosophy and Averroism', in James Hankins (ed.), *The Cambridge Companion to Renaissance Philosophy*. Cambridge: Cambridge University Press, pp. 113–36.

Harvey, E. Ruth (1975), *The Inward Wits: Psychological Theory in the Middle Ages and the Renaissance*. London: Warburg Institute.

Haydon, Frank Scott, ed. (1863), *Eulogium Historiarum Sive Temporis* (3 vols). London: Longman.

Heidegger, Martin, trans. William Lovitt (1987), 'The Age of the World Picture', in *The Question Concerning Technology*. New York: Harper and Row, pp. 22–51.

Henry, Anne (2007), 'Tragedy and the Sign of the Eclipse', in Sarah Annes Brown and Catherine Silverstone (eds), *Tragedy in Transition*. Oxford: Blackwell, pp. 78–102.

Herbert, George, ed. F. E. Hutchinson (1941), *Works*. Oxford: Clarendon Press.

Hermes Trismegistus, ed. Deborah Houlding (2006), *The Centiloquium*. Accessed 20 July 2012. www.skyscript.co.uk/centiloquium2.html.

Hobbes, Thomas, ed. C. B. Macpherson (1968), *Leviathan or, The Matter, Forme and Power of a Common-Wealth Ecclesiasticall and Civill*. Harmondsworth: Penguin Books.

Holinshed, Raphael (1587), *The Chronicles of England, Scotland, and Ireland* (2nd edn, 3 vols). London: Henry Denham.

Hollis, Martin (1985), 'Of Masks and Men', in Michael Carrithers, Steven Collins and Steven Lukes (eds), *The Category of the Person: Anthropology, Philosophy, History*. Cambridge: Cambridge University Press, pp. 217–33.

Hollywood, John of, ed. Lynn Thorndike (1949), *The Sphere of Sacrobosco and Its Commentators*. Chicago: University of Chicago Press.

Howard, Henry, Earl of Northampton (1583), *A Defensative against the Poyson of Supposed Prophecies*. London: John Charlwood.

Husserl, Edmund (1956) [1924], 'Das reine Subjectivität und Intersubjective Bewusstsein', in Rudolf Boehm (ed.) *Kant und die Idee der Transcendentalphilosophie: Erste Philosophie (1923/24), Husserliana, 7*. The Hague: Martinus Nijhoff.

Impey, Oliver and MacGregor, Arthur (eds) (1985), *The Origins of Museums: The Cabinet of Curiosities in Sixteenth- and Seventeenth-Century Europe*. Oxford: Clarendon Press.

Jagodzinski, Cecile (1999), *Privacy and Print: Reading and Writing in Seventeenth-Century England*. Charlottesville: University of Virginia Press.

James VI and I, ed. Neil Rhodes, Jennifer Richards and Joseph Marshall (2003), *Selected Writings*. Aldershot: Ashgate.

Jonson, Ben, ed. Stephen Orgel (1969), *The Complete Masques*. New Haven: Yale University Press.

Jonson, Ben, ed. Felix E. Schelling (1910), *The Complete Plays* (2 vols). London: Dent.

Kastan, David Scott (1986), 'Proud Majesty Made a Subject: Shakespeare and the Spectacle of Rule', *Shakespeare Quarterly*, 37, 459–75.

Keats, John, ed. Miriam Allott (1970), *The Poems*. London: Longman.

Kemp, Martin (1998), 'Temples of the Body and Temples of the Cosmos', in Brian Baigrie (ed.), *Picturing Knowledge: Historical and Philosophical Problems Concerning the Use of Art in Science*. Toronto: University of Toronto Press.

Kiefer, Frederick (1978), 'Seneca's Influence on Elizabethan Tragedy: An Annotated Bibliography', *Research Opportunities in Renaissance Drama*, 21, 17–34.

Klibansky, Raymond, Erwin Panofsky and Fritz Saxl (1964), *Saturn and Melancholy*. London: Nelson.

Kolve, V. A. (1972), '*Everyman* and the Parable of the Talents', in Jerome Taylor and Alan H. Nelson (eds), *Medieval English Drama: Essays Critical and Contextual*. Chicago: Chicago University Press, pp. 316–40.

Kristeva, Julia, trans. Margaret Waller (1984), *Revolution in Poetic Language*. New York: Columbia University Press.

Ladurie, Emmanuel L. Roy, trans. Mary Feeney (1981), *The Carnival at Romans: A People's Uprising at Romans 1579–1580*. Harmondsworth: Penguin Books.

Langland, William, ed. A. V. C. Schmidt (1978), *The Vision of Piers Plowman: A Complete Edition of the B-Text*. London: Dent.

Lapidge, Michael (1979), 'Lucan's Imagery of Cosmic Dissolution', *Hermes*, 107, 344–70.

Laroque, François (2002), 'Popular Festivity', in Alexander Leggatt (ed.), *Cambridge Companion to Shakespearean Comedy*. Cambridge: Cambridge University Press, pp. 64–78.

Leenhardt, Maurice, trans. Basia Miller Gulati with preface by Vincent Crapanzano (1979) [1947], *Do Kamo*. Chicago: University of Chicago Press.

Levy, David H. (2011), *The Sky in Early Modern English Literature: A Study of Allusions to Celestial Events in Elizabethan and Jacobean Writing*. New York: Springer Books.

Linden, Stanton J. (1996), *Darke Hieroglyphicks: Alchemy in English Literature from Chaucer to the Restoration*. Lexington: University of Kentucky Press.

Long, Pamela (2002), 'Objects of Art / Objects of Nature', in P. Long and P. Findlen (eds), *Merchants and Marvels: Commerce, Science, and Art in Early Modern Europe*. London: Routledge, pp. 63–82.

Longfellow, Erica (2006), 'Public, Private, and the Household in Early Seventeenth-Century England', *Journal of British Studies*, 45, 313–34.

Lowes, John Livingstone (1914), 'The Loveres Maladye of Hereos', *Modern Philology*, 11, 491–546.

Macdonald, Michael (1981), *Mystical Bedlam: Madness, Anxiety, and Healing in Seventeenth-Century England*. Cambridge: Cambridge University Press.

Maisano, Scott (2007), 'Infinite Gesture: Automata and the Emotions in Descartes and Shakespeare', in Jessica Rifkin (ed.), *Genesis Redux: Essays in the History and Philosophy of Artificial Life*. Chicago: University of Chicago Press, pp. 63–84.

Mandeville, Sir John (1677), *The Voyages and Travels*. London: R. Scott, T. Basset, J. Wright and R. Chiswel.

Marlowe, Christopher, ed. David Bevington and Eric Rasmussen (1995), *Doctor Faustus and Other Plays*. Oxford: Oxford University Press.

Martin, John Jeffries (2006), *Myths of Renaissance Individualism*. Basingstoke: Macmillan.

Maus, Katherine Eisamen (1995), *Inwardness and Theater in the English Renaissance*. Chicago: University of Chicago Press.

Mauss, Marcel, trans. Ian Cunnison (1969) [1923], *The Gift: Forms and Functions of Exchange in Archaic Societies*. London: Cohen and West.

Montaigne, Michel de, ed. Alexandre Micha (1969), *Essais* (3 vols). Paris: Garnier-Flammarion.

Montaigne, Michel de, trans. M. A. Screech (1987), *The Complete Essays*. London: Penguin Books.

Murphy, James J. and Katula, Richard A. (1995), *A Synoptic History of Classical Rhetoric* (2nd edn). Davis, CA: Hermagoras Press.

Nance, Brian (2001), *Turquet de Mayerne as Baroque Physician: The Art of Medical Portraiture*. Amsterdam: Rodopi.

Nancy, Jean-Luc, trans. Peter Holland, Lisa Garbus, Michael Holland and Simona Sawhney (1999a), *The Inoperative Community* [*La Communauté Désoeuvrée*]. Minneapolis: University of Minnesota Press.

Nancy, Jean-Luc (1999b), 'Of Being-in-Common', in Miami Theory Collective, (ed.), *Community at Loose Ends*. Minneapolis: Univerisyt of Minnesota Press, pp. 1.12.

Newcomb, Lori Humphrey (1994), '"Social Things": The Production of Popular Culture in the Reception of Robert Greene's *Pandosto*', *ELH*, 61, 753–81.

Ong, Walter J. (1958), *Ramus: Method and the Decay of Dialogue*. Cambridge,MA: Harvard University Press.

— (1982), *Orality and Literacy: The Technologizing of the Word*. London: Methuen.

Orgel, Stephen and Strong, Roy, (eds) (1973), *Inigo Jones: The Theatre of the Stuart Court* (2 vols). Sotheby: London.

Orlin, Lena Cowen (1998), 'Gertrude's Closet', *Shakespeare-Jahrbuch*, 134, 44–67.

Palfrey, Simon (2005), *Doing Shakespeare*. London: Arden Shakespeare.

Parker, David R. (1998), *The Commonplace Book in Tudor London: An Examination of BL MSS Egerton 1995, Harley 2252, Lansdowne 762, and Oxford Balliol College MS 345*. Lanham: University Press of America.

Patterson, Lee (1990), 'On the Margin: Postmodernism, Ironic History, and Medieval Studies', *Speculum*, 65, 87–108.

— (1991), *Chaucer and the Subject of History*. Madison: University of Wisconsin Press.

Paylor, W. J. (ed.) (1936), *The Overburian Characters*. Oxford: Blackwell.

Péres-Ramos, Antonio (1988), *Francis Bacon's Idea of Science and the Maker's Knowledge Tradition*. Oxford: Oxford University Press.

Plotinus, trans. Stephen Mackenna (1991), *The Enneads*. London: Penguin.

Post, Jonathan F. S. (2006), 'Donne's Life: A Sketch', in Achsah Guibbory (ed.), *The Cambridge Companion to John Donne*. Cambridge: Cambridge University Press, pp. 1–22.

Pricket, Robert (1606), *Times Anotomie*. London: George Eld[er].

Ptolemy, ed. and trans. F. E. Robbins (1940), *Tetrabiblos*. Cambridge, MA: Harvard University Press (Loeb).

Quilligan, Maureen (1979), *The Language of Allegory: Defining the Genre*. Ithaca: Cornell University Press.

Quintilian, ed. Donald A. Russell (2001), *The Orator's Education* [*Institutes*]: *Books 6 to 8*. Cambridge, MA: Harvard University Press (Loeb).

Rapport, Nigel and Overing, Joanna (2000), *Social and Cultural Anthropology: The Key Points*. London and New York: Routledge.

Rist, John.M., ed. (1978), *The Stoics*. Berkeley: University of California Press.

Roach, Joseph R. (1985), *The Player's Passion*. Newark: University of Delaware Press.

Roberts, Jeanne Addison (1991), *The Shakespearean Wild*. Lincoln: University of Nebraska Press.

Rosenmeyer, Thomas G. (1989), *Senecan Drama and Stoic Cosmology*. Berkeley: University of California Press.

Rotman, Brian (1999), *Signifying Nothing: The Semiotics of Zero*. Basingstoke: Macmillan.

Schmitt, Natalie Crohn (1978), 'The Idea of a Person in Medieval Morality Plays', *Comparative Drama*, 12, 23–34.

Schramm, Matthias (1963), 'Aristotelianism: Basis and Obstacle to Scientific Progress in the Middle Ages', *History of Science*, 2, 91–113.

Schoenfeldt, Michael C. (1999), *Bodies and Selves in Early Modern England: Physiology and Inwardness in Spenser, Shakespeare, Herbert, and Milton*. Cambridge: Cambridge University Press.

Seneca, ed. and trans. John G. Fitch (2002), *Hercules, Trojan Women, Phoenician Women, Medea, Phaedra*. Cambridge, MA: Harvard University Press (Loeb).

— (2004), *Oedipus, Agamemnon, Thyestes, Hercules on Oeta, Octavia*. Cambridge, MA: Harvard University Press (Loeb).

Shakespeare, William (1968) [1609], *Shake-Speares Sonnets*. London: G. Eld; Facsimile. Ilkley: Scolar Press.

Shakespeare, William, ed. René Weis (1993), *King Lear: A Parallel Text Edition*. London: Longman.

Shakespeare, William, ed. E. A. J. Honigmann (1996), *Othello*. London: Arden Shakespeare.

Shakespeare, William, ed. Stephen Orgel (1996), *The Winter's Tale*. Oxford: Oxford University Press.

Shakespeare, William, ed. René Weis (1997), *Henry IV Part Two*. Oxford: Oxford University Press.

Shakespeare, William, ed. Charles R. Forker (2002), *King Richard II*. London: Arden Shakespeare.

Shakespeare, William, ed. David Scott Kastan (2002), *King Henry IV, Part 1*. London: Arden Shakespeare.

Shakespeare, William, ed. Keir Elam (2008), *Twelfth Night*. London: Arden Shakespeare.

Shakespeare, William, ed. John Pitcher (2010), *The Winter's Tale*. London: Arden Shakespeare.

Sidney, Sir Philip, ed. Katherine Duncan-Jones (1973), *Miscellaneous Prose*. Oxford: Clarendon Press.

— (1989), *The Major Works*. Oxford: Oxford University Press.

Simpson, James (2007), *Burning to Read: English Fundamentalism and Its Reformation Opponents*. Cambridge, MA: Belknap Press of Harvard University.

Smith, Pamela H. (2008), 'Collecting Nature and Art: Artisans and Knowledge in the *Kunstkammer*', in Barbara A. Hanawalt and Lisa J. Kiser, (eds), *Engaging with Nature: Essays on the Natural World in Medieval and Early Modern Europe*. Notre Dame, Indiana: University of Notre Dame Press, pp. 115–35.

Snead, James A. (1981), 'On Repetition in Black Culture', *Black American Literary Forum*, 15, 146–54.

Spearing, A. C. (2005), *Textual Subjectivity: The Encoding of Subjectivity in Medieval Narratives and Lyrics*. Oxford: Oxford University Press.

Spenser, Edmund, ed. A. C. Hamilton (2001), *The Faerie Queene*. London: Longman.

Spenser, Edmund, ed. William A. Oram, Einar Bjorvand, Ronald Bond, Thomas H. Cain, Alexander Dunlop and Richard Schell (1989), *The Yale Edition of the Shorter Poems*. New Haven: Yale University Press.

Spargo, Tamsin (1997), *The Writing of John Bunyan*. Aldershot: Ashgate.

Spicci, Mauro (2012), '"After an Unwonted Manner": Anatomy and Poetical Organization in Early Modern England', in Matthew Landers and Brian Muñoz (eds), *Anatomy and the Organization of Knowledge, 1500–1850*. London: Pickering and Chatto.

Springborg, Patricia (2000), 'Hobbes and Historiography: Why the Future, He Says, Does Not Exist', in G. A. J. Rogers and T. Sorell (eds), *Hobbes and History*. London and New York: Routledge.

Spufford, Margaret (1981), *Small Books and Pleasant Histories: Popular Fiction and Its Readership in Seventeenth-Century England*. Athens, Georgia: University of Georgia Press.

Stewart, Alan (1995), 'The Early Modern Closet Discovered', *Representations*, 50, 76–100.

Stock, Brian (2010), *Augustine's Inner Dialogue: The Philosophical Soliloquy in Late Antiquity*. Cambridge: Cambridge University Press.

Stone, Lawrence (1977), *The Family, Sex and Marriage: England 1500–1800*. London: Weidenfield and Nicholson.

Stone, Walter W. B. (1953), 'Shakespeare and the Sad Augurs', *Journal of English and Germanic Philology*, 52, 457–79.

Taylor, Charles (1989), *Sources of the Self: The Making of the Modern Identity*. Cambridge, MA: Harvard University Press.

— (2007), *A Secular Age*. Cambridge, MA: The Belknap Press of Harvard University Press.

Teskey, Gordon (1996), *Allegory and Violence*. Ithaca: Cornell University Press.

Thomas, Keith (1971), *Religion and the Decline of Magic*. London: Weidenfield and Nicholson.

— (1986), 'Literacy in Early Modern England', in Gerd Baumann (ed.), *The Written Word: Literacy in Transition*. Oxford: Clarendon Press.

— (2010), 'Bodily Control and Social Unease: The Fart in Seventeenth-Century England', in Angela McShane and Garthine Walker (eds), *The Extraordinary and the Everyday in Early Modern England*. Basingstoke: Palgrave Macmillan, pp. 9–30.

Tolkien, J. R. R. and Gordon, E. V. (eds), revised Norman Davis (1967), *Sir Gawain and the Green Knight*. Oxford: Clarendon Press.

Tomlinson, Gary (1993), *Music in Renaissance Magic*. Chicago: University of Chicago Press.

Tralau, J. (2007), 'Leviathan, the Beast of Myth', in Patricia Springborg, (ed.), *The Cambridge Companion to Hobbes's Leviathan*. Cambridge: Cambridge University Press.

Turner, Henry S. (2006), *The English Renaissance Stage: Geometry, Poetics, and the Practical Spatial Arts*. Oxford: Oxford University Press.

Turner, Victor W. (1969), *The Ritual Process: Structure and Anti-Structure*. London: Routledge & Kegan Paul.

Underwood, Robert (1605), *The Little World* [*internally title: A New Anatomie*]. London: William Jones.

Vico, Giambattista, ed. Fausto Nicolini (1911–14), *La Scienza Nuova* (3 vols). Bari: Laterza e Figli.

Vico, Giambattista, trans. Thomas Goddard Bergin and Max Harold Fisch (1968), *The New Science*. Ithaca: Cornell University Press.

Virgil, trans. H. R. Fairclough and G. P. Gooch (1999), *Eclogues, Georgics, Aeneid 1–6*. Cambridge, MA: Harvard University Press (Loeb).

Volk, Katharina (2006), 'Cosmic Disruption in Seneca's *Thyestes*: Two Ways of Looking at an Eclipse', in K. Volk and Gareth D. Williams (eds), *Seeing Seneca Whole: Perspectives on Philosophy, Poetry, and Politics*. Leiden: Brill, pp. 183–200.

Vondel, Joost van den, ed. R. N. Roland Holst et al. (1927–37), *Werken* (10 vols). Amsterdam: Goedkoope Lectuur.

Wall, Cynthia Sundberg (2006), *The Prose of Things: Transformations of Description in the Eighteenth Century*. Chicago: University of Chicago Press.

Wells, Stanley and Taylor, Gary (1987), *William Shakespeare: A Textual Companion*. Oxford: Clarendon Press.

White, Hayden (1972), 'The Forms of Wildness: Archaeology of an Idea', in Edward Dudley and Maximillian E. Novak (eds), *The Wild Man within: An Image in Western*

Thought from the Renaissance to Romanticism. Pittsburg: University of Pittsburg Press.

Whitfield, Peter (2001), *Astrology: A History.* London: British Library.

Wilson, Stephen (1980), *The Magical Universe: Everyday Ritual and Magic in Pre-Modern Europe.* Hambledon and London: London and New York.

Winkler, John J. (1990), *The Constraints of Desire: The Anthropology of Sex and Gender in Ancient Greece.* New York: Routledge

Wolfe, Jessica (2004), *Humanism, Machinery, and Renaissance Literature.* Cambridge: Cambridge University Press.

Woolf, Francis (2007), 'The Three Pleasures of Mimesis According to Aristotle's *Poetics*', in Bernadette Bensaude-Vincent and William R. Newman (eds), *The Artificial and the Natural.* Cambridge, MA: MIT Press.

Wright, M. R. (1995), *Cosmology in Antiquity.* London: Routledge.

Yates, Frances A. (1966), *The Art of Memory.* Harmondsworth: Penguin Books.

Yeats, W. B. (1961), *Essays and Introductions.* London: Macmillan.

Index